I0759513

NEW YORK GIANTS

A Curated History of Big Blue

JORDAN RAANAN

Library of Congress Cataloging-in-Publication Data available upon request.

This book is available in quantity at special discounts for your group or organization. For further information, contact:

Triumph Books LLC
814 North Franklin Street
Chicago, Illinois 60610
(312) 337-0747
www.triumphbooks.com

Printed in U.S.A.
ISBN: 978-1-63727-762-1
Design by Preston Pisellini
Page production by Nord Compo

To Abby, Kylie, and Brody
You're my rocks...always and forever

CONTENTS

Part 4 2007

Part 5 2011

Foreword

Back when I was making the decision to sign as an undrafted free agent with the New York Giants, I was taking a leap of faith. I was just like, *Man, I want to do this at home.* The potential of living out my dream in my backyard, where my mom could come to every game and where my dad could look down at me from heaven was too much to pass up. My dad's the one who taught me how to play the game. The fact that I got to live it out every single time I put that jersey on, every single time I went to practice, every single piece of merchandise I get to this day, I'm just so proud to be part of this team. It's really a next-level feeling to be a part of this history, something that can never be taken away from me.

Being a Giant was everything to me. It made me join a litany of high-character guys who understood what it was like to represent the team, players, and people that came before us. Being introduced to and becoming friends with legends like Harry Carson, Lawrence Taylor, Phil Simms, and, of course, Eli Manning is so significant to the history of my career. And then to be mentioned in the same breath as those guys and included in the Giants' history is special. Giants legends are a specific type of athlete, one that understands how to carry himself in public, one that knows how to talk to people, knows how to galvanize their team. They're real leaders.

I love being a part of that history, which Jordan Raanan so nicely recaps and illustrates in this book. I can't go anywhere without being reminded that the Giants are a huge part of my narrative. To this day, when I do anything, I think about how the Giants are going to feel about me doing this. *Am I representing them in the best light? Am I making the best decision in something that they would be proud of? If I was still a player, would they be proud of it?*

To be able to do what I did in the New York market, oh, it has been incredible. The benefits have been tenfold off the field. Between being a successful player, doing things on the field that excited fans, and being a beloved figure in my Hispanic community for doing the iconic salsa dance in the end zone that brought my culture to the football field, I've been able to create a respectable career off the field. My daughter now has a legacy to live up to. These are the things you dream of; and to have acquired those things because of this game and the Giants, it's a dream come true.

When I was a young kid, I didn't have any former pros that came back to talk to us. I didn't have any guys who would come back and create programs or organizations that would directly give back to the kids in Paterson, New Jersey. Today, I'm proud that my work through my charity is able to raise funds that develop programs, provide technology donations, allow coaches and teachers to come in and teach new information alongside principles I was brought up on. I host an annual youth football camp so that they can get to know how to play the game the right way. I'm able to impact my community with intentions to do things bigger and better however I can.

I want to continue to develop programs I support in my old high school, which is now a full STEAM high school. Now I can watch kids grow throughout the program, go to college, and be successful. And the plan is for them to come back home and do the same thing, help the next generation. Hopefully, that cycle is what breeds a new generation of dreamers, a new generation of successful young adults who are excited to pay it forward. That's the ultimate goal for me.

It's extremely surreal that kids can say, "Oh, Victor Cruz was from here. He played for the Giants, won a Super Bowl with the Giants. I can do it." Seeing these kids' eyes light up when I come in the room is inspiring. And let's be honest, it's been almost a decade since I've retired. It's been almost 15 years since the Super Bowl. Most of these kids were six and seven years old. So the fact that they still know who the hell I am—God bless YouTube and all of these highlights—that's what really keeps us alive, right? It keeps those moments alive, and those kids look back at those things and are like, "Holy crap, this guy Victor Cruz was really doing something, Eli Manning was really doing something."

They can go back and look at those videos and say, "Oh, I see what all the hoopla was back then." And not only that, but they also become fans all over again in their own right at eight years old, those formative years when they're learning the game. If you would've told nine-year-old me that 15 years later I'd be a Super Bowl champion who comes back to his hometown to inspire others, I wouldn't have believed it. The Giants had a poll on social media asking current players which former legend they'd want to have dinner with. And one of the guys said, "Victor Cruz." Me? Of all the guys?

L.T. played here, and Eli played here. *Are you aware of the real yellow jacket that Hall of Famers got?* That's the beauty of the Giants. *You sure you want to talk to me?* It's humbling, man, and I don't take it for granted. And I want to make sure that I can continue to pay it forward and continue to be the same guy. I don't anticipate changing or being any different than the humble guy who was given a chance by the Giants organization. Every day I wake up and think about my legacy. It just keeps getting better and better.

When I tell kids I'm from Paterson and went to Paterson Catholic and to UMass Amherst, which isn't a powerhouse like LSU, and I grinded my way up to the New York Giants' roster, everyone can relate to that for sure. And my story is probably the most indicative of the grind. It's all because I'm a Giant. I owe so much to the franchise and can't wait for you to relive it all and read about its outstanding history.

—Victor Cruz

Prologue

Origin Story

WALK INTO 1925 GIANTS DRIVE, AND THE RICH HISTORY IS on full display, beginning with the address, which commemorates the year the historic organization was founded. There stands a trophy case some five feet high and 20 feet long. Inside tells the story of the modern history of the New York Football Giants, one of the National Football League's golden franchises.

It begins with a framed plaque from the 1986 NFC Championship Game: Giants 17, Redskins 0 with pictures of running back Joe Morris and linebacker Carl Banks from that blustery but memorable day. Next to it sits the George Halas Trophy from that afternoon flanked by a Super Bowl XXI plaque.

Then it's on to the 1990 NFC Championship Game with a plaque commemorating that memorable win against the San Francisco 49ers in what coach Bill Parcells thought was one of the greatest games he ever witnessed. The pictures are of Matt Bahr kicking the game-winning field goal with quarterback Jeff Hostetler the holder and of star linebacker Lawrence Taylor celebrating at the expense of 49ers future Hall of Fame quarterback Steve Young. Next to it is another George Halas Trophy flanked by a Super Bowl XXV plaque.

Then you get to the true gems, the centerpieces of the impressive collection of hardware housed inside the trophy case—the Lombardi Trophies. All four of them sit in the lobby of the Giants' facility, called the Quest Diagnostics Training Center. They are in order: Super Bowl XXI, XXV, XLII, XLVI. Each glistens brilliantly in the well-lit foyer as if polished daily, sitting as a reminder of the success of the storied franchise.

They are the showpieces that sit in the lobby of the Giants' modern palace, which is spattered with history. There are old newspaper clips of memorable days and moments on the walls throughout the facility from their time at the Polo Grounds to their run under longtime coach Steve Owen to the exploits of owner Wellington Mara and his father, franchise founder Tim Mara, to the Super Bowls in the '80s to more conquests with Eli Manning and Co. in 2007 and 2011. There are pictures and murals of legendary players such as Taylor, Frank Gifford, Roosevelt Brown, Harry Carson, Phil Simms, Sam Huff, and Manning, to name a few. There are artifacts left behind by the Maras and their eventual partners, the Tisch family. Framed newspaper clippings line the walls commemorating some of the greatest moments in franchise history. There are even pictures of the team's most recent wins.

It's all there at 1925 Giants Drive. The Quest Diagnostics Training Center is a Giants museum of sorts. It's apropos for a franchise that has now been in existence for a century, a full 100 years.

It all began with a purchase in 1925 by Tim Mara, a known bookie and businessman in New York who had friends in high places. He eventually had a fuel company and a law book binding company. His professional football ownership came about when the National Football League was looking to put a team in the nation's largest city. NFL president Joe Carr went to fight promoter Billy Gibson and offered him the franchise. He declined but introduced him to his friend, Tim Mara. It was an offer Mara couldn't refuse. The cost? A mere $500. Mara's famous line was: "An empty storefront with a couple folding chairs in New York is worth $500." So he invested.

It wasn't always a great investment in the early days. In fact, there were times where it was a losing financial proposition, and Mara contemplated bailing on the Giants and the National Football League. His friends told him it was never going to amount to anything. But Mara's sons, Wellington and Jack, were so in love with the Giants that selling or folding wasn't an option. "My grandfather said, 'I would've broken their hearts that night.' So he kept it, thankfully," John Mara, Tim's grandson, said almost a century later.

The NFL in the '20s was hardly the gold mine it has become in the 21st century. Tim Mara had his hands full trying to build the game and a fan base in the busy metropolis of New York City. During their inaugural season, he brought in the legendary Jim Thorpe, a two-time Olympic gold medalist who also played professional baseball and basketball. That only lasted a few games. The Giants even tried to sign college star Red Grange later that year only to lose out to the Chicago Bears. But when Grange came with the Bears to the Polo Grounds in December 1925, it was reported to be a sellout crowd that netted Mara $143,000.

At that point the Giants were off and running. They went 11–1–1 and won their first championship in 1927 in only their third season. They were also involved in some of the league's most memorable games in the early years of the franchise. One of those was "The Sneakers Game" in 1934. It was the NFL Championship Game that year, and the Giants were hosting the Bears at the Polo Grounds in a rematch of the previous season's title game. Chicago was heavily favored after winning that previous year's encounter and having beaten the Giants twice in the '34 season. The Bears were also undefeated. They were supposed to win walking away.

Only they could hardly walk, nevertheless run, because the conditions didn't cooperate. They weren't prepared for the frozen, icy field they were about to encounter. The Giants were because captain Ray Flaherty remembered a game at Gonzaga University where he wore basketball shoes instead of cleats. This kept him from slipping uncontrollably in the conditions. As one version of the story goes, locker room attendant Abe Cohen went to Manhattan College and grabbed the basketball team's sneakers during the game. This allowed the Giants significantly better traction that gave them a decided advantage on the field. It helped turn a seven-point halftime deficit into a 30–13 win. Cohen returned the famous sneakers to Manhattan College the following day. Perhaps a more realistic version of the story is that Giants trainer Gus Mauch worked at Manhattan College and had the sneakers waiting in standby. Cohen had them ready, and it was widely considered the difference in the game. Either way, "The Sneakers Game" was born.

Another monumental game in New York and NFL history was the 1958 Championship Game between the Giants and Baltimore Colts. This one the Giants didn't win, but it was a turning point for the league. It helped transform the NFL into the behemoth it is today. That game between the great Johnny Unitas, one of the best quarterbacks of his generation or ever, and his Colts against the Charlie Conerly–led Giants and starring the great Gifford was the first sudden-death overtime game in NFL history. "What happens now?" Giants kicker and eventual Hall of Fame announcer Pat Summerall famously asked receiver Kyle Rote at the end of regulation.

What happened was the Giants got the ball, punted, and Baltimore drove the length of the field for an Alan Ameche game-winning touchdown run. It was as dramatic a finish as the NFL had ever witnessed—and seen by an audience bigger and wider in scope than ever, spilling into the nightly news. The 1958 Championship Game was a nationally-televised contest during a time when TV was taking off and becoming exponentially more popular. It was the perfect mix for NFL commissioner Bert Bell and the game—two great teams (featuring 12 future Hall of Famers), stars galore, down to the wire, sudden death. The game had it all right there for the entire nation to see. It was incredible drama. Football was on its way to the moon after that.

That contest was eventually labeled "The best football game ever played" by *Sports Illustrated*'s Tex Maule. It has over time evolved into the "The greatest game ever played." The impact it had on professional football and its checkbook was immense. That matchup between the Giants and Colts is credited with helping grow the game to levels Tim and his cronies never thought possible. The American Football League (AFL), which would eventually merge with the NFL to make it what it is today, was established within two years of that 1958 Championship Game. By the mid-1960s the three behemoth networks—ABC, NBC, and CBS—were jostling to broadcast games. They still are today—along with streaming companies—some 60 years later, but it now costs billions of dollars.

The overarching success of the league didn't happen by accident. A lot of it has to do with the Giants and Wellington Mara, who dedicated his working life to the game of football. Wellington was so influential in the history of the NFL that his nickname "The Duke" is inscribed on every official football used in games today. He not only coined the term "Once a Giant, always a Giant," it was a way of life. He was that invested in the team and in the game. He was actually instrumental in introducing Polaroid pictures to NFL sidelines. It was Wellington, the owner of the Giants, who was the one in the upper deck at Yankee Stadium sending the pictures down to the field to offensive coordinator Vince Lombardi. "That was a hand-me-down from Vince Lombardi," he said. "They did that when he had been at West Point, and when he joined us, the first thing he wanted to do was take some pictures...So I volunteered. I used to take those pictures and put them in a sock, weigh it down with some cleats, and throw them down from the upper deck to the bench."

In-game adjustments haven't been the same since.

Wellington, along with his older brother Jack, took control of the Giants following their father's death in 1959, just a couple months after "The greatest game ever played." Jack died in 1965, and that is when Wellington took over as team president, a role he held until his death in 2005. By then the Giants had already won two of those Lombardi Trophies that currently sit in the lobby at 1925 Giants Drive.

Wellington became a key figure in the NFL—not just with the Giants. Ultimately, his willingness to share revenue with other owners from smaller markets (such as Green Bay, Buffalo, or Kansas City) was crucial to the long-term growth of the league. He believed the NFL was only as strong as its weakest link. "He thought what was good for every team in the NFL was good for the New York Giants," said Susan McDonnell, Mara's oldest daughter.

His oldest child, John, is currently the team's president and CEO. John and Susan are the oldest of Wellington and Ann

Mara's 11 children. They run and operate the organization in the 21st century along with the Tisch family, who bought 50 percent of the franchise from Wellington's nephew, Tim, in 1991 for $75 million. "It's one of the great franchises in the sports world," Loews Corporation president and owner Preston Robert Tisch said at the time of the purchase.

Bob Tisch, as he was known, previously had other opportunities to get into the NFL. Options included the New England Patriots, Dallas Cowboys, and Cleveland Browns. They just never were the right option. They weren't New York. Tisch was born in Brooklyn and was Mr. New York, knowing everybody in the city after having invented the Power Breakfast at the Regency Hotel, which he owned and where he lived. Nobody worked a room quite like Bob. He was the ultimate schmoozer. At Super Bowl XXXVII, he wanted to attend one more party off premises before the actual game, and it took his family 45 minutes to talk their way back into the stadium and get to their seats. Tisch knew everybody, and everybody loved him.

Given that innate talent, it's no surprise the Tischs eventually became intimately familiar with the Maras, football aristocracy, and the Giants in the early '60s when they moved to Scarsdale, New York. Their neighbor at the time was Allie Sherman, then the Giants coach. Through Sherman, Bob and Joan Tisch met the Maras. Joan Tisch's father, Dr. Howard Hyman, was also embedded with the Giants since he arranged for years to have veterans attend football games at everywhere from Yankee Stadium to the Yale Bowl to Giants Stadium to MetLife Stadium.

But the ultimate lure to the NFL came when Bob later moved to Harrison, New York. It was there that he befriended a man who lived three-fourths of a mile down the road named

Pete Rozelle. The NFL commissioner became one of his closest friends. In fact, the Tischs were part of a group they called Rozelle's Raiders that would encamp at Super Bowls no matter where they were around the country. It provided Bob a first-hand look at the business and the ownership fraternity. It was ultimately something he coveted.

When Tisch heard that Tim Mara's 50 percent of the Giants was on the market, it was a no-brainer. The deal was basically done in the fall of 1990, but it dragged, and the decision was made not to announce it until after the Giants ended up winning Super Bowl XXV. Even though he wasn't technically an owner, Wellington gave Bob a Super Bowl ring after they beat the Buffalo Bills in January 1991. He was in the fraternity, incredibly meaningful for a young Jewish boy from Brooklyn who grew up with modest means and earned his way into this elite business circle. "We knew that for a guy that was so embedded in the fabric of New York City, a guy that was truly Mr. New York, to be able to own 50 percent of his hometown football team was incredibly special and meaningful for him," said Jonathan Tisch, the youngest of his three children.

The transition was rather seamless. Bob made himself useful where needed. He had extensive business experience and knowledge, which was of use to the Giants. They were a marquee franchise in the budding NFL. Bob and Wellington were hardly absentee owners. The opposite really. They were both there regularly at practice, watching but never making themselves a distraction. They reached the Super Bowl in 2000 and set them up for two more not long after their deaths. Bob and Wellington ran the Giants successfully for 14 years. They passed within weeks of each other in 2005.

The Giants remain the only NFL franchise with a 50/50 ownership split. "I think one of the important elements is the partnership between Wellington Mara and Bob Tisch and the respect that the two families have for each other...it really was a partnership," Jon Tisch said. "Wellington and Bob were partners, and Wellington, he's obviously one of the greatest names in the history of the NFL and the Mara family going back to 1925. And Bob Tisch, highly respected business leader, civic pride in New York City, they were partners for 14 years until each of them passed away."

The late Preston Robert Tisch passed the team down to his children Steve, Laurie, and Jon at the time of his death in 2005. Steve is the executive vice president and chairman of the Giants, Jon is the treasurer, and Laurie is a board member. What the Tischs bought into was an organization steeped in history. The Giants made six NFL championship games from 1956 to 1963. With players like Gifford, Huff, Conerly, Alex Webster, Brown, Rote, Andy Robustelli, Emlen Tunnell, and Rosey Grier, they captured and inspired a whole generation of fans.

Among those fans was one Duane "Bill" Parcells, whose love for that team would later draw him to the organization as a coach. Players like Conerly and Huff caught the attention of Parcells, the New Jersey native. Those were his guys. "Yeah, I loved them when I was young," Parcells said.

Huff was one of the first defensive players to start getting significant recognition. It didn't happen by accident. Huff spent countless nights at the home of defensive coordinator Tom Landry, watching film on the coach's living room wall as they redefined the middle linebacker position.

That Giants defense in general was beloved and well known with Huff, Grier, Tunnell, Dick Modzelewski, and Jim Katcavage. But the group was led by Robustelli, who was nicknamed "The Pope."

The defense became so big and beloved that it was the unit introduced before games. And that unit inspired the "Dee-fence! Dee-fence! Dee-fence" chants that were created by Giants fans. It was a symphonic anthem that echoed throughout Yankee Stadium in that era. The chant still lives to this day and has spread to all fan bases.

The Giants moved from the Polo Grounds to Yankee Stadium in 1956. It was considered a massive upgrade at the time. They played there until the mid-1970s when they went to the Yale Bowl and Shea Stadium while they waited for their new place in New Jersey to be built. That was eventually Giants Stadium, which has since been replaced by MetLife Stadium in the same complex.

It was at Yankee Stadium where the Giants of the '50s and '60s did their winning. John Mara, a young kid at the time, can still remember sitting in those stands (always the sunny side thanks to a demand from his mother after the first game there) and seeing famed politician Bobby Kennedy standing and cheering in one of the front rows. Kennedy was a big fan of the Giants and became friendly with Grier.

The Giants of that era also shared a locker room with the Yankees, those same Yankees who had Mickey Mantle, Roger Maris, and Whitey Ford. Their nameplates were right there above the great Giants players from that era. Even the clubhouse attendants were the same. Big Pete and Little Pete would tell tales of Babe Ruth and Lou Gehrig to the Giants players. It was a step up in class. Players would walk out of the locker room through the Yankees dugout and onto the field on gamedays. "That was a pretty cool thing," John said. "Walking out of that locker room into the dugout and then onto the field on a game day was...I still get chills in my spine thinking about that."

Many of those Giants players during that era were there in the first place as a result of Wellington. He immersed himself in the football side of the business by that time. Scouting was his obsession. He compiled background on college players and even shared his list with other teams. The way they used to conduct the draft, different owners would meet in a hotel conference room where there would be a blackboard. On the blackboard Wellington wrote the names of the top prospects around the country, and some teams would draft off that. Even when he was off fighting as a Naval officer in World War II, he would send letters home detailing the prospects of college players. Scouting was his passion, so much so that he sat through the entirety of the team's draft meetings. The owner of the Giants was there from start to finish—whether it was to talk about the No. 1 overall pick or the 17th-round offensive guard from South Dakota State. (The NFL draft back then could be 30-plus rounds.)

After the glory days of the '50s and '60s, Wellington's Giants hit a wall. The mid-'60s through the '70s were the dark ages for the team. They struggled to get draft picks right, and everything they touched seemed to go wrong. New York won just one home game during its two years at the Yale Bowl. It reached the point in 1978 where fans flew a plane over the stadium with a banner that read: "15 Years of Lousy Football... We've Had Enough." That same year fans hung a dummy from the third deck at Giants Stadium with a sign indicating it represented Wellington.

It almost certainly would have never reached this point if Wellington had been able to keep their offensive or defensive coordinator from the mid-'50s teams. From 1954 to 1958, New York had Lombardi running the offense and Landry guiding the defense under head coach Jim Lee Howell. Lombardi went on to become a legendary head coach for the Green Bay Packers. Landry built the Dallas Cowboys into a champion and the most valuable football franchise in the world. Both are in the Hall of Fame and considered among the greatest coaches of all time. "They appreciated one another," Wellington said. "There was a rivalry, to be sure, but they meshed together very well and had the benefit of having a head coach, Jim Lee Howell, who recognized their abilities."

Landry, a cerebral former defensive back who played for the Giants, is credited with inventing the 4-3 defense with four defensive linemen and three linebackers. He would have been the more difficult of the two coordinators to keep long term. Howell wasn't going anywhere since he had a winning season every year he was the Giants coach from 1954 to 1960. Landry, meanwhile, was born and raised in Mission, Texas. When the Cowboys were established in 1960 as an expansion team, it was an opportunity for him to go home.

It was Lombardi, a Fordham classmate of Wellington's, who seemed born to be the next head coach of the Giants. Mara thought he could send Lombardi to Green Bay for a year or two until Howell stepped aside from coaching. A good plan in theory. The only problem was that Lombardi went to Green Bay and was geared up to win the NFL championship by the end of the 1960 season. He wasn't going anywhere. (The Packers won the NFL title in 1961, '62, '65, '66, and '67.) And Green Bay wasn't going to just let him come back home. That's the thing. Lombardi was a native of New York. The Giants would have been home for him. It would've been the perfect fit with the Giants. He could have coached under Wellington, who became his golfing buddy over the years, too. "I used to say to my dad jokingly, although he didn't necessarily see the humor in this,

'If you just kept one of them, Lombardi or Landry, I would've had a much happier childhood,'" John Mara said.

It got bad after the Giants quickly became old and started to fall apart in the mid-'60s. They weren't able to turn it around for quite some time. And then in the late '70s there was a feud between Wellington and his nephew, Tim. That would create some problems and lead to the hiring of general manager George Young, which was engineered by Rozelle in 1979. But it was perhaps the most unfortunate moment in team history that ironically set the Giants up for the turnaround and for the first two Super Bowls in franchise history. It was November 19, 1978, when the unthinkable happened in a game between the Giants and Philadelphia Eagles.

The Giants were winning 17–12 in the final seconds. All they had to do was run out the clock. The Eagles had exhausted their timeouts, and New York seemed destined to win—except the Giants could find a way to mess up anything in those days. They inexplicably fumbled the ball while trying to run a play in the waning seconds. Quarterback Joe Pisarcik went to hand it off to running back Larry Csonka, and it clanked off his hip and dropped to the ground. Eagles cornerback Herman Edwards scooped it and ran to the end zone for the winning score. It was dubbed the "Miracle at the Meadowlands," a famous play more because of how pathetic it was for the Giants than it was amazing for the Eagles.

It was also, ironically, John Mara's last day in the television business. He used to work for the CBS broadcast as a spotter and did a ton of games with Summerall. He would pass along to the former Giants kicker who made the catch or tackle, how many yards each play gained or lost, and all the requisite information the play-by-play announcer or analyst would need in the moment. The last game John ever worked was that "Miracle at the Meadowlands" with Don Criqui and Sonny Jurgensen on the call. At the time John was generally able to keep his cool—even during Giants games—which was necessary because a spotter isn't supposed to be noticed. But on this instance with such an extraordinary and frustrating finish and given his ties to the organization, John couldn't contain his disgust. "God damn it!" he said as his fist pounded the table.

The microphones at the time were propped up on stands. They tumbled over. As he liked to tell people, he and CBS came to a mutual understanding that was not the best place for him during games. (It didn't stop the same scenario from unfolding years later, though it wasn't in the TV or radio booths. During a frustrating late-season loss at the Detroit Lions in the 2013 season, he pounded the table in the press box after the Giants offensive operation repeatedly had trouble getting plays called.) "God damn it," he mumbled as those nearby looked to see who broke the cardinal rule of no cheering in the press box.

Shortly thereafter, he no longer sat in the press box. He would always be tucked away in a suite to avoid another "God damn it" moment. Still, that loss in Detroit was nothing like the "Miracle at the Meadowlands." Not even close. That was a new low even for that pathetic era of Giants football. Except little did they know that miscue turned into a blessing. It led to New York getting the seventh pick in the following year's draft. With that selection they grabbed a quarterback out of little-known Morehouse State by the name of Phil Simms. He was actually the second quarterback taken that year behind Washington State's Jack Thompson, who went third to the Cincinnati Bengals. And while Simms' success wasn't immediate, the pick would eventually pay dividends beyond anyone's imagination.

Simms was Young's first selection as general manager. He turned into one of the best quarterbacks in franchise history, a champion, and Super Bowl MVP. Nobody knew it at the time (and it took a few years to get things rolling), but that would be a major turning point for the Giants in the Super Bowl era. They were about to be on their way to a new golden age.

PART 1

1986

1

The Ride

The 1986 campaign began for the New York Giants the moment the previous season crashed to a miserable end in Chicago. Actually, on the plane ride home for coach Bill Parcells.

His team came up short against the Chicago Bears and their dominant defense in the playoffs on January 5, 1986. They lost 21–0, and Parcells was ticked that his team had blown an opportunity to reach the NFC Championship Game and more. Even more so, the Giants coach felt he had let down veteran defensive end George Martin and linebacker Harry Carson, the team's two longest-tenured players at the time and his trusted leaders.

It was to the point that Parcells wasn't really speaking to anyone from the moment the divisional round playoff game in Chicago ended until he was a few beers deep on the flight home to New Jersey. He went through his postgame press conference and exchanged half-hearted pleasantries with players and team personnel while wallowing in a malaise of regret. It wasn't until the Giants were halfway home, somewhere over Pittsburgh, where Parcells' mentor and high school coach Mickey Corcoran provided a much-needed dose of reality. "You got to figure out a way to beat those God damn guys!" Corcoran said.

Parcells knew he was right—even if it was easier said than done. The Bears were the Monsters of the Midway. The San Francisco 49ers were on the brink of a dynasty. The Washington Redskins were in their division and won the Super Bowl as recently as 1982, and more were on the horizon. But from that point on, Parcells and the Giants were singularly focused on their shared goal of getting over the hump in the 1986 season before the opportunity passed. Parcells owed it to Martin and Carson, who were in their thirties. Who knew if they would have many more chances. Martin and Carson wanted to make the most of this relatively young and supremely talented team that they knew could do damage. It was now—or possibly—never.

Parcells and the '86 team weren't going to forget the way that previous season ended. No chance. It was that ugly and disappointing. *The New York Times* summed it up in the lede of their game story: "The Giants' season ended today in wind and cold and embarrassment and a 21–0 loss to the Bears."

Embarrassment. That word spoke volumes considering the biggest play of that game was a punting miscue. As trusted punter Sean Landeta went to kick the ball in the first quarter, a strong gust blew it away from his foot. Landeta barely got a piece of the ball, and it trickled only a few yards. Chicago backup safety Shaun Gayle scooped it and ran in for an easy touchdown—the only score of the first half. It was the price of the Giants needing to play a playoff game in the Windy City rather than at home. The play officially went for a punt of minus 7 yards and a five-yard punt return for a score on a day where there were freezing conditions. The actual temperature was 14 degrees, but with winds of at least 15 miles per hour, it felt as if it was 13 degrees below zero. It was cold and blustery, to say the least, making it almost impossible to muster consistent offense against that Bears defense. The wind was such a factor that the botched punt was more inclement-weather-induced than individual failure. "The wind was blowing so hard that it affected the six-inch drop to his foot," linebacker Carl Banks insisted years later.

That punting debacle was more than enough to beat the Giants that day. Nobody was going to score against that '85 Bears defense, especially in those conditions. That great defense led by Hall of Famers Mike Singletary and Richard Dent was too much when handed a lead.

New York managed 181 yards of total offense on that January afternoon in Chicago. Phil Simms and Co. went a woeful 0-for-12 on third down. The better team had won, and it left a nasty taste in everyone's mouth. "With the lead up to that game, we're in our hotel in Chicago, and it's all about who's the better team, who's the better defense," Banks said. "And it's player for player. They're making these comparisons, and we knew it was going to be a fistfight. They were brash, they were confident, they were arrogant, and they were bullies. And so things didn't get off to a good start early on, and it just snowballed. But after that game was over with, nobody had to say a word. We knew our mission."

It wasn't to get revenge against the Bears or even to get past the divisional round of the playoffs. It was to fully commit the next season and...win the Super Bowl! The Giants were on a mission from that point forward, and it would take everyone and everything to make it happen. Star outside linebacker Lawrence Taylor went to rehab for substance abuse that offseason. He had a down '85 season (13 sacks) by his standards, and

Parcells later admitted he could see some slippage. Taylor came back in '86 and had the best season of his career, recording 20.5 sacks and winning the NFL MVP. There really weren't any great additions or subtractions to the '86 roster. Parcells had already cleared out some of the bad influences when he revamped the shape of the team prior to the 1984 season. Now it was about extracting every last bit of blood, sweat, and tears from what was at his disposal.

General manager George Young drafted defensive reinforcements in linebacker Pepper Johnson, defensive end Eric Dorsey, nose tackle Erik Howard, and cornerback Mark Collins. They would serve primarily as depth that season. The Giants really were counting on growth from their previous two drafts to take that next step in 1986. It was Banks, guard William Roberts, and linebacker Gary Reasons from the '84 draft. From the following year, it was tight end Mark Bavaro—known as Rambo because of his physicality and resemblance to Sylvester Stallone—who was about to become one of the league's best tight ends. "Well, quite frankly, our '86 draft was pretty good in terms of we had a first-round pick and four second-round picks," Parcells said. "And those players now from '85 were in their second year, and so we were expecting help from the younger players, and I think that kind of rounded us out depth-wise. We were pretty deep at almost every position."

Banks, Roberts, and Reasons were also coming into their own from the '84 draft. It was all starting to add up. The Giants had a renewed commitment level that began in the offseason. There was a general focus on playing and winning as a team. It just felt different to those in the building. They were no longer a team on the rise, an organization that was building. They were a group that was willing to do whatever necessary to get to the top of the mountain even if it involved more time, more focus, more energy.

This was a different time in professional football, where players weren't making millions and didn't live in exclusive tax brackets. Defensive lineman Leonard Marshall may have been a second-team All-Pro in 1985, but he still had an offseason job to supplement his income after that season. Marshall was working at the Meadowlands Racetrack in the marketing department prior to the '86 campaign.

He still remembers calling strength and conditioning coach Johnny Parker to set up a schedule. Marshall came to the stadium every morning that offseason before work. He would work his job at the racetrack in the afternoons from 1:00 PM to 9:00 PM. He would go home, sleep, wake up early the next morning, and head into the Giants facility to train. Marshall would bring his work clothes with him to the complex. He would shower there and head over to the track.

"I put a lot into it from '84 to probably '88. And once I figured everything out, I said, 'Okay, I think I can give up this second job and focus on school and focus on my career,'" Marshall said. "And everything turned out the way I wanted it to turn out. [It] made me a better person, made me a better father, a better parent, a better player, a better everything."

Marshall wasn't the only one putting everything into 1986. Carson remembers not being able to sleep at the Woodcliff Lake Hilton in anticipation of playoff games that season. Before playing the 49ers in the NFC divisional round and Washington in the NFC Championship Game, he went home around 1:30 AM to watch more film. It was never enough for the '86 Giants.

The day before the matchup with Washington at Giants Stadium, Simms was talking in the training room about also not being able to sleep. He had a similar story to Carson. That is what it meant to this crew after the loss to the Bears the previous year. They went through those games—both resounding victories over difficult rivals—on adrenaline alone. That is how determined they were to win it all, no matter what it took. "The most important thing that sticks out as far as I'm concerned is the way that everybody within the organization checked their egos at the door, and it was really a joint effort by everybody," Carson said. "It stemmed from getting so close the year prior when we played Chicago, and we thought that we could beat the Bears even in Soldier Field, and the bitter taste of losing that game played into it, and everybody came back with a different mind-set and didn't care who got credit for what as long as the job got done. And of all the years that I've played organized football, that was really the first time that I'd been a part of a group that was so committed to winning."

It took a while for the Giants to get to this point. The genesis can be traced back to the end of 1978 when John McVay was fired as coach, and Andy Robustelli stepped down as general manager. Fifty-eight days later—with an assist from NFL commissioner Pete Rozelle—Young was hired. It was a compromise pushed by the league because of a feud between Wellington Mara and his nephew, Tim Mara, who were running the team at the time.

A lot happened in those 58 days. Wellington Mara concentrated on getting the right head coach while Tim Mara wanted a general manager first. Wellington talked to John Madden, who had just stepped down as coach of the Oakland Raiders about some kind of role. It didn't work out. He contemplated bringing in then Penn State coach Joe Paterno. Getting Paterno to leave Happy Valley wasn't going to happen. Dan Reeves, the same coach the Giants would hire 14 years later who at the time was an assistant with the rival Dallas Cowboys, also flew in secretly to meet with Wellington. Perhaps it was a tad bit early for that one. Reeves would get hired by the Denver Broncos two years later and would ultimately be the final challenge for the Giants to win their first Super Bowl in 1986. Meanwhile, Tim publicly stated they should hire George Allen to be the coach if only to irritate his uncle who wasn't a fan of the former Redskins leader's tactics. "Well wants a winner, but he wants it his way," Tim said of his uncle's public objection to Allen. "His way has been holding us back for 15 years."

While the search for a coach was unfolding behind the scenes, the two sides were also trying to agree on a general manager. And trying to get them to agree on anything at the time was a challenge. Both sides of the Mara family kept submitting names. None of them matched. If Wellington made a submission, it was rebuffed in part because it came from him. And vice versa.

It wasn't until recommendations from the legendary Frank Gifford and Tom Scott, a player for the Giants in the '60s who was friendly with Wellington, that they made significant progress. Gifford and Scott are the ones who started the momentum flowing in the right direction when they endorsed George Bernard Young to be the general manager of the New York Football Giants.

Wellington did some research on Young. He saw the background—a former player, coach, and the right-hand man to Don Shula at the time with the Miami Dolphins. That alone was enough to pique his interest. But Wellington knew that if he submitted Young's name, the other side would reject it because it was *his* suggestion. That is where the relationship between the two sides stood. It was frosty. So he went to Rozelle. "Why don't you recommend George Young?" Wellington suggested.

Rozelle did. Tim was also close with Gifford and valued his positive opinion on Young. At that point the ball was rolling, and it eventually worked out to be the compromise. Young would take over the roster of the fledgling franchise on February 14, 1979. Young was a massive man (around 370 pounds at the time he was hired) with an outsized personality to match. Among his perverse hobbies was battling with the media. He loved it. But Young made the Giants a much more professional organization in terms of scouting, pro personnel, even trainers and equipment. "We became a much more credible organization with him," said John Mara, who was 24 years old and working as a lawyer at the time of Young's hiring.

Young immediately went to work on the roster. His first ever draft pick was Simms, a quarterback from Morehead State. Taylor was the team's top pick in 1981. Parcells was hired as the head coach in 1983. Marshall and running back Joe Morris were second-round picks in consecutive years. And then there was that critical draft in '84 with Banks and Roberts as first-round picks, quarterback Jeff Hostetler as a third-round pick, Reasons in the fourth, and Lionel Manuel in the seventh that really set the stage to get over the top in '86. It certainly didn't happen overnight. It was a gradual build for the Giants to get to the point where they could compete with the San Franciscos and Chicagos of the world. "It wasn't just bang all of a sudden," conceded Parcells, whose job was in jeopardy after his first year as head coach in 1983.

Young and Parcells were hardly best buds, but they eventually built a dominant defense that featured Martin, Carson, and the secret weapon, Taylor. New York finished fifth in scoring defense during the 1985 season. The offense and special teams weren't half bad either. The Giants had Simms at quarterback playing at a Pro Bowl level by this time, and Morris emerged during the '85 season to give him the kind of running game he never quite had before. They were becoming a well-rounded and capable offense.

With all this at their disposal, the sole focus became getting to the Super Bowl in the 1986 season. It wasn't going to be easy. They would need to beat the dominant teams of that era—the 49ers, Bears, and Redskins—in order to accomplish their goal. Those were great teams loaded with talent from top to bottom in the pre-salary cap era that had legendary coaches with a winning pedigree. Parcells and the Giants wanted all of that, and they knew it would take becoming champions to get that type of recognition and praise.

The group Young gave him was singularly focused that year on making it happen. Just making the playoffs as they had done in 1984 for the second time in 21 years wouldn't be enough. They lost that year to the 49ers, the eventual Super Bowl winner. Winning a playoff game for the second straight season like they did in 1985 wouldn't be satisfying either. It didn't matter that the '85 Bears also won the Super Bowl. That didn't make anyone with the Giants feel better. New York felt it was its turn in 1986. The Giants had the Super Bowl in their sights the moment they were dominated and embarrassed in Chicago to end the previous season. "Coming out of those games, we felt like we could compete with them, and we just needed to turn it up a little bit ourselves and kind of make a little greater commitment," Parcells said. "And that's kind of what I think was the beginning of the '86 run. We were kind of not going to be satisfied with just getting in the playoffs. We had done that. We were looking for bigger fish."

The biggest catch for the coach affectionately nicknamed the Tuna would be the Lombardi Trophy that now sits prominently displayed in the foyer at 1925 Giants Drive in a stacked trophy case. That is because 1986 would be *their* year. It may seem hokey, but it was bigger than just the people in the Giants building. There was a sense of desire to do it for a bigger cause, especially from ownership. Giants fans had been through a lot. They were intensely loyal and vociferous despite a 17-season stretch of misery from 1964 to 1980. New York failed to make the playoffs during that time. It finished in last place in its division nine times, and the fans hadn't seen a championship since 1956. Martin made it a point to consistently remind the young players, who had just joined the team, that it wasn't that long ago that fans were sitting in the stands with bags over their heads. They owed it to them to do better.

Martin and Carson were there for the end of that extended rough stretch. They helped the Giants dig out of the New Jersey dumps. They passed along the responsibility that winning was for a cause bigger than just the players or coaches. "My bridge to Giants history was George Martin and Harry Carson," Banks said. "And they, above all other things, talked about the fans, what the fans deserve."

It takes Banks back to a moment from his rookie season in 1984. The Giants were playing poorly one afternoon, and the fans were giving it to them. Banks was on the bench sitting next to Martin, and Carson was flanked on the other side. The boos continued. "Listen. You hear them? We deserve it," Martin said. "We're not playing worth a damn! They deserve better than this."

Carson, who had been with the team since 1976, and Martin, who had been there since 1975, were the conduits to that previous era. They had been there for the bad years as the franchise wandered through the wilderness of weekly defeats. It was sad. It was dire. It understandably left the fan base hopeless and ownership irate. This was once a proud, winning franchise.

They didn't resemble that same organization during this stretch. Martin and Carson knew what it meant to the fans and owner Wellington Mara. He wanted to win in the worst of ways and was preoccupied with providing a quality product that would make the fans proud.

Even if Wellington couldn't get out of his own way, his players truly felt that. It was among the reasons the Giants never in their history had cheerleaders. Tim Mara passed along to his son Wellington that he wanted the focus to be the product on the field. That was the most important things for the fans to come and see. The product on the field wasn't good for more than a decade, but it was about to be the best it had been in years for the fans during the 1986 season.

2

Big Blue Wrecking Crew

THE '86 GIANTS WERE BUILT AROUND THEIR DEFENSE, dubbed the Big Blue Wrecking Crew. It would ultimately carry them to a place they had never been before. They were dominant up front with George Martin and Leonard Marshall as the defensive ends and Jim Burt at nose tackle. Lawrence Taylor and Carl Banks were the outside linebackers in their 3-4 defense with Harry Carson and Gary Reasons the inside 'backers. There were no weaknesses with that group. They weren't too shabby on the back end either with Elvis Patterson or Mark Collins and Perry Williams at cornerback. Kenny Hill and Terry Kinard were the safeties. It was a group that finished second in total defense and only allowed 14.8 points per game.

They were coached by Bill Parcells and his defensive coordinator, Bill Belichick. Two legendary coaches. Perhaps the greatest coach of all time, Belichick was 34 years old at the time, a geeky football savant. Despite being perceived as a lacrosse guy, he earned the respect of his players because of his intense work ethic and smart schemes. He had the answer to any question they could ask about a specific defense.

The '86 Giants under Belichick relied on the front seven. He let them work. They primarily played zone defense on the back end. They were also disciplined to the point that they knew everything about every coverage—even its biggest weaknesses and what could be exploited. Belichick made sure to point that out every week. You could not run the ball against this Giants front in 1986. The right side with Marshall and Taylor backed generally by Carson was basically impenetrable. It's no wonder they finished first in the NFL, allowing only 80.3 rushing yards per game.

Marshall was the final addition to that right side of the defense when he was drafted in the second round of the 1983 draft. Disappointed he wasn't selected higher despite being a dominant player at LSU, Marshall was motivated. He felt there was something to prove. When Parcells asked where he wanted to be situated in the Giants locker room, Marshall pointed toward the area where Taylor and Carson were seated. He wanted to see what those guys did or didn't do to be successful; that way he could try to replicate it. "Eventually that became a three-legged stool of our locker room because it became a three-legged stool of our defense," Marshall said. "You couldn't run the football at the right side of our defense. You couldn't challenge the right side of our defense. And if you didn't plan for us, we're going to make you pay for running, especially on that side of the defense. I felt like the three of us became a driving force behind the success or failure of our football team every weekend. If we played well, the team [followed]. If we didn't play well, the team didn't go well. So I took a lot of pride in that."

Marshall became a two-time Pro Bowl selection and two-time All-Pro. His greatness almost gets overlooked because of playing in such a great defense and with Taylor overshadowing them all. Marshall had a remarkable 15.5 sacks from the defensive end spot in 1985. He followed that up with 12 in '86. It was the beginning of a seven-year stretch where he averaged 10 sacks per year.

Marshall and the rest of the defense took pride in sucking the will out of their opponents on a weekly basis. It was something they talked about on the sideline and in meeting rooms. Each player they forced to quit was a notch on the belt. It was sort of a competition. Get recognition by dominating your opponent to the point where you sucked out their will until they had thrown in the towel. "Our big thing is by the third quarter of every game, every game, we wanted to know who quit, whose player quit on the other team," Banks said. "And we would be on the sideline and we'd come off after a series. Leonard might say, 'My guy just quit!' or Jim Burt, 'He just quit. My guy just quit!' And that was our thing. If he didn't, it was going to be a fight. It was just going to be a battle. But our goal every single game is to count how many players quit. We were just pounding, pounding, pounding. And so that mind-set we carried throughout the season."

This was the best defense of the Parcells era, and it traced back to the Chicago Bears game the previous season. That '85 Bears defense is considered one of the best (if not the best) of all time. The Giants were good, but they were not quite at that level. The way the 1985 divisional round loss to the Bears played out, it showed the Giants that they could get to another level. They did it the follow season. "We were determined to go there and beyond," Banks said.

It, however, didn't start out all the promising for the '86 Giants defense. They allowed 31 points in the season opener on Monday night to the Dallas Cowboys. They allowed a shade under 400 total yards to quarterback Danny White and Co. It was not what this group expected. It was not what Taylor expected. After an offseason where he spent time in rehab, he wasn't football-ready for the first game. He wasn't his normal dominant self—even if he had 1.5 sacks in the contest. The game-winning run came when Cowboys running back Herschel Walker waltzed passed a winded Taylor late in the fourth quarter. "I was tired," Taylor said. "It wasn't pretty."

In retrospect it was exactly what Parcells and the Giants needed. Only one team topped 20 points against their defense the rest of the season, and that was in a blowout win—55–24 over the Green Bay Packers—in Week 16. "We were a little bit full of ourselves coming out of preseason," Parcells said, "and they used the term wake-up call. That was a wake up."

The Giants had five interceptions and forced seven total turnovers the following week against Dan Fouts and the San Diego Chargers in Week Two. They had six interceptions of Washington Redskins quarterback Jay Schroeder later in the season.

Taylor went on to have what many consider the best defensive season in NFL history. He finished with 20.5 sacks, 105 tackles, five passes defended, and two forced fumbles. He was so dominant it earned him the league MVP. This was Taylor at his very best. "Lawrence was in his maturing stage as a player," Parcells said. "He wasn't a rookie anymore. He'd been in the league five years. He was one of the top guys in the league, and with his ability, that's what he should be doing and that's what he did."

Those are undoubtedly lofty expectations. Not everyone can do that. Even Taylor couldn't do what he did in 1986 every year. Defensive players aren't supposed to win the NFL MVP award. Taylor was the first defensive player since Minnesota Vikings defensive tackle Alan Page in 1971 to do so. Nobody has done it since Taylor in 1986. "I mean, we knew what Lawrence could do, and we were able to play off of him or have him play off of us," Carson said. "And if we wanted somebody to make a play, we all could make plays. Lawrence did more than his share of improvising and sort of doing his own thing and, if something did not go exactly as he had planned it, he either had me or George Martin or his teammates to back him up, Carl Banks, Gary Reasons, etc. He created situations for us to exploit and kind of threw the opposing team out of whack sometimes. The reality is, when we played in '86, teams knew that. And I hate to put it like this, but they were going to get their ass kicked."

3

L.T.

The fate of the New York Giants ultimately changed with one pick near the top of the 1981 NFL Draft. Only it wasn't the slam dunk you would think it should have been in retrospect. In fact, it came against the will of some of the team's top players, including the respected Harry Carson and George Martin. They were not alone either because the Giants needed a running back, and George Rogers was universally lauded as a prospect and was going to be one of the top picks. He was the Heisman Trophy winner out of the University of South Carolina.

The New Orleans Saints selected first that year. Off a 4–12 campaign with Ray Perkins as the coach, the Giants were picking second and loved a young man out of North Carolina named Lawrence Taylor. He was considered a little bit of a "goofball" as Chris Mara, a Giants scout at the time, said years later. More importantly, Taylor was a rare combination of speed, explosion, and intensity. A monster off the edge wearing No. 98 for the Tar Heels, it was as if he had the power of a bulldozer and the energy of the Energizer Bunny. "A blue chip, a No. 1 all the way," Giants director of player personnel Tom Boisture said.

The Saints would ultimately do the Giants a favor and take Rogers. He would become an All-Pro back as a rookie, but he wasn't Taylor. He lasted four years in New Orleans and had four 1,000-yard rushing seasons in his career.

But Taylor to the Giants still almost didn't happen. It was known that a top pick would command at least a three-year contract worth about $750,000. A salary of $1 million was rumored. That was a hefty number that didn't sit well with the Giants' veterans, many of whom were making less, even though they were significant players. They made their displeasure known publicly, and there was talk of a potential walkout. Taylor responded by sending a telegram to the Giants on the Monday before the draft telling them he would rather not be selected by them. General manager George Young, however, was in love with Taylor's ability. Later that night Taylor got calls from some players and coaches. They made him feel wanted and told him it was nothing personal. It greased the skids for Taylor to come to New York. "They said there was nothing to the story, and there would be no walkout," Taylor said. "They said they wanted me here. That made me feel better."

Taylor became the No. 2 overall pick in the 1981 NFL Draft by the Giants, and that selection changed the franchise forever. "I remember going into that year and I remember how desperately we needed a running back and I was kind of hoping for George Rogers. I had heard of George Rogers. I had seen him play," said John Mara, a young lawyer at the time. "He gets drafted ahead of us by New Orleans, and we take Lawrence Taylor and, okay, great. Little did I realize he'd become the greatest player in the history of the franchise. And that was pretty evident from very early on, from the first few practices, that he just stood out. So relentless and such a combination of power and speed unlike anything I had ever seen."

The rookie linebacker signed a six-year, $1.35 million contract. That came out to $225,000 per season, which made him the highest-paid Giant. It wouldn't ultimately matter. Taylor's teammates immediately came to realize what they were dealing with. This was a special player and character, one that would help take them to levels they had only dreamed about. It didn't take long either. Perkins was a big believer in making rookies earn their spot. Except Taylor was different. John Skorupan, a linebacker who played eight seasons in the NFL with the Buffalo Bills and the Giants after starring at Penn State, had a fair read on the situation. He became the backup, and Taylor was the first-team right linebacker at his very first practice. There was no reason to waste anybody's time.

But Taylor was joining a bad team, one that hadn't won in decades. The Giants had just endured eight straight losing seasons and hadn't made the playoffs since 1963. They hadn't even won a division title, nevertheless sniffed a Super Bowl. Taylor didn't know what he was stepping into in New York. He was an energetic and brutally honest young man from Williamsburg, Virginia, who had just spent the past four years in Chapel Hill, North Carolina. He didn't know much about the New York Football Giants or the Big Apple, the pressures that came with the job, and the temptations he was about to encounter. "Absolutely nothing," Taylor said. "My team was the Washington Redskins or Dallas Cowboys. When I first came to the Giants, I'm like, 'Who the hell is that?' We made up for that."

It didn't take long for Taylor to become the legendary L.T. He was Lawrence the person, L.T. the player/character.

Lawrence was a relatively naïve young man learning the benefits of living in the New York metropolitan area; L.T. was an All Pro, NFL Defensive Rookie of the Year, and NFL Defensive Player of the Year as a rookie. The Giants made the playoffs that season for the first time in 18 years in large part because of the boost this rookie, who fell into their lap thanks to the Saints taking Rogers. That is the kind of instant impact that Taylor had. He could rush the passer, cover receivers, stop the run. He did it all right from the jump when he had an estimated 9.5 sacks (it wasn't an official stat until 1982) and an interception in 1981.

His linebacker coach that year was Bill Parcells. That would come into play later on down the line when Parcells became head coach. He already had the respect of several of his top players, including Carson and Taylor. That room that Parcells coached in 1981 would ultimately label themselves the "Crunch Bunch." It was Carson, Brad Van Pelt, Brian Kelley, and the final piece was Taylor. They were the mostly hard-partying, fast-playing strength of the team from 1981 to 1983, which is memorialized by the famous "Crunch Bunch" poster. It featured the four of them on a John Deere bulldozer in their blue Giants jerseys, white football pants, and blue construction helmets with their respective numbers emblazed on them. That poster still lives on today, making appearances whenever they do autograph signings. It reads "The Crunch Bunch: Board of De Wreckers."

With the addition of Taylor, the Giants not only made the playoffs during that 1981 season, but they also won a playoff game. He wasn't the sole reason, but his presence certainly made a difference. The playoff win came against the Giants' division rival, the Philadelphia Eagles, and Taylor had four tackles and a sack while they limited Ron Jaworski and Co. to just 226 total yards in a 27–21 victory at Veterans Stadium. It was a big deal, especially considering the Giants hadn't beaten the

Eagles since 1975 prior to that season. They beat them twice in 1981, including in the playoffs.

It was a statement. They were no longer the bumbling, fumbling Joe Pisarcik Giants. They were now Lawrence Taylor's Giants, and they were winning playoff games. It was the start of something big, and Taylor was a massive driving force even if there would be some setbacks for team and player. They stumbled through the 1982 strike year. Perkins was eventually replaced by Parcells, and the Giants went 3–12–1 in his first year as coach. Taylor was excelling on the field but slipping off it. He admitted in his autobiography to using drugs as early as his second year in the league. He went to rehab in the offseason before the 1986 season. He tested positive when they began drug testing in 1987 (receiving a warning) and was suspended in 1988 after another positive test. In between all that, he was the MVP of the entire league in 1986 when he had 20.5 sacks, 105 total tackles, five passes defensed, and two forced fumbles. That monster year helped him become the first defensive player to win MVP since 1971.

Taylor brought a ferocity that stood out even amongst the toughest of players on one of the toughest of defenses. He once played through a torn pectoral muscle against the New Orleans Saints in 1988. All he did that day was have seven tackles, three sacks, and two forced fumbles while wearing a harness. He later came back from a ruptured Achilles in 1992 in L.T. fashion to play all 16 games in his final professional season.

The way that Taylor chopped at the ball to dislodge it from the quarterback was game-changing. It was ferocious. He wasn't just out to get sacks; he was out to get the ball. Taylor forced 33 career fumbles. That right-hand chop from his shoulder to his knee was reminiscent of Paul Bunyan swinging his axe. Only Taylor's arm was his weapon.

The greatness of Taylor wasn't just the supreme physical talent—he was a football savant. His understanding of the game and what needed to be done took him to a level that was never before seen. Banks recalled getting ready for a game against the Redskins in 1986. It was a Friday, and they were putting in the pass rush plan after lunch before they went out to practice. In typical Taylor fashion, he didn't show up until after lunch. When he finally did, the rest of the group was watching film. L.T. showed up with sunglasses on and crawled under the table. "He's fucking asleep!" Banks said years later with a chuckle.

The meeting had been going on for 30 minutes already. Defensive line coach Lamar Leachman was drawing up plays and trying to figure out how they were going to rush the Redskins. He was going through all these scenarios and breaking it all down through the film. It was not making much sense to the guys in the room. Leachman was generally really good with the gameplan. But he was frustrated this wasn't going so smoothly. Reaching his boiling point, Leachman cut the lights and stood over Taylor. "God damn it! You would think you'd want to be awake for this part of the meeting," Leachman said.

Taylor sat up and took off his glasses. "What the fuck are you talking about?" he retorted.

Taylor demanded they run the film. It rolled for one play and didn't rewind at all. Taylor stopped the film, got up, grabbed the chalk, and drew everything up as needed on the board. "'Here's what we're going to do here. Here's what we're going to do here,'" Banks recalled Taylor saying. "The defensive line coach is like this [jaw dropped]. Everybody is. He nails it because he's like, 'Joe Jacoby's going to do this, Mark Schlereth is going to do this, and if he does this, we're going to run these three stunts.'"

It was an incredible display of football acumen outsiders wouldn't expect from him. Leachman was amazed too in this instance. "God damn it, boy, you pretty smart," he said.

Taylor smiled. "Can I go back to sleep now?" he asked.

This was the sneaky genius of Taylor. For all the talent, all the bluster, all the off-the-field shenanigans that came with him, this was what put him over the top. And Taylor would do this type of stuff regularly.

Most importantly, Parcells and defensive coordinator Bill Belichick were amenable to Taylor's approach. As long as he produced and played at a level nobody had ever seen, they seemed fine with it all. "It was easy to coach him. It really was," Parcells said. "I have always said it, 'You just had to show him where the competition was.' If you could point out a player or a thing or a team or just something that he could relate to, 'Hey, I hope you're watching this tight end this week on the film. I hope you're watching him close because if you're not ready for this, this guy's going to give you a lot of trouble.' Little statements like that. 'This team, they're going to double team you on the pass rush, and you just can't get discouraged. You just got to keep forcing them to maximize their attention, and if you do that, that's going to help us win.' And that kind of thing. So that was easy with him. It really was."

The way Belichick looked at it, Taylor never actually freelanced. When he did something that wasn't planned during the game, it just became part of the playbook. It became the gameplan. No wonder Belichick, who went on to win six Super Bowls as the head coach of the New England Patriots, rejects the premise that anybody even be compared to Taylor. "Wait a minute," Belichick said. "We're talking about Lawrence Taylor now. I'm not putting anyone in Lawrence Taylor's class."

4

Gatorade Bath

THE 1986 SEASON DIDN'T START OFF MAGICAL. THE GIANTS allowed 31 points in a season-opening loss to the Dallas Cowboys on a Monday night, an evening where quarterback Danny White and running back Herschel Walker amassed almost 400 total yards against them. Walker ran for a pair of touchdowns, and the Giants defense was hearing it from coach Bill Parcells. He knew his unit wasn't ready all summer long. "I told you guys, 'This was coming,'" Parcells said. "But you didn't want to listen. Maybe you guys think you're the defending champions of the world. Well, go look it up. You're not. If you don't get your asses in gear, and I mean right now, it's going to be a very long year around this team."

The following week the Giants were hosting the San Diego Chargers. That was still a high-octane Chargers offense quarterbacked by Dan Fouts. San Diego may have been past its heyday, but it had dropped 50 points on the Miami Dolphins in Week One and was a capable offense, to say the least.

All week long Parcells rode the Giants defense hard. This was a massive game for the Giants. They couldn't go 0–2. They had the Los Angeles Raiders the following week and had to be careful not to end up in an early hole. So Parcells was relentless, reminding his defense over and over about what happened in Dallas, about what happened when it cruised through the summer and didn't prepare themselves properly for the opener. It made the Chargers game in Week Two that much more important.

The tension only intensified when Harry Carson received a racist letter that week. The team leader understandably took it to heart. He went to the training room and read it to the team over the public-address system in Giants Stadium. "They said that we stink, and you have too many n-----s on the team," Carson said. "And they said that the White guys aren't any better than the n-----s."

It created a heavy feeling going into that matchup with the Chargers. The letter stuck with Carson. The loss from the previous week was on his conscience as well. Carson knew there weren't going to be many more chances for him to win a Super Bowl after the '86 season and he couldn't squander this season. He couldn't let it slip away early. After the defense painted a masterpiece with five interceptions in a 20–7 win against San Diego, Carson felt an extra sense of joy. At that point a spontaneous decision was made to accentuate the celebration. He decided to let out his remaining frustration. He got the Gatorade bucket and dumped it on Parcells.

It was a joke or gag to release the tension and get back at the coach who had spent the week reminding the defense of how bad they had been against the Cowboys. Not that they didn't agree. They did. But Carson needed to wait for the right moment. He judiciously waited for Parcells to take off his headset, snuck up behind him, and dumped the contents of the bucket on his head coach. "And so it became basically a symbol of the '86 season," Carson said. "And that was it."

At that point there was no way Carson could stop either. Parcells was Mr. Superstitious. If you did something one week and it worked, he demanded you kept on doing it. That was the case with the Gatorade bath. It continued throughout the season and into the Super Bowl. There would be a confetti version at the Super Bowl celebration in freezing temperatures at Giants Stadium, and there would be a knockoff popcorn dump on President Ronald Reagan during their visit to the White House. This was the Giants shtick that season.

The Gatorade dump became the 1986 Giants' thing—even if it had been done before. It traces back to two years earlier when defensive lineman Jim Burt was believed to be the originator, and Carson was his accomplice. It's a similar story—only the previous time Parcells was riding Burt hard, not the entire defense. The Giants were entering a game against the Washington Redskins, a team that had owned them at that point. Parcells needed to get the most out of Burt and his entire defense. He did what he did best—pushing buttons in the most crude way imaginable. Washington was a tough team under Joe Gibbs (perhaps Parcells' biggest rival) and had been to the Super Bowl the previous two seasons. The Redskins were essentially a lock to win double-digit games every season during that time.

But the Giants had been closing the gap. They knew this was going to be a difficult game, having lost six straight to Washington heading into that Week Nine matchup in 1984. Parcells had fixated on Burt as his target of the week. He did it in front of the entire team. “That Jeff Bostic, he’s going to kick your ass, and everybody’s going to be laughing at you,” Parcells said to Burt, according to Carson. “If you don’t play well, you’re going to be embarrassed.”

Burt took it personally. He wasn’t going to let Parcells pick on him. This was his opportunity to fight back—on the field and off it afterward. So it was actually Burt who came up with the idea of the original Gatorade bath. He just needed the support of Carson, the kind of respected veteran who could help pull off such a vindictive move. Burt recruited the team captain to make sure the gag went off properly. If Carson participated, it gave the act some legitimacy.

Burt, who had four tackles and two assists from his nose tackle position, went first after the 37–13 victory against Washington. Carson came over the top with a second dumping seconds later. Parcells took it like a champ and with a sly smile. The way Burt viewed it, he was making a statement. “You have to rise to the occasion with [Parcells] because if you don’t rise to the occasion with him, he’ll bully you,” Burt would say years later in an interview with Giants broadcaster Bob Papa.

For Burt, it was personal. For Carson, it was fun and games. Burt had made his point—don’t mess with me, and if you do, expect to get it back in some way, shape, or form. Parcells was all right with that. He knew if he dished it that he had to be able to take it. This was how he operated. In a way, he almost respected it more if you were willing to fight back. If you were going to just lay down and die, you probably weren’t long for the Giants.

At that point, the Gatorade dumping was a one-off. It wasn’t until two years later in 1986 when Carson took the stunt to the next level. He did it out of jubilation after the win against the Chargers, and it took on a life of its own from there. It became a thing after every Giants win that season. Fans and players were basically waiting to see what Carson and Co. were going to come up with next. "I wasn't thinking down the line. I wasn't thinking the next game. I was just thinking about that game and throwing Gatorade on the coach," Carson said. "And so I got him, and that was it. And then the next week we won, and I'm shrewd enough to understand that if it happens one week, you got to keep doing it. So then I started doing it after each win, and that's kind of how it went down. Parcells never said anything about doing it. He left it to me. I was a captain, and he knew me on a different level. I mean, it wasn't like I was trying to do this or that with him. We were just having fun. And as a captain, I had my ways of doing stuff that might be different."

In fact, Parcells understood. He was hard on his defense heading into that Week Two game with the Chargers. He wasn't happy with the way they were whipped by the Cowboys on national television in the opener. Perhaps it was, in a way, at least a little bit deserved. "That was probably a little retribution on the part of the players based on what my attitude had been after that loss to Dallas," Parcells admitted.

Once the Gatorade baths started that season and the Giants started rolling, there was no way it could stop. San Diego was the first of five straight wins. In fact, the Giants would lose just once more that season (Week Seven at the Seattle Seahawks' noisy Kingdome) on their way to the first Super Bowl in franchise history. There were 17 wins that season...and a lot of Gatorade baths. "Well, I'm superstitious," Parcells said. "Some of the players are superstitious, too."

It reached new levels in the postseason. Carson, hiding behind a tan overcoat and hat from the team doctor, got Parcells after their divisional massacre of the San Francisco 49ers. Defensive coordinator Bill Belichick got his own mini dumping after that 49–3 win against the 49ers, too. Carson then got Parcells in the howling winds and freezing cold when they beat the Redskins in the NFC Championship Game. Parcells unsuccessfully fought that one, dancing a two-step trying to avoid the cold yellow bath. It was still all with a smile as the Giants were headed to their first ever Super Bowl.

The Super Bowl dump was perhaps the most iconic of them all given the enormity of the game and the optics. The legendary John Madden, working at the time as a CBS analyst, used the telestrator on the Gatorade buckets. He labeled one as the father, the mother, and the third smaller one as their offspring. Then there was Carson wearing a yellow Rose Bowl security jacket, sneaking up behind Parcells, and dumping the orange Gatorade on his head. Madden was having fun breaking it all down. "Well, there are two kinds. There is plain water and the sticky stuff," Madden said. "When it has color in it, it's still sticky. And I'll tell you, Bill Parcells loves this one."

Carson doubled back and dumped a bucket of water on his coach as Madden was still breaking down the first bath. "A Super Bowl is worth a double bucket," Madden added. "It really is."

The players loved it, the coach soaked it all in, and it became a sensation that still exists to this day. The 1986 Giants accomplished a lot that season, including popularizing the Gatorade dump. Gatorade couldn't have asked for any more free publicity. It was so good that its head of marketing, Bill Schmidt, later said he sent Carson and Parcells $1,000 gift cards to Brooks Brothers. Parcells later got a three-year, $120,000 deal from the company, and Carson got $20,000 to be included on a poster.

To this day, Parcells, Carson, and the Giants are associated with the invention of the Gatorade bath. It's a tradition for the Super Bowl–winning head coach to get doused on the sideline as the clock ticks toward zero. Even more so, it's commonplace in sports at all levels. Burt was the actual innovator, Carson took it and ran with his idea, and Parcells was the willing subject. The 1986 Giants popularized something that has serious longevity. "It's something that's always done in fun, and I'm happy that it's something that anybody could do," Carson said. "I like seeing guys who are playing, or girls who are playing a sport, enjoy what they're doing and celebrating."

5

Super Season

THE GIANTS WENT 14–2 DURING THE 1986 REGULAR SEASON, their best record ever in the modern era. But it still wouldn't have been a successful season had they won a playoff game or two and lost to one of the other NFC powerhouses in the divisional round or championship game without reaching the Super Bowl. This particular Giants season was about one thing and one thing only—winning the Super Bowl.

After a first-round bye, the Giants had to face the San Francisco 49ers in the divisional round of the playoffs. The same 49ers team, which had eliminated them in the postseason of the '81 and '84 seasons, had to come to Giants Stadium this time. That made it infinitely more difficult for them to face the Lawrence Taylor–led defense in the winds of the Meadowlands. Even though they weren't in the same division and 3,000 miles away, the 49ers were becoming a rival of the Giants. In fact, they were considered the Giants' Achilles' heel heading into the '86 playoffs, according to nose tackle Jim Burt, who would create the lasting image from this matchup and then ironically switch sides in the rivalry later on in his career.

San Francisco, which had lost a hard-fought 21–17 game to the Giants in Week 13 of that season at Candlestick Park, didn't know what they were in for on that Sunday afternoon in New Jersey. In fact, nobody saw what was coming after that tightly-contested Monday night contest several weeks earlier. It was a demolition of epic proportions that began with a rare drop from second-year 49ers wide receiver Jerry Rice that likely would've been a touchdown. The Giants defense, which drove the march through the regular season and carried it into the postseason, took over from there.

They knocked out All-Pro 49ers quarterback Joe Montana on a famous hit from Burt that exemplified New York's dominance in the contest. He nailed Montana, who had returned from back surgery earlier that season, so hard as he was releasing the ball that he flew into the air. Burt had hit the quarterback under his throwing arm, almost in his armpit, and sent him flying. Montana landed on the ground headfirst and was out with a concussion. (He did not return, and Jeff Kemp finished the game at quarterback.) Meanwhile, that Montana pass fluttered in the air and out to the flat. It was intercepted by Taylor, who returned it 34 yards for the touchdown and a 28–3 Giants lead before halftime. It was his first interception returned for a touchdown since his famous Thanksgiving interception in 1982 against the Detroit Lions.

At that point, it was over, but it would only get worse for the 49ers. The final tally was 49–3. "We were shattered by a great team," legendary 49ers coach Bill Walsh said after the game.

The Giants had played almost a perfect game to reach the NFC Championship Game. Four of quarterback Phil Simms' nine completions went for touchdowns. Running back Joe Morris ran for 159 yards and two touchdowns. "We scored 49 on them," Burt said. "And I wish we would've scored 89 on them." That is how the Giants felt at the time about the 49ers.

Bill Parcells and Co. had slayed their first dragon, but they knew there was still work to be done. They would have to get past the Washington Redskins on a blustery afternoon in East Rutherford, New Jersey, in order to reach the first Super Bowl in franchise history. The weather was similar to what the Giants encountered the previous year in Chicago—cold and windy to the point that it was going to be difficult to throw the football against the wind even if it was John Elway or Dan Marino out there. Instead Washington had Jay Schroeder, the same quarterback who was picked off six times by the Big Blue Wrecking Crew earlier that season. He stood no chance. Instead of the Giants being on the road like they were in Chicago the previous year, this time they were the home team with the dominant defense in an environment where newspapers and garbage were visibly whipping through the air because of the crazy winds. It was almost as if confetti was being dragged in circles inside Giants Stadium throughout the game.

While it affected the Redskins, the Giants seemed oblivious to the conditions. It was obvious Washington was in big trouble when the previous year's goat, punter Sean Landeta, atoned for his past miscue. He quickly became the hero in the NFC Championship Game one year later. Landeta was cutting the ball through the high winds as if it was nothing while the Redskins were unable to adjust. The Giants jumped out to the early lead, and Washington had little chance of scoring in those conditions against the Big Blue Wrecking Crew. "The elements were so prohibitive that day, and they were just a little more prohibitive for them than they were for us," Parcells said. "And our defense was just a little stronger than their offense. I kind of felt at the halftime they were going to have a hard time beating us...It would've been difficult for any team in any situation to come back with those elements."

That 17–0 shutout on January 11, 1987, is considered—along with the NFC Championship Game blowout victory against the Minnesota Vikings in 2001—among the greatest games in Giants Stadium history. This afternoon was a celebration only to be topped by what would be seen in the coming weeks when the Giants brought home the Lombardi Trophy.

Their Super Bowl XXI opponent would be the Denver Broncos, a team the Giants had played (and beaten) in the regular season 19–16 in Week 12 at Giants Stadium. That gave them confidence. "I felt like we had better personnel," Parcells said. "If we just played a good solid game, we'd win."

But the same coach that Wellington Mara met with secretly eight years earlier and almost hired, Dan Reeves, brought a complex offense with a star quarterback to the table. This time they had to face Elway in a neutral site and with no crazy prohibitive wind. The Broncos would not make things easy for Parcells and Co.

The Giants were happy they had made it to the Super Bowl, but it was clear they had more business to take care of at the Rose Bowl in Pasadena, California. They were adamant the season would not have been a success if they fell short at this point. They set the bar supremely high the moment the previous season ended in Chicago and made it clear anything less was a failure.

It was win the Super Bowl or bust for this group, especially for veterans such as Harry Carson and George Martin. "I kept saying, 'It's just another game. It's just another game.' And it wasn't until the morning of the Super Bowl that Sunday I allowed myself to go there. And when I woke up, I said to myself, *This is the biggest game of my life*," Carson said. "Now, if I had said that to myself prior to that Sunday morning, I don't know if I would've been able to function because there's a lot that's on your mind. I'm already playing the game in my mind because we had played Denver during the course of the season and so I'm thinking about the talent that they have. I'm thinking about John Elway. I'm thinking about who's going to be singing the national anthem. I'm thinking about military flyovers. I'm thinking about all of this stuff."

Professionally, everything was at stake for Carson. He was the heartbeat of the Giants and one of Parcells' all-time favorite players. He had been with the organization since being a fourth-round pick out of South Carolina State in 1976. Carson had been through the bad times. He had seen when there was no hope, and the fans were left distraught and helpless. He was there for the ups and downs at the quarterback position with Simms, the beginning of Parcells when he was his defensive coordinator and linebackers coach dating back to 1979, the hiring of George Young, the drafting of Taylor, and the building of what became this championship team.

Carson, who eventually was recognized for his greatness by being inducted into the Pro Football Hall of Fame in 2006, epitomized what it meant to be a Giant. He had done everything right every step of the way. Parcells wanted to win for Carson and Martin almost as badly as he did for himself. Martin, who had been with the Giants since 1975, recorded a safety when he tackled Elway in the end zone in the first half of Super Bowl XXI.

There was nothing that was going to stop the Giants at this point. They were a team on a mission, a team of destiny. That didn't stop entering the big game. Carl Banks, who had one of the best Super Bowls in history with 14 total tackles including four for a loss, could feel it before the game ever began. "I'm looking at the entire film, everything, and just things start to pop out, how they like to do things. And during the game, I don't think they ran a single play that I wasn't subconsciously prepared for," Banks said. "And I don't know, I might've made the first eight tackles of the game, but run or pass, it was just like I kind of felt how they wanted to play the game, and I just mentally prepared for it. I was in the zone. And so there was nothing they could do that was going to take me by surprise."

That was evident by the way the game started. Banks had three tackles on the opening drive, including a key third-down stop when he stuffed Sammy Winder at the line of scrimmage, forcing the Broncos to settle for a field goal. Early in the second quarter, he pummeled Winder behind the scrimmage on third down on a goal-line stand for a four-yard loss.

That goal-line stand epitomized these Giants. Taylor sprinted out with Elway on first down and tackled him for a one-yard loss. Carson, the steady team captain, met Broncos running back Gerald Willhite up the middle on second down. Banks then tracked down Winder on the left side for the loss on third down. It forced Denver, which had a 10–7 lead, to settle for a field goal. This time kicker Rich Karlis missed a 23-yard field goal. It changed the game. You couldn't provide these Giants with extra opportunities. They were too good.

The Broncos were giving the Giants trouble in the first half, just like they did in the regular-season matchup. But they held just a 10–9 lead at halftime. The Broncos allowed the Giants to stay in the game, which was a big mistake.

That is when Parcells gave what still has to be the shortest halftime speech in Super Bowl history. It was because there was no panic in these Giants. They were confident the job would get done. “We came in the locker room. Bill called everybody up, says, ‘You know what you got to do. Go get with your coaches,’” Banks recalled. “That was the halftime [speech]. That’s it. That was it. We went out and we just took control of the game, won it.”

That was all the Giants needed. Simms and the offense came out on fire in the second half. They drove 63 yards on nine plays, and Simms hit tight end Mark Bavaro for a 13-yard touchdown. It was all part of the most efficient performance in Super Bowl history. Simms went 22-of-25, passing for 268 yards with three touchdowns and no interceptions as the Giants exploded offensively in the second half when they scored on their first five possessions of what turned into a 39–20 rout.

Simms didn’t throw an incompletion in the second half on his way to the Super Bowl MVP. “I’m gonna go to Disney World,” Simms said to the camera as he walked toward the center of the field after the final whistle. He was the first MVP to get the Disney treatment, and it has become a tradition ever since. For Simms it was the ultimate full circle moment. Just four years earlier in Parcells’ first act as head coach, he benched Simms in favor of Scott Brunner. Then they reached the pinnacle with Simms the star of the biggest game of both their lives.

It ended with what has become a fun tradition: the Gatorade bath for the Super Bowl-winning head coach. Parcells was predictably drenched by Carson. So there was the gruff Giants coach, enjoying the greatest day of his professional life in the locker room with his gray Giants V-neck sweater with a white collared shirt underneath still dripping. It had a red stripe wrapped around his chest and back and “Giants” stitched in blue under his heart. The sweater had different shades of gray in multiple spots because of the Gatorade and water that Carson dumped.

Parcells didn't care. He gathered his team one last time in this magical season. "One thing, fellas: listen to me," Parcells said. "'I'll tell ya, the rest of your life, the rest of your life, men, nobody could ever tell you that you couldn't do it...because you did it!'"

For the first time in franchise history, the New York Football Giants were Super Bowl champions.

PART 2

1990

6

San Francisco Beast

Bill Parcells viewed the New York Giants' biggest rivals during the 1980s as the Washington Redskins and San Francisco 49ers. The Giants were constantly chasing those teams, and he was chasing their coaches—Joe Gibbs and Bill Walsh, respectively.

It didn't matter that the Niners weren't in the same division, the NFC East. It was simply that they were the standard for much of the decade with Joe Montana at quarterback throwing to Jerry Rice in their fancy, new, spread-'em-out West Coast Offense. With everything based off timing, it was a thing of beauty. Rice would turn around, and the ball would hit his hands without breaking stride. But San Francisco was more than that. It was a really good well-rounded team that looked almost unbeatable during the 1990 season. So did the Giants, who started that season 10–0.

Still, San Francisco was the heavy favorite. Every time the playoffs came around, it was the 49ers who seemed to stand in the Giants' way. They met in the postseason to cap the 1981, '84, '85, '86, and '90 seasons. San Francisco won the first two meetings; the Giants took the last three. And it was the final matchup that was the most memorable. "That was one of the great games I was ever involved in," Parcells said of the Giants' 15–13 triumph in the NFC Championship Game at Candlestick Park.

It's not possible to understand the enormity and intensity of that game on January 20, 1991, without understanding the full context of the situation. The 49ers were looking to three-peat. They had won the two previous Super Bowls and were attempting to become the first team ever to win three in a row. Only one thing stood in their way—the New York Football Giants, the same franchise that beat them 49–3 in their previous playoff meeting after the 1986 regular season.

The Giants and Niners were mighty familiar with each other. They met earlier during the 1990 regular season in a much-hyped *Monday Night Football* matchup that featured the two-time defending champs against the 10–1 Giants, who were actually undefeated before losing the previous week to the Philadelphia Eagles. It was a physical, intense game that the 49ers won 7–3, but it was afterward when the fireworks erupted that set the stage for what was to come later in the season.

It was there for the entire football world to see when Giants quarterback Phil Simms and San Francisco safety Ronnie Lott went face to face after the game, shouting insults. There was clearly no love lost between them and their respective teams. The story behind the spat is the stuff of legends. It stemmed from a contrived controversy courtesy of Jim Burt, the same nose tackle who once played for the Giants and knocked out

Montana in the '86 playoffs. But Burt was on the other side this time around. He had switched sides in the rivalry by this time, joining the 49ers in 1989 after Parcells tried to push him into retirement. That didn't go over well. To spice it up before playing his former team, Burt told Lott that Simms had some choice words for the future Hall of Fame safety. "Simms said, 'You're overrated,'" Lott wrote in his book about what he was told by Burt outside the team hotel hours before the Monday night game. "He says, 'You're washed up, that you're turning down hits. He claims you don't want to hit anybody.'"

After squeaking out the hard-fought victory, Lott unloaded on Simms as they stood nose to nose. Never one to back down from a verbal confrontation, Simms fired back. Later after things settled, Simms went into the San Francisco locker room to explain that Burt had made up the whole thing. He never said any of those things. But it didn't matter. The bad blood already existed between the teams from their years of playoff battles. "It was a close game, but Ronnie and Phil going at it, jawing at each other. It just pissed everybody off," Giants linebacker Carl Banks said. "And I'm sure Joe Montana probably preferred Ronnie not talk because he's got to come out and face [our defense]. So we knew the next time around what it was going to be."

Things only amplified when they met later that season in the NFC Championship Game. It was going to be another last-man-standing type of game; that much was certain. It was just going to come down to whether the Giants could play without Simms and starting running back Rodney Hampton and still outlast the two-time defending champs. Simms and Hampton were injured in a Week 15 game against the Buffalo Bills. So the Giants had to go to San Francisco for the NFC Championship

Game with Jeff Hostetler at quarterback and Ottis Anderson reinstalled as the featured running back.

A Pro Bowl player with the St. Louis Cardinals a decade earlier, Anderson was a proven player in the league. Everyone knew what he could do. Hostetler came with more questions. He had been stuck on the bench behind Simms seemingly forever. But he did add a new element to the Giants offense that the 49ers hadn't yet seen firsthand. "He was elusive," Parcells said. "He could scramble."

It made all the difference in the world after the Giants received a mini-miracle when 49ers running back Roger Craig fumbled with just more than two minutes remaining and his team holding a one-point lead. Defensive lineman Erik Howard forced the fumble, and it fell into the hands of Lawrence Taylor. On the very next play, Hostetler, who hurt his knee badly earlier in the game, managed to hobble right while being chased by none other than Burt and fire a pass to tight end Mark Bavaro for a gain of 19 yards. Aided by a few runs, the Giants got in field-goal range. Matt Bahr, a journeyman kicker wearing the old single-bar facemask, snuck a 42-yard kick inside the left upright as time expired for a 15–13 win that would send the Giants to the Super Bowl.

Parcells had his team ready for the big game in Tampa Bay even before the 49ers win. With Super Bowl XXV scheduled for the following Sunday and with no bye week in between, the Giants had packed their suitcases for two weeks and went straight to Florida. The flight was, as one might expect, a massive 2,800-mile celebration. When the Giants arrived, it was almost as if they were an unexpected visitor. The 49ers were supposed to be there. "[The 49ers] were so cocky that they had sent all of their equipment pertaining to training the following week," said Anderson, the eventual Super Bowl MVP, "all the equipment, the tickets, practice stuff, everything down to the hotel."

He remembers the Giants getting off the plane and heading to the hotel. It was early in the morning since they took a red-eye flight across country. When they arrived the people working at the hotel were looking for the 49ers. "Bill said, 'They freaking ain't coming,'" Anderson said before adding that the city looked ready for a matchup between the 49ers and Buffalo Bills.

Around lunchtime there was a sense of normalcy. All the flags and signs around the hotel and town that said 49ers and Bills were changed to Giants and Bills after the Giants were able to beat that great 49ers team in the NFC Championship Game. Banks attributes that to knowing San Francisco's weakness. It wasn't that they were soft, but they were a finesse team. They looked big and tough. It's just that sometimes looks can be deceiving. San Francisco was built on precision. Their passing game, their runs to the outside with Craig were based on timing. They ran like a well-oiled Cadillac. But how did they handle potholes and obstacles? That is what the Giants knew they had to present. "They were a tough-minded team, but they didn't have all tough guys. And so that kryptonite was that adjustment. The second game, we were going to pound Jerry Rice because he was a free-release guy. A great route runner, get the ball, and he's out-and-gone guy," Banks said. "And so we either played some form of Cover Two or some form of two-man, and then we just turned Mark Collins on him, and Mark just pounded him. He jammed him, and Jerry started whining because it was just uncomfortable for him. He never really had that piece of it."

It was the same for Craig. The 49ers with Walsh and then in 1990 with George Seifert as coach schemed him into space. He high-stepped down the field and thrived in those situations. The Giants plan in the NFC Championship Game was to run a linebacker into the flat to limit his space. When Craig got the ball, he either would have to avoid the linebacker immediately or absorb the big hit and try to make yards after contact. This was defensive coordinator Bill Belichick at his finest.

San Francisco's lone touchdown came on a 61-yard touchdown pass from Montana to John Taylor early in the third quarter. The Giants actually knocked Montana out of the game again in the fourth quarter when Leonard Marshall hit him from behind as he was about to throw. It forced a fumble that was somehow recovered by the 49ers. Still, Montana was done. New York's defense had delivered such a punishment to Montana that he sat on the bench most of the final few minutes in a daze. Announcer Pat Summerall informed the television audience at one point: "The report from the 49ers bench is that everything hurts." It seemed appropriate given the physicality of the game. That game actually was pretty much the end of Montana in San Francisco. He would later go on to have success with the Kansas City Chiefs, but he would play just one more game with the 49ers. That NFC Championship Game loss was his final playoff game in San Francisco.

It also was the end of the Giants–49ers rivalry as we knew it. Parcells would be gone several months after winning the Super Bowl. The Giants and 49ers would meet again in the 1993 playoffs with Taylor and Simms in their last professional seasons. But that Giants team wasn't the same. In fact, that game was essentially the end of an era for the Giants. San Francisco beat them 44–3 in the divisional round that year.

7

Wide Right

SAY TWO WORDS: "WIDE RIGHT," AND IMMEDIATELY FANS know. It's all you need to describe the New York Giants victory in Super Bowl XXV. "Wide right" is right up there with "Helmet Catch" among the most recognized phrases in team and NFL history. In fact, they're probably the two most famous Super Bowl phrases, and both can be attributed to specific moments in the big game involving the Giants. If you're a football fan, you can remember exactly where you were when these indelible moments led to a Giants championship.

"Wide Right" incontrovertibly describes how Super Bowl XXV ended. It was the result of Buffalo Bills kicker Scott Norwood missing a 47-yard kick as time expired in Super Bowl XXV. It was the call of announcer Al Michaels as the ball sailed past the post, and the Giants team poured onto the field in celebration at Tampa Stadium. "Norwood will try to kick his longest ever on grass, 47 yards. Eight seconds left. Adam Lingner will snap it," Michaels said to set the scene. "No good! Wide right!" The tumbling football dipped to the side of the right upright.

Still, 30-plus years later, that barely registers when asking about the most memorable part of that Super Bowl experience. The popular answer pertains to the rare atmosphere around the game. That is because Super Bowl XXV was actually the backdrop to something much bigger.

The United States was involved in the Gulf War—its first war in decades—in January 1991. It was at the forefront of the nation's mind, to the point that there were rumors about potentially cancelling the Super Bowl because of the security concerns.

The game eventually went on but not without extreme precautions. Teams were told to stay inside much of the week and travelled with extraordinary security everywhere they went. As players entered the stadium, they had their cameras with the old-school film emptied to make sure there were not bombs inside. They had to go through magnetometers—machines used to detect metal objects such as guns and weapons—just like everybody else upon arriving for the actual game. Everywhere the teams looked, there were signs this was not your normal Super Bowl. "I remember seeing my first machine gun with troops walking around the streets with guns. I'm thinking to myself, *What in the world is going on? Are we going to play this game?* That really stood out to me," Giants tight end Howard Cross said. "We were happy. We were excited, but it was a little jarring to see that."

At the game there was a sea of red, white, and blue representing the patriotism of the moment and the colors of the teams involved. Both the Giants and Bills had red, white, and blue as their colors. It blended in seamlessly among the crowd with everybody waving the small American flag that was distributed upon arrival. As it turned out, fans were treated to perhaps the most dramatic and patriotic Super Bowl of all time. It also appropriately had the best Super Bowl national anthem. "I remember the wonderful flyover, the unbelievable presentation before the game with the 'Star-Spangled Banner' with Whitney Houston," former Bills coach Marv Levy said years later. "The best I ever heard."

That was a common recollection of the event. The flyover and Houston's rendition lives on in Super Bowl lore. It was the kind of moment that left everyone in the building and those watching from home throughout the world with chills.

Everything about this Super Bowl was different. Giants quarterback Jeff Hostetler was about to complete one of the most unexpected stories the Super Bowl had ever seen. He was stuck as a backup for years until a few weeks before the big game when starter Phil Simms broke his foot. Hostetler's opportunity came and almost disappeared the previous week when his knee was severely damaged in San Francisco.

Yet there was Hostetler—on the verge of becoming the first backup to step in and win a Super Bowl as a starter—ready to run out the tunnel, and his core memory all these years later had little to do with his story and the actual game. It was something much bigger. "Probably my fondest memory of the entire thing was waiting in the tunnel to be introduced," he said. "Just standing there, I was next, and looking out and seeing that stadium just rocking with all these red, white, and blue flags and just knowing here it is. Six weeks earlier I had already made up my mind I was retiring, and being on that stage, knowing the whole world was watching, and then to run out and have Whitney Houston sing and have that flyover, it was such a great thing to be part of."

Bills linebacker Cornelius Bennett admitted years later this was actually an abnormal experience. The Bills would know. They would get the more traditional experiences the next three years when they also made it back to the Super Bowl. Unfortunately for that great team and the city of Buffalo, the result was the same in each. They lost all four. This being their first, they didn't know what they were in for at the time of Super Bowl XXV. In an event that always seems to supersede sports, there was a clear concentration on things other than the game. "We came out for warm-ups, and they were playing Lee Greenwood's 'God Bless the U.S.A.,'" Bills offensive lineman Jim Ritcher said. "There was a sweet, sweet spirit."

The game itself was still almost as memorable as the peripheral events associated with this specific Super Bowl. It's still considered one of the best Super Bowls, if not the best, of all time that featured the most dramatic final moment in history. That is because of all the incredible storylines and the ending, including Norwood missing the 47-yard kick.

Hostetler was among the most amazing stories in any Super Bowl, setting the stage for Nick Foles with the Philadelphia Eagles almost 30 years later. The Giants weren't supposed to be there once they lost Simms late in the year (interestingly during a loss to the Bills) let alone win the game against what linebacker Carl Banks later said was the best team to never win a Super Bowl.

Running back Ottis Anderson wasn't supposed to win the MVP either—even if he seemingly willed it into existence. Anderson rushed for more than 1,000 yards in 1989 and thought he would fulfill his prediction of winning a Super Bowl and the MVP in his home state of Florida that season. That year's Super Bowl would be played at Joe Robbie Stadium in Miami, not far from where Anderson grew up in West Palm Beach and then attended college at the University of Miami. But the Giants were eliminated in the playoffs that season in dramatic fashion on an overtime touchdown by Los Angeles Rams receiver Flipper Anderson, who ran out of the stadium after making the grab. That was a tough one for New York to swallow. Parcells thought that team was good enough to win it all. Ottis Anderson viewed it as a missed opportunity to make his prediction come true. That was until fellow running back Maurice Carthon reminded Anderson there would be another opportunity—the following year's Super Bowl would also be played in Florida. "I said, 'Dude, we're going!'" Ottis Anderson recalled. "No doubt about it."

The only problem for Anderson was that his role would be slightly reduced in 1990. The Giants drafted Rodney Hampton in the first round of that year's draft. He was going to be a big part of the mix along with Anderson. By the end of the regular season, Hampton was the primary back, and Anderson was serving as more mentor than workhorse. His role had been reduced to barely a handful of carries each week.

Except Hampton fractured his leg trying to recover a fumble in a 31–3 divisional-round win against the Chicago Bears. That opened the door for the cagey veteran Anderson—practice pants and all. The way Anderson remembers it, he arrived early for the divisional-round game against the Bears that was being played at Giants Stadium. He was so early that his uniform wasn't even laid out in front of his locker yet. So Anderson went back into the equipment room and took what he thought were his gameday pants. Only problem was they weren't. Anderson noticed during warm-ups his pants were different. *Whoops!* He was wearing what turned out to be his practice pants. "I run out to pregame, and I look around and I realized that, *Oh shoot, my pants ain't like everybody else pants!*" Anderson said. "And

I realized that I made the mistake and had put on my practice pants."

At that point, it was too late. He had already had his cleats taped up around his ankles so the shoes didn't come off easily. It would have taken too much time to take them off, get the new pants, get retaped, etc. So Anderson made the executive decision to keep the practice pants on for the game. He wasn't expecting to play much, if at all, anyway. *Nobody would really notice,* he thought. That was until Hampton got injured early in the win against the Bears. Anderson was called off the bench to play a significant role not only in the remainder of the game, but also throughout the remainder of the playoffs and in the Super Bowl. He had 20 carries for 80 yards against the Bears. It would be the first of three straight playoffs games Anderson would have at least 20 carries...in his practice pants. "Well, Bill [Parcells] was superstitious, so well, what happened was Rodney gets hurt. I'm standing on the sideline, and Bill yells to [offensive coordinator] Ray Handley, 'Get me O.J.' And I was like, *Oh, freaking no, I got on these practice pants. Oh, shoot,*" Anderson said, "because the commissioner had always sent letters out doing the playoffs about uniforms and uniform being to code. So here I am with my practice pants on, and the back of the pants was cut so that my knee pad wouldn't be tight on my legs. I had basketball knee pads underneath that, and I was a mess. I was just a mess."

Not surprisingly, Anderson got a letter from the commissioner the following week before the Giants played the San Francisco 49ers in the NFC Championship Game. It said the pants were not to uniform code, and the next time he did it, there would be a fine. Anderson picked the letter off his chair and brought it to Parcells. "I don't give a crap what they are going to do," the superstitious Parcells said. "You're wearing those pants next week."

Anderson practiced in those pants all week. The equipment team washed them before the San Francisco game, he wore them during the contest, they washed them again, he wore them for practice and again in the next game. Lather, rinse, and repeat for the Super Bowl. Anderson even recalled a conversation on the flight from San Francisco to Tampa for the big game. He was called to the front of the plane by Parcells. Surely, the coach was going to tell him what a great job he'd done and so forth. Parcells did tell him he was proud of him before getting to the most important order of business heading into the Super Bowl. "Do I have to tell you?" Parcells said.

Anderson was trying to figure out what exactly his coach was talking about. Perhaps it was a specific play from the classic NFC Championship Game that just concluded. Or maybe it was about the run-heavy gameplan the Giants were about to install for the Bills. "What do you mean?" Anderson said.

"Wear them!" Parcells said. "God dang it, the practice pants."

"Well, you know I'm getting fined," Anderson said.

"I don't give a crap. I'll pay the fine," Parcells said. "Don't think about it anymore."

Magically, the fines never came out of Anderson's check. He wore the practice pants on his way to a 21-carry, 102-yard performance that included a touchdown run against the Bills. It earned Anderson Super Bowl MVP honors in his home state just as he'd predicted would happen 12 years earlier when he was coming out of Miami.

It wouldn't have been possible without the dramatic "Wide Right" ending. The MVP almost certainly would have gone to Buffalo running back Thurman Thomas if the kick had been made. He had 190 total yards and a touchdown in the contest thanks to the gameplan of defensive coordinator Bill Belichick unimaginably funneling the ball into the hands of the Bills' star running back.

Thomas helped the Bills get into field-goal range in the final minutes of a game the Giants dominated. New York held the ball for more than 40 minutes; Buffalo had it for less than 20. The Norwood miss helped produce what the Giants believe was the deserving result. "I was thinking it would be a shame if we lost this game because we had outplayed them," Parcells said. "My kicker, Matt Bahr, had told me before the kick, 'Coach, he hasn't made one from 47 yards on grass this year. He's going to overkick the ball.' That's exactly what happened."

The ball spun through the air and drifted wide right of the upright. The Giants—with a great defense; with a backup quarterback; with a coach who they would find out later would be coaching his last ever game for the team he grew up rooting for; with a 34-year-old running back who would start only one more game in his career—had won the Super Bowl in the most dramatic fashion.

While the underdog Giants had taken advantage of the opportunity, the Bills felt they let one slip away. It would hurt even more as time elapsed, and their Super Bowl window eventually closed without a Lombardi Trophy making its way to Buffalo. Bills lineman Will Wolford discussed it with fellow lineman and friend, center Kent Hull. "We felt like," Wolford said, "we brought our C game all the way around, coaching, playing, everything."

Parcells, Belichick, and the Giants had brought their A game to the biggest stage even if it almost became an afterthought amidst an ongoing war. As a result for the second time in four years, there would be no parade down the Canyon of Heroes in Manhattan. This group of Giants would never get to enjoy that kind of celebration. That would have to wait for Eli Manning and Co. 17 years later. Owner Wellington Mara just didn't think it was appropriate in the time of war for such a parade. Four years earlier it didn't happen because New York mayor Ed Koch didn't want the New York taxpayers paying for a celebration for what he viewed as a New Jersey team.

In the grand scheme of things, the "Wide Right" Super Bowl was a win for the 1990 New York Football Giants. And in the big picture, it was a win for the entire country because the game went off without a hitch.

8

The Hoss

It was the fourth quarter of a late September game in 1990 when coach Bill Parcells did the unpredictable. He called for his backup quarterback to enter the game with the New York Giants ahead 24–10. There was still an entire quarter remaining, but Parcells had something specific in mind. It included surprisingly removing starter Phil Simms from that game against the Dallas Cowboys and seeing what Jeff Hostetler could do on short notice. "Jeff?" Parcells screamed on the sideline. "Where's Hostetler?"

The backup with whom he'd butted heads with numerous times over the years came running with his helmet. Hostetler, the Giants' third-round pick in the 1984 draft, was about to enter a game the Giants ultimately won 31–17.

It was eye-opening because Hostetler had not played much up until that point. He wasn't known as a "Parcells guy" by any stretch of the imagination and, in his first five professional seasons, he had started just two games and thrown 68 passes. In Hostetler's first career start, which came against the New Orleans Saints in 1988, Parcells pulled him at halftime and questioned his sensitivity level and ability to handle adversity and criticism. Mind you, Hostetler had just thrown an 85-yard touchdown pass before halftime.

It wasn't normal for Parcells to call for Hostetler at any time—let alone in the middle of a game. But perhaps there was a sixth sense element to it all. This would be the year that the Giants were finally going to need Hostetler, and there he was in a Week Four contest getting called into action. "You never know when you're going to be called. So if you get a chance, you better be ready," Hostetler said. "When there's a situation, the quarterback goes down, and you don't get any time to prepare, you're in. And you never know when that time's going to be, and so it was a test, and I did real well. Again, it built up confidence—my confidence but also his confidence in me, the rest of the team's confidence in me, knowing that just out of the blue you're in, and you're able to do it."

Hostetler, who was 29 years old at the time, immediately led a scoring drive, rushing for a 12-yard touchdown. But after that early regular season game, it was back to the bench. Hostetler was called upon again in a Week Seven contest against the Arizona Cardinals when Simms got hurt. This time he led two scoring drives in the final 5:38 to erase a late nine-point deficit. The Giants won 20–19 on a Matt Bahr field goal as time expired. Afterward, it was again back to the bench. "What's new?" a frustrated Hostetler said at the time.

This only added to the years of dissatisfaction. Hostetler wanted to play, knew he could play. In fact, he would do nearly anything possible to get on the field. The Giants used him over the years on special teams and even at wide receiver at times to try to satisfy that competitive itch. It wasn't enough. Hostetler remembers going home one night during that 1990 season and telling his wife, Vicki, that this was it for his football career. They would go home to West Virginia after the season, and he would find something else to do. He couldn't take another year of being stuck on the Giants bench.

At this time there was no free agency, but Hostetler tried numerous times to get himself released or traded by the Giants. He had conversations with Parcells about wanting to leave, wanting to play. Those back and forths, as you can imagine, could get nasty. Parcells and general manager George Young had no intention of complying to his wishes. He gave them depth at the most important position. "It wasn't great," Parcells said years later of their relationship. "He was wanting to play and he wasn't playing, but he had been with us a long time. I had confidence in his ability. I don't think he knew that."

With the Giants and everywhere the head coach went, there were always "Parcells guys." And then there was everybody else. That is at least how it was perceived by many of the players. The non-Parcells guys would often have the coach ride them relentlessly. He rarely eased up. It was evident in 1985 with nose tackle Jim Burt, which led to the birth of the Gatorade Bath. Parcells was all over his nose tackle. Except Burt knew that if he just allowed it to persist, it might never stop. So he made his displeasure known and retaliated with the Gatorade Bath. In Burt's mind his willingness to respond and fight back earned him a spot in the circle of trust.

Hostetler tried everything to get there, including playing special teams, which is hardly the norm for a quarterback. But he wasn't playing regularly, so it was hard to do, especially considering he expressed his disapproval to Parcells' tactics. "I was definitely on the outside along with a lot of other guys," Hostetler said. "And so we all used that in our own different ways. But I just did let Bill know, 'Listen, if you want to motivate me, you don't need to tell me what I did wrong. I already know what I did wrong. I'm harder on myself than you'll ever be. So that's not the way to motivate me.'"

It seemed to have reached a boiling point during that 1990 season when Hostetler made the internal decision that this would be his last year. He wasn't going to return if things remained unchanged. Only they didn't, through no part of Parcells or Hostetler's doing. It was during a much-hyped early December game against the Buffalo Bills. With both teams sitting at 11–2 in what would be a Super Bowl preview, Simms went back to pass and fell to the ground. He reached immediately for his right leg. He had broken his foot on the third-quarter play. His season was over. Hostetler entered the game, which the Giants lost 17–13, and would be the starting quarterback for the remainder of the season.

The prevailing thought was that without their starting quarterback, the Giants' season was effectively over. They weren't real Super Bowl contenders anymore. The San Francisco 49ers were in their conference, and they seemed destined for a three-peat. They had won the two previous Super Bowls with the great Joe Montana as their quarterback surrounded by a star-studded supporting cast. The Bills were the heavy favorites in the AFC and on their way to the first of four straight Super Bowls. How could the Giants compete with all that without Simms?

Nobody but the Giants themselves thought they had a chance with Hostetler despite being 11–3. "When Phil got hurt, I went into the team meeting the next day and everybody's, 'Oh, wow, you've got a backup quarterback, and nobody's ever won with one,'" Parcells recalled. "And I stood up right in front of the team and I said, 'I'm going to tell you guys something right now: we're not going to lose in these playoffs because of Jeff Hostetler. It'll be one of you other'—and I used a bad word—'but it'll be one of you other guys. It won't be him.' That let the team know where my confidence level was on him. And then we tried to design some things that we knew he would do well, and he did. That's just the way it worked out."

The Giants players also believed. They had seen it on the field and in games earlier that season. They saw it every day in practice—not just when Hostetler was finally installed as the starter in the final few weeks. There were crumbs left on the practice field from the previous six years that suggested he could play. Hostetler did everything during that time to show his toughness. He was a gunner on the punt team. He was used as the end rusher to try to block punts. He was the fullback on the punt team at times. He played wide receiver. He was the holder. He really was willing to do anything to get on the field.

The starting Giants defense had their hands full that season with Hostetler at quarterback, veteran Ottis Anderson at running back, and wide receiver Stephen Baker taking scout team reps for a chunk of the year. They ended up not only playing key roles in the Super Bowl, but also being the heroes. It was proof that the Giants were *a team* in the greatest sense of the term during that 1990 season. It wasn't just the stars from the '86 title team that ultimately carried them to another championship. They received contributions from everybody. "[Hostetler] did everything right. He did everything that they asked him to do," Anderson said. "He threw good passes in practice. He gave good looks. I mean, we both were running scout team plays...so he just transitioned. He and I got to be together and play in Super Bowl. We knew each other very well. He knew Baker because he was our receiver. It was Hostetler, Stephen Baker, and me. It was the three guys that did a lot of the special teams. I mean, we weren't the only ones but the Three Amigos: Hostetler, Baker, and [Anderson]."

Hostetler went from backup to Super Bowl–winning quarterback, something that nobody at the time had previously done. Anderson went from forgotten backup to Super Bowl MVP. Baker went from pretty much a non-contributor the first few weeks of the season to the team's leading receiver who caught a game-changing touchdown right before halftime of the Super Bowl against the Bills.

It was quite the run that the Giants made after Hostetler and Anderson entered the lineup. Both Simms and starting running back Rodney Hampton were injured in that same regular-season matchup with Buffalo. Hostetler and Anderson entered the lineup for wins against the Cardinals and New England Patriots to close out the regular season. New York finished the regular season 13–3. It was still only good enough for the second seed in the NFC as the 49ers (14–2) earned home-field advantage.

The Giants beat the Bears in the divisional round 31–3 with Hostetler throwing for a pair of touchdowns and running for another. Anderson rushed for 80 yards. But it really was in the classic NFC Championship Game in San Francisco when the legacy of Hostetler was made. Hostetler took a controversial low hit to the knee from former teammate Jim Burt early in the fourth quarter. Hostetler can still remember hearing the pop. The pain was excruciating—so bad that he couldn't hear the medical team as they attended to him on the field. He describes it as if someone had pressed the mute button. It hurt even more because Hostetler had waited so long for this opportunity to play and start. This was his opportunity of a lifetime. And this was the NFC Championship Game. How could it all get taken away just like that? Could this really be how the opportunity he had waited all these years for was going to play out?

That is when Hostetler believes some sort of minor miracle took place. "I came from a real strong Christian family and a mom that was constantly praying for us. And I'm out there on the field and I'm going to tell you this because this is the truth and what happened. I'm out there in all kinds of pain and then, all of a sudden, I just felt a little bit of tingling across me, and it's just like all the pain kind of just disappeared," Hostetler said. "And they helped me up, and I'm thinking, *Well, I think, I don't know, maybe I can [play].*"

Hostetler walked slowly over to the sideline. Little by little, his knee felt a tinge better while third-string quarterback Matt Cavanaugh nervously commanded the huddle. It wasn't going to work with Cavanaugh against that great 49ers team. Parcells and the Giants needed Hostetler. New York trailed 13–9 and knew what was necessary if they had any chance to win the game. "Can you go?" Parcells asked. "Can you go?"

"I knew I could go," Hostetler said 30-plus years later. "I felt like I could have enough stability there to go do it and was able to get back in and lead a drive down to make a couple throws on the run."

Hostetler led two scoring drives in the final 10 minutes after hurting his knee. He made a key throw to tight end Mark Bavaro to get them into field-goal range and then was the holder on the game-winning kick from Bahr to knock off the two-time defending champion 49ers. "They all said it couldn't be done, and here we are: we're going the Super Bowl," Hostetler said. "It's pretty special."

They called it a hyperextended knee at the time. Hostetler spent the whole week leading up to the Super Bowl tending to his left leg. It wasn't great, but there was no way he was going to miss the biggest game of his life. All these years later, Hostetler said he had suffered a torn ACL. He actually played the end of the NFC Championship Game, the Super Bowl, and the rest of his NFL career with no intact ACL in his right knee!

"I'm one of the very few that had enough other things going on structure-wise that I was able to continue to function," he said.

To this day he maintains it has never been fixed. He's had MRIs since, and doctors will look at the knee and mention the ACL is gone. It's something he already knows, but it's also nothing one can really tell without doing a thorough evaluation.

Anyway, Hostetler and the Giants still had one more difficult task in front of them to create the storybook ending. They were underdogs again in Super Bowl XXV to the Bills, which would end with the famous wide-right field-goal attempt off the right foot of Scott Norwood.

In order to get to that point, Hostetler had to do his part. Perhaps his biggest play came while the Bills recorded a safety in the second quarter. Ferocious Bills pass rusher Bruce Smith came around the edge and got to Hostetler in the end zone. Smith swiped at Hostetler's cocked arm, hitting his wrist with all his might. Somehow, Hostetler held onto the ball. The play went for two points for the Bills, but it easily could have turned into seven if Hostetler hadn't had that cobra grip on the football.

It was as much a miracle that he held onto the ball as it was that he was playing in the game with a torn ACL. Hostetler credits all those years where he and his younger brother were getting the tar kicked out of them by their two older brothers, both of whom went on to play linebacker at Penn State. "It was always my younger brother and I against the two older ones, and I give them the credit," Hostetler said. "It was in the backyard toughening us up and on the farm, being farm strong."

It wasn't long after the almost-fumble that Hostetler led a long scoring drive before halftime. He hit his scout team buddy Baker for a monstrous 14-yard touchdown that cut the deficit to 14–10 before halftime. Anderson scored on a one-yard touchdown run on the opening drive of the second half to give the Giants the lead.

When the final kick sailed wide right, Hostetler sat there on the sideline, kneeling on one knee. Frozen, he didn't move for what seemed like minutes, even though it was probably only 20 to 30 seconds. He was absorbing everything that had just happened—from the struggles (personal and on the football field) to finally getting his opportunity to almost having it taken away to nobody believing the Giants could get this done to wishing it all into existence. "To have that opportunity to perform and [win the Super Bowl]," Hostetler said 34 years later, "it's something that follows me all the time."

The relationship between Parcells and Hostetler didn't magically heal because of the Super Bowl. But Hostetler knew that Parcells respected his work ethic. Hostetler insists they didn't have a real conversation afterward to discuss his role moving forward. It ultimately didn't matter because Parcells was gone a few months later. Hostetler stayed two more years in New York, starting 21 more games, and played another five seasons with the Los Angeles Raiders and Washington Redskins after free agency was introduced to the sport. It wasn't until long after his career ended that Parcells and Hostetler made amends.

The two crossed paths after Hostetler's playing career ended, and Parcells told him nobody knows how difficult of a spot he was in as the backup quarterback in New York behind Simms. He noted what a great job Hostetler did handling it all those years. Parcells, whose toughness played a large part in his success, told him there was some regret about how he handled the situation with his backup quarterback and that he wished he would've done some things differently in retrospect. Several years later, Parcells even called Hostetler about a coaching job.

Though not exactly close friends, they have a mutual respect for each other to this day. "Those were huge things for me," Hostetler said. "There was respect there, and you have to earn it. And I felt like I did and I felt like he recognized that, too. Those were some pretty encouraging words and actions from him."

9

Belichick's Masterpiece

It was Tuesday afternoon, and the first media session from Super Bowl XXV was already in the books. The New York Giants defensive players shuffled from their rooms on the third floor of the team hotel in Tampa, Florida, down one level. Meetings were held on the second floor throughout that week. That is where players like Lawrence Taylor, Carl Banks, Leonard Marshall, Erik Howard, Everson Walls, and Myron Guyton filed into the room, not knowing the evil genius they were about to hear. Defensive coordinator Bill Belichick was about to divulge a gameplan that seemed antithetical to who they were. He was about unleash upon his group that Buffalo Bills running back Thurman Thomas would run for 100 yards in the biggest game of their respective lives.

This was lunacy in the eyes of the Giants defensive players. Nobody ran the ball against their defense. They took immense pride in that fact. Not Barry Sanders, not Emmitt Smith, not even Thomas when they played earlier that year. Just handing an opposing running back 100 yards rushing sounded absolutely absurd to them. It went against their core morals and beliefs.

The "Evil Genius" or "Little Bill" knew better. His famous gameplan was so crazy and brilliant that it now sits in the Pro Football Hall of Fame. The Giants executed it to perfection while holding Buffalo's fast-break K-Gun offense to four touchdowns less than it averaged in its first two playoff games that season. "That first [defensive] meeting was one for the ages because that defense didn't like giving up a lot of yards," Banks said. "And Bill started the meeting by telling us that Thurman Thomas is going to get 100 yards. 'In order for us to win the game, Thurman Thomas is going to get 100 yards!' And we're like, 'Screw that. We ain't giving up 100 yards to anybody.' And this is before we knew what the gameplan was."

In a way Belichick had to know this was going to be the reaction. His proud defense would have reservations with this plan if the players digested it solely on the surface without further explanation. But in typical Belichick style, he had to detail the why in order for it to truly work as intended and to get the full buy-in from L.T. and the guys. Belichick had spent the previous 24 hours before that legendary meeting studying every bit of tape of the Bills from that season when they went 13–3 and pummeled the Los Angeles Raiders and Miami Dolphins in the playoffs by a combined score of 95–37 to reach the Super Bowl.

Belichick started his gameplan meeting with the defense by explaining that he normally studied the past four games to determine tendencies, but the Giants coaches went back eight games with the Bills. So now they were no longer talking tendencies; they were talking trends.

He saw a trend that Buffalo didn't run the football much. Pretty much their only running plays were draws to Thomas and some swing passes. In order for the Giants to win the Super Bowl, their focus needed to be on taking away Buffalo's passing attack.

With the help of defensive line coach Romeo Crennel and linebackers coach Al Groh, Belichick drew up defenses using 2-4-5 or 2-3-6 personnel groupings. That meant just two defensive linemen with either three or four linebackers and five or six defensive backs. Belichick and Co. were going to dare the Bills to run. "Our goal was to let them have Thurman Thomas run. He could have had 300 yards. We didn't care," Marshall said. "As long as he didn't get in the end zone, we were good with that."

Thomas finished with 135 rushing yards and a touchdown on just 15 carries. He had the monster game that Belichick permitted with his scheme. It still wasn't enough. The Bills offense led by quarterback Jim Kelly was lethal, using short crossing routes to wide receivers Andre Reed and James Lofton that regularly carved up opposing defenses. In the AFC Championship Game, when Buffalo won 51–3, the Raiders linebackers weren't able to get back in coverage quickly enough. By the time they dropped back, the ball was already downfield and caught. They couldn't get back fast enough to limit the space for the Bills' receivers. So instead of putting pressure on the Giants linebackers to drop in coverage so quickly, Belichick decided to line them up in coverage. And because they were already in coverage, it would help them see the draw play or swing pass in front of them. Still, the most important aspect was that it would allow the Giants linebackers to punish the Bills' receivers when they caught the ball on those short crossing routes. "We want to be as physical as possible," Banks said. "We want to pound this fucking Andre Reed."

It was feasible because the Giants basically had nine defensive players in coverage. Reed, Lofton, and Thomas would be surrounded by New York's swarming linebackers or defensive backs the second they caught the ball. They would ultimately be pummeled into submission.

Belichick had effectively created speed bumps all over the field. The Porsches could never get over 60 mph. Every time Reed made a catch, he was pounded. It was almost as if the Giants were taking turns with the debilitating hits. Sit back, wait to see who is crossing, and hit the man with the ball. That was the approach. "I mean, we hit [Reed] so much," Banks said. "I remember one of his teammates said that he couldn't sit down on the flight home. And then I saw him because he lived in Orlando at the time and I saw him, and he said, 'Bro, I thought you broke my hip on one crossing route.'"

That play came on a third-and-7 late in the second quarter. Reed caught the ball underneath and was met immediately by Banks, who exploded forward into the defenseless receiver just as Belichick had drawn it up. Reed made the catch while Banks' helmet banged incidentally into Reed's hip. You could tell it hurt. Reed remained on the ground for a few extra seconds. Meanwhile, a content Banks could see the pain in his face. He remembers Reed rolling over and hobbling back to the huddle. The gameplan was working to perfection. "I knew when I hit him," Banks said, "that was going to hurt."

Near midfield the Bills were forced to punt. It was a massive play. The Giants went down and scored a touchdown in the final seconds of the second quarter on a 14-yard touchdown pass from quarterback Jeff Hostetler to wide receiver Stephen

Baker. They also received the ball to start the third quarter and had a 14-play drive that took almost 10 minutes and resulted in a one-yard touchdown run by eventual MVP Ottis Anderson.

In all, the Bills didn't have the ball for nearly two hours of real time, including the extended halftime show, which was "A Small World Salute to 25 Years of the Super Bowl" and included a performance by boy band New Kids on the Block. The plan that Bill Parcells and Belichick concocted was working to perfection.

It wasn't always a given that Belichick was the right choice as defensive coordinator in 1985. Taylor threw a fit when Parcells originally made the appointment. He stormed up to the head coach's office and has admitted multiple times over the years that he called Parcells "fucking crazy" for the decision. How could this guy who never played football and not so long ago was a special teams assistant be running the defense? Parcells told him to give it a chance. Belichick already was the one who was putting together their schemes and coverages leading into that season. Still, Belichick needed to prove himself, just like he did from the moment he was hired as a lower-level assistant. "Belichick was a lacrosse player," linebacker Harry Carson said. "He didn't play football, and Parcells had played at Wichita State or some place, but he played football. And so he looked at things from a football player's perspective, whereas Belichick was very cerebral, and he was a guy who never really experienced maybe the trauma of getting the shit knocked out of you when you played. And so when he would ask us to do certain things, our attitude was like, *Wait a second, this is not the way that things are done when you've got two defensive linemen.* And you want to do something a certain way. And it wasn't until he was able to show us the benefits of doing things his way that we bought in."

The Giants were a top 10 scoring defense every year that Belichick was the defensive coordinator, aside from the strike season in 1987. Their success was immediate. The respect was ultimately earned. When Belichick spoke, they listened.

It didn't mean the players loved Belichick. He was hard on them and demanded excellence. He was thorough beyond anything they had seen before. Belichick made a habit of explaining the ins and outs of each week's schemes to the point that it could become mind-numbing. He would back everything up with data and film. That at least gave it some validity. He knew each defensive call came with weaknesses and would point them out as well so that his players would be aware of what they were trying to avoid. There didn't seem to be anything that wasn't covered in a Belichick practice. He ran drills and then flipped them, running it to the other side. Players basically needed to be ambidextrous in their techniques if they wanted to earn the full trust of their coordinator. If it wasn't drilled right, he'd make them do it over and over again until they were fundamentally sound.

This was imperative for a Belichick defense. These were the details that made the Giants defense great under Belichick. Parcells seemed to approve of it all to the point that he gave his defensive coordinator full autonomy. "Bill was young. So he was relatable," Banks said. "He also was a fucking asshole. He was very demanding. I don't know what Parcells was like as a defensive coordinator, but they seemed to be in lockstep on a lot of things."

Belichick didn't become the greatest coach of all time by accident. Limiting the Bills to 19 points in a 20–19 upset victory in Super Bowl XXV just added to his resume as an assistant. That gave him two Super Bowl victories and the respect of not only his players, but also the entire league. This was before he even took that next step in his career. Belichick was hired to be the head coach of the Cleveland Browns several weeks after the 1990 season ended. He was 38 years old at the time but had been building to that point since he started watching and breaking down film with his dad at seven years old. He—at the very least—grew into the greatest head coach of his generation, passing even his mentor Parcells while building a dynasty later on with the New England Patriots.

Still, those Giants years are something he has never forgotten. He reflected on them years later during an emotional visit to Giants Stadium before it was torn down. "I probably wouldn't have thought it would turn out like this," Belichick said. "[I] was just trying to establish my coaching career, win some games. We won a lot of them here. This is a great organization. It's hard not to get choked up about it. I loved it here."

10

Parcells Era

BILL PARCELLS ALMOST DIDN'T MAKE IT OUT OF THAT FIRST year as head coach of the New York Giants. He was convinced that general manager George Young tried to hire Howard Schnellenberger to replace him in 1984. Young had worked under Schnellenberger previously with the Baltimore Colts as an assistant coach. They were friends, and Parcells had a rough first season with the Giants. It ultimately didn't happen, and Parcells got a reprieve.

It may not have always been obvious at the start, but Parcells was the right choice at the right time to be the head coach of the Giants. He was the perfect mix of character, leader, football smart tactician, and disciplinarian to whip the struggling franchise into shape. Born and raised in New Jersey, Parcells wanted nothing more than to be the Giants head coach. He made it his mission to get the iconic franchise back to where it belonged.

The Hasbrouck Heights, New Jersey, native grew up a Giants fan. He went to games at the Polo Grounds and was a Giant at heart, and still is to this day. He splits his time between Saratoga County in New York and Florida. His formative years were spent close to the future site of Giants Stadium, and he rooted for the team back in the '50s, when his favorite players were linebacker Sam Huff and quarterback Charlie Conerly. Huff, in particular, resonated with the young Parcells. He was strong and tough, one of the first defensive players to gain significant recognition in pro football. Huff in a way represented so many of the hard-working, blue-collar fans who watched that successful era of Giants football. It's not a coincidence so many years later when Parcells led the organization to its first championship since the '50s that an emotional and nearly teary-eyed Conerly was there, celebrating with Parcells and the team.

Even though the organization was in bad shape when Parcells took over, having not been a serious contender for several decades, it was a no-brainer for Parcells to be the man who would turn it all around. "It was personal to me," he said.

While Parcells climbed the coaching ladder—with stops at Hastings, Wichita State (his alma mater), Army, Florida State, Vanderbilt, Texas Tech, and Air Force—there was never a Sunday afternoon or Monday morning where he wouldn't check in on the Giants. It didn't matter where he was throughout the country. He was a true fan at heart and still invested in the team's success or lack thereof. The Giants may have stumbled through the '60s and '70s, but Parcells remembered the good years. This was his dream job—no matter the struggles of the organization leading into his tenure. "Once I got into coaching, I couldn't think of anything else," Parcells said. "Maybe one of those top Ohio States or something like that, but your chances of getting one of those is so remote. I just felt like when I went to pro football, if I did a good job, it's a smaller circle of people, and they recognize things very quickly. So I was very lucky to get a chance. The Maras took a chance on me with George Young, and it didn't start out too well, but once we got going..."

It helped that in Parcells' first two years with the Giants (1981–82) he was the defensive coordinator and linebackers coach. He earned the trust of key players such as defensive lineman George Martin and linebackers Harry Carson and Lawrence Taylor. Several years later, when he was sputtering through a 3–12–1 campaign in his first season in 1983 as head coach, having their support mattered—even if Young might have been looking elsewhere. It was integral in being able to turn it around the following year to start something special. "Parcells was one of us. So it was me and Brad Van Pelt and Brian Kelley and Lawrence, and he was one of us," Carson said. "But then when [Ray Perkins] left and went back to Alabama, and then Parcells was elevated to head coach, then we had to kind of make a distinction as to how we were going to deal with Parcells because if we had continued to treat him like he's one of us, then the younger guys were going to follow suit. So we had to give him a certain amount of respect and go from there."

It made a world of difference. If Parcells could get on Carson or Taylor or any of the other big-name Giants in a way only he could and they were able to handle it, then how could anyone else question the approach? It's similar to what was said later about Parcells' protégé Bill Belichick, who years later in New England handled Tom Brady and many of the Patriots stars the same way.

Parcells hit a fork in the road early in his Giants head coaching career. There was serious doubt he was ever going to survive after that '83 season, his first as an NFL head coach. Parcells believed wholeheartedly from his connections throughout the league that Young was trying to replace him with Schnellenberger. It made his personal relationship with Young frosty, but it didn't affect their ability to work effectively together. Ultimately, getting Schellenberger to New York didn't happen, and Parcells went into the 1984 season determined to do it his way. If he was going down, it was going to be under his terms, rather than trying to please somebody else, specifically Young.

Things changed entering that '84 season. Parcells didn't leave anything open for interpretation. He gathered his team at the start of training camp that year at Pace University in Westchester, New York, and put everything on the table. "I remember it like it was yesterday," linebacker Carl Banks said. "It was probably the most vulnerable I've ever seen Bill Parcells."

Parcells called the team up and delivered a crystal clear message. "If we don't win, they're going to fire my ass," he said. "There's going to be a lot of guys that are not going to be here that are some of your friends, but what I need from you, the guys that are going to be here, I need you to be my guys, and I'll give you everything I got if you give me everything you've got."

Right there was the birth of the Parcells guys. If you put it all on the table for him on and off the field, he wanted you around at all costs. If not, *see ya!* There were more than a few players jettisoned that offseason as he tried to clean out the roster and locker room, which was dealing with a drug problem. Given this approach it's probably no surprise that in some of his later stops in Dallas, New England, or with the New York Jets that many of the players, who were Parcells guys through the years, followed him. This is the way he worked. If you were part of that circle of trust, you were golden. If not, *good luck!*

But it was that vulnerability that Parcells had heading into the '84 season that many of the players believed brought the team together. It was a make-or-break situation, and the roster had been turned over that offseason, including some unpopular moves. Among those exiled players were longtime Giants linebackers Brian Kelley and Brad Van Pelt. In were rookies Banks, Gary Reasons, Lionel Manuel, William Roberts, and Elvis Patterson. This was now Parcells' team filled with Parcells' guys—even if they were picked by Young. "[Parcells] knew that his time was now or never," Banks said, "because they were going to fire his ass."

Parcells was unapologetically himself that season and beyond. What that meant is he could be a grade-A hard ass. It worked—even if at times it ruffled feathers. Parcells and quarterback Phil Simms famously went back and forth during practices and games. Parcells credits that to them being too similar and equally stubborn. It still didn't matter who you were in the eyes of the head coach. It could be a star player, a fringe player, or an assistant coach. Heck, Parcells fired Belichick too many times to count. He cut Banks and Simms and Taylor. Then they kissed (metaphorically) and made up. "I played under him for eight years," Simms said. "When he went and told me he was leaving the Giants, I went and got my birth certificate to see if my first name started with a P or an F because I was F'in Simms for eight years."

There was one instance that Parcells remembers when it got especially intense. It was during a Monday night game in Indianapolis against the Colts during the 1990 season. The Giants had a third-down package where they put two halfbacks into the game, and there was what they called a "read pattern." But Simms threw it to the tight end instead. It went for an incompletion. Simms jogged off the field and went past Parcells—but not before his coach had a few choice words that didn't exactly sit well with the quarterback, even though they had been together for years and already won a Super Bowl at that point. "What do you think I put that [play] in for?" Parcells said with authority.

"Well you go out there and throw it!" Simms snapped back.

At that point, all hell broke loose. The things that came out of their mouths were harsh and vile. It ended with Parcells telling his quarterback to "sit the fuck down."

Not that the play mattered much in the end. The Giants won the game easily 24–7, though Simms didn't throw a touchdown pass. As they walked off the field at the end of the contest, Parcells saw his quarterback. "Well, what are you going to say now?" he asked.

"I'm going to say it's less filling," Simms answered.

"Well, I'm going to say it tastes great," Parcells responded, riffing off the old Miller Lite commercials.

That was the relationship they had. They could yell and scream and get everything off their chests. In a way it was healthy. It created clarity. They knew how one another felt. There was never any gray area. It was all part of the brilliance of the motivational mastermind of Duane Parcells, who only became "Bill" when he moved to Oradell, New Jersey, and started attending River Dell High School. His classmates there confused him with another boy named Bill. Hence, the legendary Bill Parcells was born.

His accent, brutal honesty, and outspoken nature made him one of a kind. "Parcells would use you as an example because he wanted to send a message to the team. He would come to me prior to practice, and he would say, 'Okay, I'm going to be a little rough on you today. Don't take it personally,'" Carson said. "And it was between me and him, and he would chew me out for this or that. And when it initially happened, I would ask, 'Well, why do you want to fuck with me? I'm doing my job.' And he would say, 'Well, the guys know that if I chew you out, then they better get their asses in gear.' And so it was like I'm doing this for the betterment of the team."

Not that it was always that good-natured. There were times when Parcells' fiery side would lead to legendary explosions. It would create combustible situations. It wasn't uncommon for him to fire Belichick for a call that didn't work during a game. Belichick was not alone. Banks remembers a time when he was cut during a wild-card game his rookie season against the Los Angeles Rams. The Giants were getting killed by penalties, and Parcells warned that the next guy who received a penalty would be "fucking cut."

Well, Banks thought he was cheap-shotted on a special teams play. He retaliated and got caught. Like usual, the guy who retaliated received the penalty. That was the case in this instance as well, and it left Banks the recipient of Parcells' wrath. "I am walking off and Bill says, 'Go sit your ass down. You're cut!' I don't know what to think of it," Banks said. "I'm sitting there by myself, and Romeo Crennel was the special teams coach then, and he was coming over to talk to me, and Parcells says, 'Don't fucking talk to him! He's making stupid fucking plays.' And I was like, 'Fuck you!' He says, 'What did you say? Fuck you?' But that was the give and take we had with Bill."

The beauty of Parcells was that he could have that type of back and forth with players. Then, Monday morning he sat down with Banks in the middle of the locker room to talk. He told him he appreciated the fight and all, but the team couldn't afford for him to do that. Banks didn't get cut. Most of the time, the threats were hollow. But Parcells was still able to get his points across despite his loud and often over-the-top approach. He had that ability to break down his players and build them back up to get the most out of them.

Most of the time, it worked, assuming you had the personality and mind-set that could handle the often harsh approach. But it wasn't for everybody. Backup quarterback Jeff Hostetler for one was not much of a fan of Parcells for most of his career. It's not hard to understand why either. The things that would come out of the head coach's mouth could be anywhere from obscene and inappropriate to humorous and joking—sometimes in between or all of the above. One of his most famous incidents came when he was coaching the Dallas Cowboys later in his career, and he called wide receiver Terry Glenn "she" as Glenn dealt with an apparent injury. This was typical Parcells. "If you don't make a play, he would say all kinds of crazy funny things," tight end Howard Cross said. "Bill cannot coach in today's society. He just couldn't. I think that today's society would never be able to...no one takes criticism to begin with, right? No one will be able to take someone directing them or calling a guy 'Missy' or 'Sunshine' or something. Yeah, today's world, Twitter, and all that stuff, they'd have had him canceled a thousand times over."

But this was a different generation, and there was also that other side of Parcells that was often not seen publicly—even with the media. Although most of the times he was seen as cantankerous and grumpy in his interactions, behind the scenes there was a softer and fairer version of the Hall of Fame coach. Legendary reporter Peter King, then working for *Newsday*, one of 19 daily newspapers covering the team in 1985, was nicknamed "Relentless" by the coach for his dedication and approach. But Parcells respected it and told King if he ever really needed anything he could meet him at his parking space at 5:45 AM. King took him up on the offer on several occasions. Once Parcells even had the "Relentless" reporter in his office for 45 minutes.

It wasn't only King. Parcells knew the importance of the media, especially considering it wasn't so long ago that his job was in jeopardy. He would come down to the media room on Thursday evenings and answer all the reporters' questions off the record. It was such a paradox from his reputation. This was the same coach who once called the media "commies" and insisted they were "subversive from within," trying to stir up drama.

It seemed as if Parcells was the perfect coach for that era, for that group, and for that team. But his Giants tenure came to a screeching halt only months after winning a second Super Bowl. There were talks of him going to the Atlanta Falcons to become their coach and general manager. That idea was squashed by commissioner Pete Rozelle who ordered both sides cease negotiations because Parcells was still under contract with the Giants.

How close was it to becoming a reality that Parcells would join the Falcons? "Not real close," Parcells said years later. "Things happened that get out of your control. It's just something got out about that. I don't remember any direct offer. I just knew that there was something there, but I really wasn't inclined at that time."

Some five months after winning a second Super Bowl on May 15, 1991, Parcells resigned as head coach of the Giants. He had medical problems and was trying to figure out what was wrong. He would eventually have heart bypass surgery and two angioplasty procedures. Belichick had already left to take the coaching job for the Cleveland Browns, and wide receiver coach Tom Coughlin had landed at Boston College. The Giants promoted Parcells' offensive coordinator, Ray Handley, to head coach. That didn't work out.

Parcells returned to coach the Patriots beginning in 1993 and almost landed back with the Giants four years later. Young and Co. were searching for a new head coach in 1997, and Parcells wanted to return to the franchise he had already led to two Super Bowls. But Young didn't want Parcells back—just like after that first season in 1984. This time it wasn't because Young questioned whether Parcells was a good head coach, but he wasn't convinced Parcells was still as dedicated and willing to put in the same time and energy as he did a decade earlier. There was also a belief that the coach would want more control of personnel, minimizing Young. That's not crazy, considering what Parcells famously said regarding the responsibilities of the coach and general manager when taking the Patriots job. "They want you to cook the dinner—at least they should let you shop for some of the groceries," he uttered with a smile.

The way that all unfolded, Young interviewed Nick Saban for the job. He declared it the best interview he ever conducted. Saban's intelligence, the way he saw the game and understood personnel and schemes was unmatched. Young viewed Saban, then the head coach at Michigan State, as the complete package. So the Giants—Wellington Mara, John Mara, Bob Tisch—interviewed him as well and were impressed. They decided Saban would be their guy. But during discussions that lasted about a week, they couldn't come to an understanding of what his powers would be. Young, who had built two Super Bowl winners with the Giants, was still the general manager. He would be the final decision maker. The head coach would provide all the input in the world, but if there was a disagreement in New York's setup, the onus would fall on the GM.

That is how the Maras and Tischs structured their organization, and they weren't about to change that for Saban or anybody else. It had worked for them for almost two decades at this point. So, eventually, it was a mutual decision for Saban and the Giants to go their separate ways.

"We parted on good terms after that," John Mara said.

At this point Parcells was still angling for the Giants job. He had the support of Wellington Mara. Young, though, was pushing for Jim Fassel, who had been an assistant with them in the past. "Faze-el," as Young used to say, was waiting in a hotel room as the Giants' general manager tried to expedite the process. Young quickly went and made the hire. Not moments later Tisch had come around and given the go-ahead to hire Parcells. It was too late. Young had already offered Fassel the job. The Giants would not renege on an offer. So he was their guy.

Parcells would not return to the Giants. He did however get back to New Jersey. Parcells landed with the New York Jets some three weeks later. His Giants legacy would always read: head coach (1983–90), two-time champion (Super Bowls XXI, XXV), and AP Coach of the Year (1986). "I'm just a guy that got to be part of that great Giants tradition, and it's the team that I grew up loving," he said. "I was very fortunate to have that opportunity to do it and then to help win championships. One thing I know about New York, the metro area—once you win, they never forget you."

PART 3

2000

11
Chips on the Table

It was the day before Thanksgiving in 2000 when New York Giants head coach Jim Fassel stepped to the podium in that windowless media room beneath the stands at the old Giants Stadium. It didn't matter that nobody outside those 30 or so people stuffed in that rectangular box could see him in the moment. By the time Fassel was done, his words and actions were so out of character and provocative for an NFL head coach—especially one who had a reputation of being more Mister Rogers than Kenny Rogers—that they would soon be broadcast across the world and plastered as headlines especially in the always sensationalized New York tabloids.

"Fassel: Pencil Us In!" the *New York Post* wrote.

"A GIANT CHALLENGE," said the *Daily News*.

"Fassel Fuel," wrote *Newsday*.

Engulfed by the blue-painted cinderblock walls as his team was in the midst of a two-game skid that dropped the Giants to

7–4 on the season, Fassel stood at the podium that day. From a distance the team was still in good shape. But through the microscope of their own estimation and the New York media, the Giants were eerily close to falling into another late-season collapse.

There was a podium—about five feet in height—at the front of the media room, where just a few days earlier Fassel stood trying to explain a miserable all-around effort in a 31–21 loss to the Detroit Lions. There were two bathrooms in the back. This was in the bowels of the old Giants Stadium when the 24-year structure was a decade from becoming extinct. The bells and whistles, amenities, and luxuries that come with new-age stadiums didn't exist here. It was cold and damp in the innards of the oval-shaped edifice that opened in 1976 and moved the Giants out of New York and across the river to New Jersey. At the time that was a big deal.

It would have been unfortunate if anyone had been in those restrooms at the time when Fassel began speaking because he hardly wasted any breath before getting straight to his pre-planned talking point. He sprinted unprompted into a speech that would have made John "Bluto" Blutarsky from *Animal House* proud. It was so legendary that it still lives on in Giants lore as one of the ballsiest, yet finely calculated gambles in sports history. It sits only behind Joe Namath and Marc Messier in the best of New York sports guarantees. "Get off my coaches' backs. Get off my players' backs. I'm responsible for the whole thing," Fassel said as part of his 25-minute press conference on that Wednesday afternoon. "I'm raising the stakes right now. This is a poker game. I'm shoving my chips to the middle of the table. I'm raising the ante. Anyone wants in, get in. Anyone wants out, get out, okay? This team is going to the playoffs, and that is my whole goal in life right now. I'll set the course, and I'll set the expectations, and they'll have to live up to them."

And so this went on for 25 minutes following Fassel's eye-opening playoff guarantee. It was especially surprising because those in the room were stunned to see this side of the head coach who earned Coach of the Year honors in 1997, his first year with the Giants. They went 10–5–1 that season but were 8–8 and 7–9 the following two years, leaving his job security shaky heading into that 2000 season. It wasn't a secret that the Giants needed to make the playoffs, especially after a 7–2 start, or it could be the end for the head coach. He was hired by the previous general manager George Young and not his boss at the time, Ernie Accorsi.

Given all this, there was no way around the increased scrutiny on Fassel heading into the 2000 season. It came with a head coaching job in the New York market no matter the circumstance. And then there were the dynamics of this specific situation on top of that. Fassel knew the 2000 season would decide his fate and so did the players. That is because late in the 1999 season Wellington Mara made it crystal clear he wasn't happy with the direction of his beloved franchise. His New York Football Giants had fallen apart in a playoff loss to the Minnesota Vikings in '97, fighting and arguing on the sideline as they allowed a 16-point halftime lead to slip away. Things didn't get much better the next two years as the team failed to finish with a winning record.

After the Giants were officially eliminated from playoff contention in Week 16 of the '99 season when they were dismantled at home by those same Vikings 34–17 at Giants Stadium, Mara did something those in the locker room had never seen. He stood in front of the team after a game and spoke. It was as surprising as God talking to Jesus at his baptism. Mara sent a message to those Giants, which left most of those in attendance with their jaws dropped to the floor because they realized just about nobody was safe. "For those of you who tried hard, put forth the effort, I commend you," Mara said, according to those in attendance. "But for those of you that gave up, you will not be wearing a Giants uniform next year."

Ouch! To hear those words from Mara hit hard. The soft-spoken but powerful owner then walked straight out of the room. There was nothing more that needed to be added. His disgust was palpable. His feelings were clear. Crystal. Those two stern sentences were all that he needed to say. Prior to that point, Mara was always at practice. He was always standing there in the corner watching but never making himself noticed. He was omnipresent but also somewhat mysterious to those in the locker room. He shook their hands but mostly just exchanged pleasantries and *never* spoke to the team as a whole. "So then after that, we go to the offensive meeting that next week, and the coach...was like, 'Everybody, look to your left, look to your right, two out of three of you guys ain't going to be here next year,'" wide receiver Amani Toomer recalled. "And damn sure that next year, they got rid of everybody. And that's why that year [in 2000] was extra pressure because the owner was pissed off."

Only 12 of the 22 starters from that Week 16 loss to the Vikings in 1999 started Week One the following season. What turned into the 2000 NFC East and NFC champions had a very different look and feel. The offensive line, in particular, had been overhauled. They added veterans such as Lomas Brown, Glenn Parker, and Dusty Ziegler to provide stability in the trenches and solidify the locker room. New York also drafted Heisman Trophy–winning running back Ron Dayne to provide a fresh, young complement to Tiki Barber. It was also quarterback Kerry

Collins' second season with the team, allowing the offense to become less run-dependent and more balanced. These Giants were clearly improved.

It seemed to be working early that season with how the multidimensional offense added to a stout defense, which possessed a dominant front seven that teams couldn't run against. The 2000 Giants under Fassel charged out to that 7–2 record before running into the Greatest Show on Turf, the high-flying St. Louis Rams, who put 38 points on them in three quarters without quarterback Kurt Warner. That would have been palatable, but the Giants also lost to the Lions the following week at Giants Stadium, where they were down three touchdowns in the first half and looked incompetent on special teams. They allowed a 50-yard punt return, and Brad Maynard had a punt blocked. The loss was extra troubling because memories from wilting down the stretch the previous season were still fresh in everybody's minds. "We're in dire straits," Brown, the veteran offensive lineman, said after the Detroit debacle despite still being 7–4.

"We're melting," cornerback Jason Sehorn added.

The Giants' special teams, their punt team in particular, was a mess for the second straight week in that game. Maynard not only had a punt blocked, but also watched Detroit's Desmond Howard rip off two long returns. It prompted criticism...from the punter. The normally soft-spoken Maynard thought there was too much laughing and joking going on in special teams coordinator Larry Mac Duff's meetings. That, in turn, led to the poor performance against the Lions. It led to some curious comments as well. "Sometimes you wonder where guys' hearts are," Maynard said after the game. "We are supposed to come to work prepared."

The Giants appeared to have problems. Most of all, none of this reflected well on Fassel, who was ultimately the man in charge of the coaching and those meetings. The feeling afterward was that Fassel's guarantee was partially in response to Maynard's comments. What unfolded the following Wednesday with the guarantee—one day before Thanksgiving and in the middle of a week that would end with a cross-country trip to Arizona—was so incredibly shocking because it was completely out of character for Fassel. The former air conditioning salesman was generally astutely calculated. He planned his moves and rhetoric as if he were a poker player preparing for his final act on the river. In the moment this seemed more like flying by the seat of his pants—even if that was only partially true. Fassel had told his team leaders what he was going to do before actually acting on his impulses. The front office was kept out of the loop at first perhaps to keep them from talking him out of the seemingly crazed approach. Immediately after the press conference, Fassel went upstairs to the executive offices and told general manager Ernie Accorsi and executive vice president John Mara what had just unfolded in the hotbox below. "Well, I did it," Fassel said.

"Did what?" they asked.

"I guaranteed we're going to the playoffs," Fassel revealed.

The executive floor couldn't believe what they had just heard. They were in shock—much like anyone who eventually saw clips of that press conference. It stunned management, fans, and even those in the locker room who didn't see it coming. Some players think that was part of Fassel's intended result. He wanted them to know that if he was going down, it would not be without a fight. It was Fassel's last stand, and he was seeing how it was going to be perceived. "It was more of he was talking to the powers to be, so to speak," veteran tight end

Howard Cross said. "He was like, 'Hey look, if this is the way it's going to be and everybody knows, I'm going to let it all hang out.' And he did that."

It sent a message to the players as well. It suggested that Fassel was in this struggle with them. If they couldn't get back on track and to the playoffs, who knew what could happen that offseason? They had already seen that Mara meant business. Surely there would have been a new coach. With a new coach comes a new philosophical approach and schemes. That meant new players and even assistant coaches. It would essentially be a complete overhaul that wouldn't include Fassel and possibly them. So although the playoff guarantee and how it was delivered was undoubtedly unconventional, it was well received internally. "To see him do that, as a player you say, 'Heh!' You kind of giggle, but at the same time it was smart," Michael Strahan said in an interview years later. "We said, 'Okay, this guy is in the middle with us. He's going to fight with us. We're not going to quit on him. We're not going to give up on him.' And from then on, we took what he said to heart and played well."

Maybe, in retrospect, the late Fassel, who passed away from a heart attack in 2021, saw that this was what his team needed. They were a team headed in the wrong direction at the wrong time. It was an act that was all too common for his teams at this time of the year. They needed something in this instance that would galvanize a team that had a lot of talent on its roster and coaching staff. Fassel's coordinators were Sean Payton on the offensive side of the ball and John Fox for the defense. Both would become successful and respected head coaches in the league.

It was on Tuesday night of that Thanksgiving week that Fassel decided he was going to adopt a new attitude for the remainder of the season. It was the old I-don't-give-a-damn approach. If he was going down, it was going to be swinging, similar to what Bill Parcells thought when his job was on the line after one season. After his famous decree, Fassel was asked if there was any concern about putting it all on the table—his honor, pride, dignity, and professional fate—all at once. "No worries," he said. "I've got no fear. None. Zero."

He said it with the look of a fireman about to run into a burning building. Or an individual who dared not to blink while staring down the barrel of a revolver. No fear. None. Zero. Fassel did that day what most football coaches try to avoid on a daily basis—speaking in absolutes. Even worse, he unequivocally made an out-of-character guarantee. Former Giants reporter Bill Pennington described the Superman-in-a-phone-booth transformation the following day in *The New York Times*: "Jim Fassel, the Mister Rogers of football coaches, tore off his cardigan today, tied it around his head, and joined the Hell's Angels."

It was the perfect description. When asked in the following days whether there were any regrets because the move might ultimately cost Fassel his job, he made it clear. Again, none. Zero. "I don't give a fuck!" he said.

For good reason. The Hell's Angels' Fassel had a motorcycle gang that would ultimately respond to the calling. This was the impetus of what turned into a fun Super Bowl run that nobody—probably not even Fassel himself if you gave him truth serum—expected. It was so out of nowhere that Mara would later joke about being called the worst No. 1 seed and NFC champion of all time.

Not that anyone connected to the Giants cared. In fact, they seemed to embrace being considered these overachieving vagabonds. The locker room may have thought that Fassel's approach was unorthodox, but they were behind him from the moment he broached the idea during a meeting with the team's leaders. In a way it bonded and connected the team to its coach in a way they never were previously. "The first thing for me was I thought Coach Fassel was crazy when he made that prediction," Brown said. "And to be honest with you, he had kind of told us before. And when I say *us*, I was talking about the leaders on the team. I think it was myself, Jessie [Armstead], Keith Hamilton, Strahan, and a couple of more guys, the leaders on the team. He brought us in and he told us basically what he was going to say to the media and he put it on us first, and I think he was just testing us to see what our reaction would be. So Coach Fassel comes in there and said, 'Look, I'm going to tell the media we're pushing all our chips in. You guys are with me or you're not with me.' But he just made it strong in that's what he was determined to do. And he felt that if the leaders got on board and the leaders were behind him, the rest of the team would follow."

Some might suggest Fassel knew what was on deck. The Arizona Cardinals were the next opponent on that Thanksgiving weekend. They were a bad team that year, ultimately finishing 3–13. The remainder of the schedule wasn't all that daunting either. Not that it mattered. The locker room seemed to have an added respect for Fassel now that he was willing to put it all out there, including his career in New York. They knew in their heart of hearts that if they somehow stumbled down the stretch and missed the playoffs, he was going to be fired anyway. So this was in a way Fassel stating the obvious to the general public but also putting all the pressure on his brittle back rather than the players' stout shoulders. "I'm on board. I like it," Armstead recalled thinking. "Why? Because it is what it is. I mean, we don't have anything to hide. You put all the chips on the table. There's nothing sitting there saying that if we be quiet and we do this and do that, nobody will notice. Everybody will notice. Everybody is looking. They're going to see what we're going to do regardless."

It helped that Armstead, one of the true leaders of the team, came from Carter High School in Dallas and the University of Miami, where both programs had a no-BS approach. Armstead was on the famous Carter team that beat Odessa Permian in the famed state championship that was immortalized in the book and movie *Friday Night Lights.* He was a star linebacker for boisterous Hurricanes national championship teams in 1989 and 1991. None of those teams were afraid to tell it like it was, and neither was Armstead. To him, when Fassel introduced the idea, he barely blinked. If Armstead, Strahan, Collins, Barber, and Brown felt the same, it trickled through the rest of the team.

Collins, who had resurrected his career under Fassel in New York, was another player who was never afraid to speak his truth. So, obviously, he would ride with the Giants head coach who gave him a last chance for professional success. In need of help for a drinking problem and from the stench of what many believe was quitting on one of his former teams, the Carolina Panthers, and making a racist comment, Collins was borderline toxic when he signed with the Giants in 1999. But Collins was on board with Fassel's move. Strahan was, too, and so was Brown.

Off they went with every win along the way providing a new iota of assurance Fassel had made the right move. It helped that Fassel had the trust of his players. He was hard on them but also fair. And it's not like they didn't have any success with him as the coach, winning the NFC East with him at the helm in 1997. They also knew this was a talented group and perhaps the most well-rounded team they'd had in a while. They could run the football, sling it with a rejuvenated Collins and a talented receiving corps led by Toomer and Ike Hilliard, and dominate on defense. The group collectively bought into what Fassel was selling. "He knew the pulse of that team," Brown said. "He knew the heartbeat of our team, and he pushed the right buttons that year."

To say the 2000 New York Football Giants responded to Fassel's calling would be an understatement. They followed him straight through the pressure of landing on the back page to Super Bowl XXXV in Tampa. It was a ride they still cherish to this day. The Giants went to Arizona that week after Fassel's playoff guarantee and blasted the Cardinals 31–7 behind a dominant defensive performance that saw Hamilton record three sacks and the team force four turnovers. That was the beginning of something special.

In all, there would be seven straight wins, including what many consider the greatest day in Giants Stadium history in the NFC Championship Game. The run would take Fassel's crew all the way to the Super Bowl that season, where they would meet the Baltimore Ravens and their vaunted 2000 defense led by Ray Lewis.

The Giants followed the Arizona win with a hard-fought 9–7 victory in Washington behind three Brad Daluiso field goals. From there, they were off and running. Sprinting really.

A demolition of the Pittsburgh Steelers, where they held future Hall of Famer Jerome Bettis to 39 yards rushing on 17 carries, followed. But perhaps their biggest win came when the Giants clinched the NFC East title during a night game on December 17 in Dallas against the rival Cowboys with a dramatic fourth-quarter comeback capped by linebacker Michael Barrow's fourth-and-2 stop in the final minute near midfield.

It was the crowning moment of a monster first season with the Giants for Barrow.

Four games after Fassel had boisterously declared his convictions, there he was with a wide smile getting ice water dumped on his head at Texas Stadium. The Giants were NFC East champions. Fassel was a legend for his guarantee. The road to the Super Bowl in the NFC would eventually run through Giants Stadium after they took care of the Jacksonville Jaguars—coached by former Giants assistant Tom Coughlin—in the regular-season finale.

When all was said and done, the Giants won their final five regular-season games after Fassel's brilliantly-timed guarantee that not only saved his job, but also sparked an out-of-nowhere run. It ultimately extended his coaching career in New York for three more years. That is when it officially got stale and fell apart. For a variety of reasons, Fassel never got another chance at being a head coach in the NFL. But at least he had that moment, that year in 2000, when he did what so many other coaches only wished they had the guts to pull off. "It was the most genius thing as a coach on a hot seat you could ever do," Barber said. "Because if it doesn't work, you're getting fired anyways. And if it does, you look like a genius. So that lives in lore because it fucking worked."

It doesn't even matter if Fassel was aware the upcoming competition was conveniently soft. Well-timed and well-executed is one way to describe Fassel's actions that year. His words resonated in the locker room. "What you remember is the conviction he had behind it and the belief in us. I mean, that was apparent," then-second-year tight end and current Lions head coach Dan Campbell said. "You feel like you're in that moment, and that happens, and knowing what we had as a team and the type of locker room we had, I think that thrust us forward. I mean, we believed in ourselves, but when you know your coach is in, you could feel it and you could feel it as players. And I think that just confirmed what we already knew. And that was after two losses. So for him to do that, we kind of knew what type of team we were going to have. And I think that conviction bled into us as players, and it's like, *Yeah, absolutely, we're going to do this. We're too good not to let this bring us down.*"

The chips-on-the-table speech seemed in a way to liberate Fassel. In his mind it was addressing the 10,000-pound gorilla in the room. He believed it even helped him coach and lead better down the stretch that season. Whatever it was, it worked. It earned him a new contract after the season. Fassel signed a new four-year, $10.75 million deal just 97 days after his guarantee.

If his guarantee had backfired, it would have all fallen on his shoulders. He would have played the role of out-of-touch buffoon coach who didn't have any feel for his team. He would be just another failed coach rather than one of just three coaches in Giants history who have led the storied franchise to a Super Bowl. It's Parcells, Tom Coughlin...and Jim Fassel. A pretty good list to be on. Some quality company. "This team that went to the Super Bowl in 2000, we've got to give it up for Jim Fassel, RIP," Strahan said. "He was a hell of a coach, and we won the division championship, went to that Super Bowl with him—and I know we didn't win it all—but he was a big part of changing the culture of the organization. And, yeah, he pushed them all into the middle of the table. I think [he was] watching Kenny Rogers' *The Gambler,* and he got real excited. But it inspired all of us."

That Fassel directive was the impetus for the Giants' first Super Bowl run in a decade. Nobody—except maybe those in the locker room—saw it coming. "We shocked a lot of people, but we did not shock ourselves," Fassel said afterward. "In this country or playing in this league, if you've got a belief, if you've got determination, if you've got teamwork, there pretty much isn't anything you can't accomplish if you've got some talent. We have talent. You know what? We're living the American Dream. We're the American dream."

12

The Next Lombardi and Landry: Sean Payton and John Fox

THE 2000 NEW YORK GIANTS TEAM HAD TALENT, BUT IT WAS hardly the most talented in the franchise's 75 years of existence. They went into that season with modest expectations. Only five of 15 ESPN experts even predicted they would make the playoffs, and each of those five projected them as wild-card entries. None saw the NFC East title as an option.

The spotlight was actually on the Washington Redskins with Norv Turner (who was fired before the end of December) as the coach. Washington had just signed big-name veterans

Bruce Smith and Deion Sanders and had all the hype despite putting their faith in two 30-plus quarterbacks, Brad Johnson and Jeff George. All 15 of those ESPN experts had the Redskins winning the division. It's not hard to figure how it ultimately played out. Washington went 8–8, and Terry Robiskie finished the season as the interim coach.

The Giants had a good, solid young core and, equally important, one of the more impressive coaching staffs in the league—even if few at the time recognized just how good it was. Jim Fassel was a head coach with a modicum of success, but he had Sean Payton as his offensive coordinator and John Fox as his defensive coordinator. Both proved to be Super Bowl–level head coaches in addition to great coordinators. Payton eventually won a Super Bowl with the New Orleans Saints, and Fox reached a Super Bowl with the Carolina Panthers and Denver Broncos. If not for a classic Tom Brady comeback against the Panthers, Fox would also have a ring as a Super Bowl–winning head coach.

Payton was just 37 years old during the 2000 season when he officially became an offensive coordinator for the first time. He called plays late in the previous season when he was Fassel's quarterbacks coach, but this was his first time being tasked with handling a majority of the offensive gameplanning. He was rewarded for his work with Kerry Collins and the quarterbacks, and Fassel always felt it was most natural for the coach who works most closely with the quarterbacks to be the play caller. With more responsibility and latitude under the watchful eye of Fassel and assistant head coach Jim Skipper, the former offensive coordinator, the Giants quickly figured that this young coach was special. It became clear that Payton was ahead of his time using motion and movement before the snap as deception. He knew how to confuses defenses with the so-called eye-candy.

This is how Payton described it in the Giants 2000 season playbook under a section entitled "Formations, Substitutions, and Motion": "The ability to use multiple formations, substitutions, and motion allows us to manipulate our opponent's defense to our advantage. The key to this type of flexibility is to fully understand our formation system. In order to do this each player must understand our base formation, then be able to apply the multiple variations to them."

The 2000 Giants didn't have all that many running plays for Tiki Barber and rookie Ron Dayne, the Heisman Trophy winner the previous year out of the University of Wisconsin, but it looked like they did. This was the genius of Payton's early days: simplicity under the guise of complexity. "We only had maybe 10, 12 run plays," right tackle Lomas Brown said. "You know how some of these teams have all these plays? We didn't have a lot of plays. What we had was a lot of different formations, but we would run the same play. It would just look different because we were running out of a different formation."

Barber considered Payton ahead of his time. He not only didn't overload them with plays, but he also had them calling multiple plays in the huddle to check into the better of the two at the line of scrimmage. Today this doesn't seem like anything special. Much of what Payton did in 2000 wouldn't be considered out of the ordinary now. But in the moment, it was different than what most teams were doing. "Sean was ahead of his time that way," Brown said. "It simplified it for the offensive linemen. It simplified it for the offense. I remember talking to a player that played for Mike Martz when he was with [the Los Angeles Rams], and he said they would have a couple of hundred plays. And I'm like, *Oh my God! How could you even?* But with Sean, like the saying goes, sometimes less is more. That's how it was for us in 2000. We didn't have a lot of different plays, but we had a whole bunch of different formations for those plays, and that's how we had a lot of success against a lot of teams. And Tiki's right: Sean was ahead of his time doing it that way."

In his fourth professional season, Barber had his first 1,000-yard campaign under Payton. Dayne added 770 yards as a rookie. Together, they were the original "Thunder and Lightning" running back duo. Barber was the shifty, more versatile back who could do it all, including catch the ball out of the backfield as if he were a wide receiver. Payton viewed him as "another receiver who can run." Barber finished with more than 5,000 receiving yards in his career. Dayne was the powerful banger who ran for tough yards between the tackles. He more aptly fit the prototype of what a running back should be at the time. It was why Barber felt the Giants were always seemingly trying to replace him early in his career. Meanwhile, general manager Ernie Accorsi looked at it more as finding the right complement to Barber in order to maximize his potential.

Either way, it was a combination that worked that season with the innovative Payton being the one calling the plays. The Giants that year were often running what they called "dick 'em" plays. With the input of tight end coach Mike Pope, offensive line coach Jim McNally, and Fassel, these misdirection plays were a massive part of the Payton offense in 2000. "We would line up in *trips bunch left toss 38* or *39 crack scissors*...It looked like a toss," Barber explained. "You had three guys in a bunch to the left side, and we'd toss it to the left, and then I'd take three steps, stick my foot in the ground. The left guard is now pulling back the other way. And so all the flow goes to the trip side, and I'm coming out the back door with a lead blocker, and there's just nobody around. So it fit my skill set because I was fast, and I could change direction, but I wasn't big. And up to that point, it was all, 'Let's go 20 carries between the tackles.' It was that type of offense."

Not under Payton. He wanted to use Barber like the Rams were using Marshall Faulk at the time. Faulk was the MVP of the league that year with Martz's Rams. Payton had been Faulk's running backs coach at San Diego State and knew how to best utilize a versatile running back with the skill set of Barber, who was an untapped version of Faulk at that time. One of the ways was running scissors, a misdirection concept that fully commits the running back and offensive line in one direction before flipping to the other side. The front-side guard pulls to the weak side ahead of the running back. In this case it was often Ron Stone, an All-Pro right guard for the first time in his career that 2000 season for the Giants. His only other All-Pro year came in 2002 while also working in Payton's scheme.

New York's line may not have been the most athletic, but it moved efficiently enough and did an excellent job of getting to the second level. That made for a quality match with Barber's style and Payton's desired run scheme. "We called the run and then put scissors on the back end of everything," tight end and future head coach Dan Campbell said with a chuckle years later. "It was all different runs."

From there, Payton and the Giants kept building. Their offense in 2000 became modernized—not exactly the Rams but also not a pound-it-up-the-middle-every-time attack.

Under Payton they were no longer all power running game and defense. They added a more dynamic passing attack with Collins as the quarterback and a flexibility to adjust that few offenses at the time possessed. "We started doing double scissors and check-with-me. Now, it's ubiquitous. You see it everywhere," Barber said. "You're checking at the line of scrimmage and getting into a different play. You hear it all the time. 'Kill,

kill, kill!' So you'd call two plays in the huddle and you'd kill one. But in 2000 nobody was doing that, or at least not a lot of teams were doing that. I think the Rams were, but not a ton of teams were. So we were always right. And the reason we started having a good rushing season was because we couldn't be wrong on a play, whether it was a pass play or a run play. There were so many checks. And Kerry was the catalyst. He was so astute at the line of scrimmage."

But it was more than that which made Payton's offense so successful that season. The Giants could line up in a two-back set and motion Barber to quickly make it a three-receiver look. They could line up in trips right and quickly have a receiver slide over to the other side of the formation. Payton's offense in 2000 was considered cutting edge. He was trying new things and having success. "There's no question," Campbell said. "It was all the shifts, the motions. The dick 'em runs, the setups. That was Sean. Look, I was with him for damn near most of my playing career. And then I coached with him for five years. I mean, he is one of the most innovative coaches I've ever been around. His vision for a play and gameplan is awesome."

New York's offense ranked 13th overall and averaged just more than 20 points per game, but Payton's gameplan for the NFC Championship Game against the Minnesota Vikings in particular was a masterpiece. Not exactly Bill Belichick in the Super Bowl against the Buffalo Bills, but it was pretty damn close if judged on the success and outcome. The Giants did whatever they wanted in the first half of that contest before essentially just waiting for the clock to expire in the second. A large part of that was pinpointing the Vikings' Achilles' heel. Payton found Minnesota's biggest weakness and was intent on attacking it relentlessly. He was confident they could exploit and expose their cornerbacks, Wasswa Serwanga and converted receiver Robert Tate. His offense didn't have to get too cute.

It wasn't just Payton and the offense that were impressive in that championship game and season. In fact, the defense under Fox was probably the team's best unit. It capped a memorable season by pitching an impressive shutout against the powerful Vikings. Overall the Giants ranked fifth in total defense that year and allowed just 15.4 points per game. Nobody could run against their defensive front. They allowed just 72.3 yards per game, second best in the NFL. This was massive for the rehabilitation of Fox's reputation. He wasn't exactly in high demand when he came to the Giants as the defensive coordinator in 1997. He came with serious question marks because a year earlier he had gone to training camp—as defensive coordinator for the Oakland Raiders—with his son, Matthew, then 13 years of age. It didn't go well to the point that Fox called his wife, Robin, in the middle of the day. "Robin," Fox said. "Don't freak out. I quit my job. Matt and I are coming home. We'll be there in an hour."

Robin was unpacking in the new house they had just rented. She handled it like any loving wife who just heard their husband quit the most prestigious job they've ever had before that season even started. "Of course," she said in an interview with *The New York Times* several years later, "I totally freaked out."

Fox had enough of being nitpicked by Raiders owner Al Davis. After a confrontation he just got up and left without another job in his back pocket. He had to wait until the following year to get another shot at being a defensive coordinator. It didn't matter. He wasn't about to subject himself to that kind of constant second-guessing. Even then, there was a perception among some that Fox was this hothead nut who told an owner to fuck off and quit. It took conviction for Fassel to make the

42-year-old his first hire with the Giants. It certainly helped that the two had worked together in Oakland under Davis. Fassel was Fox's biggest advocate at the time and perhaps the only coach who might've hired him again as a defensive coordinator. In the end it was the right move. It proved to be a coup. "There will be things he learns on the job, but John is ready," Fassel said presciently at the time. "He'll have to prioritize his time and study some things. He's always done everything he can do to be good at his job."

Fox's football acumen was never in doubt. He was wicked smart—and not afraid to show it. In fact, there was a cockiness to him, similar to Payton. That same attribute that made him fearless could be viewed as both a positive and a negative. The former showed when he predicted the Giants might shut out the Minnesota Vikings in the NFC Championship Game in 2000.

But Fox also came with a reputation as a know-it-all. And he didn't exactly make a great first impression with some of the most important veterans in the Giants' defensive room. That cockiness was met with more than a hint of hesitation. "When John Fox first came in, we were sitting in the room, and me and [Strahan], I don't think we had even made a Pro Bowl, but he came in and said, 'I want to teach football to this room. You don't know a lot of football,'" linebacker Jessie Armstead recalled of the conversation. "We're like, *You better shut up. You just got fired yourself. You want to come over and tell us we don't know nothing?*"

Fox would have to prove himself to this group, but the reality was at that point that the Giants defense hadn't made it yet. They were still little more than talented players with potential. They weren't the All-Pros and Pro Bowlers they would become later in their careers. Armstead and Strahan were blossoming into great players, but they hadn't reached the Pro Bowl prior to Fox's arrival in 1997. Little did they know that his aggressive approach would be ideal for their careers. Soon enough, there would be individual and team success. The accolades would start flowing. "Well, John Fox was a big difference maker... John came in and started getting to know us and started teaching about the zone dogs and different kind of blitzes and things like that," Armstead said. "And we looked around and said, 'Maybe we don't know football.' And then we got comfortable in his defense...[and] all of us had good careers in his defense."

Strahan would go on to make his first of seven Pro Bowls and four first-team All-Pro teams in that first season under Fox. He would go on to become a Hall of Famer and one of the best defensive players in Giants history. Armstead would make his first of five straight Pro Bowls under Fox. All five of those Pro Bowl seasons in his career came with Fox as his defensive coordinator. The likelihood is that those two in particular, along with defensive tackle Keith Hamilton, would have been great players regardless. They were too talented not to be significant players in the league, but Fox found a way to maximize their abilities. In 2000, along with Sehorn and linebacker Michael Barrow, they were the leaders and most significant players on a top five defense.

Fox made it easy for his players. He would come up with ideas to free up his best players. When they were certain it was a pass play, Armstead and Co. would call "Thunder." That meant all bets were off, and linemen could do whatever they wanted to do. Just get after the quarterback. They found matchups that were advantageous and went to work. "Fox's greatest thing was every single Wednesday he would come in, and we'd start watching film and he'd tell the whole defense, he'd put that red laser up on the screen: 'All right, there's the weak link. That's who we're going after,'" Sehorn said. "I mean, just plain as day. So the defensive line were like, 'Okay, this is the lineman that we don't have any respect in. We're attacking that area.' And we would. We'd attack it and we're going to force them to overcome their own shortcomings."

In a way Payton and Fox were the Giants' 21st century Vince Lombardi and Tom Landry. A poor man's version, which is nothing to be ashamed of given that Lombardi and Landry are both in the conversation for greatest NFL coach of all time after they were once assistants under Jim Lee Howell in New York from 1954 to 1958. Clearly, Payton and Fox were not quite Lombardi and Landry, but they were the next dynamic coordinator duo with the Giants, which in retrospect gave Fassel one of the best staffs in the league.

It didn't last all that long though. Fox was eventually hired in 2002 to be the head coach of the Panthers, where he lasted nine seasons and reached a Super Bowl during his second year in charge. He would make the Super Bowl again a decade later as the head coach of the Broncos. Payton eventually became a head coach in 2006 with the Saints. He had a successful 17-season run, which included 10 playoff appearances, three NFC Championship Game appearances, and a victory in Super Bowl XLIV. He later became the head coach of the Broncos. But before all that happened, Payton and Fox helped Fassel and the Giants make an improbable run to the Super Bowl.

13

The Sehorn Interception

THE 2000 SEASON WAS IN THE MIDST OF A TIME WHEN THE New York Giants sat in the driver's seat of the roller coaster that is their rivalry with the Philadelphia Eagles. New York had won eight straight against the Eagles heading into their divisional round playoff matchup on January 7, 2001, including a pair in the 2000 regular season. The first was a 33–18 shellacking in Week Two when Kerry Collins said he felt "better than I ever felt" about the offense. They followed that with a convincing 24–7 victory off their bye week in Week Nine when they held Philadelphia quarterback Donovan McNabb to a woeful 10-of-31 passing.

The talk coming into the playoff matchup later that year was how difficult it was to beat a good team three times in the same season. The Eagles were coming off a convincing wild-card win against the Tampa Bay Buccaneers. The Giants still didn't seem all that concerned with the task of making it three for three that season, especially as the home team and the No. 1 seed in the NFC. "We were all like, *Fuck that. We own them,*" Tiki Barber recalled heading into the contest.

The matchup worked in the Giants' favor. At the time McNabb was a young quarterback, still growing into the passer he would become later in his Eagles tenure. In his second professional season that year, he threw a pedestrian 21 touchdown passes and 13 interceptions. Philadelphia's success was predicated on his legs and its running game. Dominant against the run, the Giants had limited Philadelphia's running backs to 14 attempts for 26 yards in the two regular-season matchups, which was good for a measly 1.9 yards per carry. That put all the onus on McNabb to carry the load.

All of this was still just the backdrop for what was about to unfold late that afternoon in a 4:15 PM (EST) start time for the NFC divisional round at Giants Stadium. The game, which saw the Giants again dominate from the opening kickoff when Ron Dixon took it to the house for a score, will still forever be remembered for the incredible play that star cornerback Jason Sehorn made as the sun set on that late winter afternoon. It came just after the two-minute warning in the first half on a second-and-10 from the Eagles' 26-yard line. The raucous crowd was buzzing at the time, waiving the white towels that were handed out before the game with fury. The "Dee-fence! Dee-fence!" chant created by Giants fans in the '50s was working to will Big Blue into another stop. Only this time they got even better. "The interception of Donovan McNabb and he takes it to the house," Barber said. "That game—I almost only remember the Sehorn thing."

It was that incredible. McNabb dropped back to pass and faced pressure from Big Blue's two best pass rushers on the now famous play. Keith Hamilton tossed left guard John Welbourn to the side and had a free run at Philadelphia's quarterback. Michael Strahan slipped inside right tackle Jon Runyan and bullied running back Brian Mitchell into the backfield. That made for 565 pounds of quarterback-killing pass rushers bearing down on the frazzled young quarterback.

The pressure forced McNabb, looking down the right hash, to speed up his process. He turned and fired toward the right sideline where wide receiver Torrence Small had settled. But Sehorn undercut the pass and dove for the ball, which was thrown low and away. Usually that is a safe spot to avoid an interception but not in this case. The pass bounced off Sehorn's arms, he batted it into the air with his right hand as he rolled over and managed to start getting to his feet as the ball landed, nestled softly into his glove-covered hands.

Sehorn, as he was trying to stand back up, actually caught the ball with one knee still touching the ground. He had to avoid teammate Emmanuel McDaniel immediately with the sideline to his left. So he slid inside of McDaniel to the right and raced toward the end zone, where he received a block from Jessie Armstead and beat McNabb to the left pylon for the most amazing 32-yard interception return for a touchdown that stadium had ever seen. It gave the Giants a 17–0 lead and set the stage for another magical afternoon the following week in the NFC Championship Game against the Minnesota Vikings. "We're playing a coverage where I have inside coverage," Sehorn later told Giants play-by-play announcer Bob Papa. "So I'm protecting the slant, post, all that kind of stuff. If you look at the play, it was on the far right hash mark. So throwing an out route isn't going to be the easiest throw. And they threw an out route, and I dove underneath. Another thing you're not ever supposed to do is go underneath because if you don't make the play underneath, he's gone behind you."

That is not what happened here. Sehorn never needed to worry because he made the right decision. Small was on his knees trying to make the catch. He never had a chance at the ball or the tackle since he was on the ground. Sehorn was able to get to the ball in time, likely preventing a completion and putting valuable points on the scoreboard before halftime. "I just felt, *Man, I might be able to get to this,*" Sehorn said. "So I dove. It was literally all the things you're not supposed to do. You're not supposed to cut underneath the receiver. You're not supposed to dive because if you don't make the play and he catches it, he's gone. I've seen it so many times that I know what happened is that as I'm reaching to catch the ball, my arms hit the ground, and it knocks the ball up. And then I'm on my side to my back and I look up and I'm like, *Well, there it is.* And I don't know what happened at that point in time. It's all kind of a blur, but clearly I tipped it up to get it going higher, sat up, caught it, got up, and then had to avoid my own man Emmanuel McDaniel so I didn't trip over him and then went back to the house."

Even for an athlete like Sehorn, this was something special. It was an interception unlike any you see on a normal Sunday of football. And it came in a massive spot (the playoffs) against a division rival. It's still a play Sehorn hears about to this day. People tell him how incredibly athletic it was. The former USC star still didn't quite realize at first. It wasn't until later when a friend was describing how he hopped to his feet without using his hands as leverage on the ground that he even noticed. "I was looking at him like, *Huh?* And so as they played the play, I was like, *Oh wow, you're right.* I stood up without ever pushing off the ground. I had the ball in my hands. I never put my hand down. I just stood straight up. I don't know if I could do that today."

The Giants sideline couldn't believe what had happened in the moment. They were just trying to prevent the Eagles from scoring some points before halftime in what was still a one-score game. Before they knew it, they had their jaws hanging on the ground in disbelief as the Giants had a three-score lead and the crowd going wild, as towels waved in incredulity because of what they had just witnessed. "Hey, I've never seen a play like that," a stupefied Jim Fassel told Sehorn moments later on the sideline. "I've never seen anything like that!"

"I told him: 'That is the best play I've ever seen,'" Strahan retorted while flashing that trademark gap-toothed smile. "That was unbelievable!"

That Sehorn interception would go down as the greatest play in Giants Stadium history. It was voted as such when Big Blue moved to MetLife Stadium a decade later. It was that kind of special play that seemed appropriate from the rockstar cornerback, whose strong play, good looks, and model/actress/girlfriend at the time, Angie Harmon, made him more than just your average football player. *Sports Illustrated* described him later that year as "arguably the most glamorous pro football player New York has known since Joe Namath quarterbacked the Jets a generation ago." It was a funny comparison because Sehorn in a way was somewhat anti-social. It made him uncomfortable to be in crowds and the center of attention.

Sehorn was the ultimate underdog story. He went from a poor, single-parent upbringing and never playing football until his senior year of high school to becoming a star football player in the bright lights and big city of New York. In between starring for the Giants and making circus interceptions like the one that occurred in that playoff win over the Eagles, he was booking modeling gigs and dating the *Law & Order* star. Sehorn married Harmon in 2001 and amicably split 13 years later. He's now remarried and has four kids from the two marriages.

The interception of McNabb in the playoff win still remains the most memorable play of Sehorn's nine-year career. In his mind it's right up there with an interception he made covering Vikings wide receiver Cris Carter during a playoff game during the 1997 season. But while the play against the Eagles was great and special in the way it unfolded, it almost seems apropos that it happened to Sehorn in that moment. "Jason Sehorn is the best athlete I've ever played with," Strahan said. "I've never seen anybody do the things that he could on the football field."

14

Giants Stadium's Greatest Game

The NFC Championship Game from the 2000 season goes down as one of the greatest games ever played in the old Giants Stadium. It's between that and the 1986 NFC Championship Game against the Washington Redskins, which New York won 17–0 in windy, wintery conditions at the old stadium to reach its first Super Bowl. It was a combination of the circumstances, result, atmosphere, and the sheer nature of the ass kicking that made the 41–0 victory against the Minnesota Vikings on January 14, 2001, so extraordinary.

The game was effectively over before Minnesota could catch a kickoff. By then the Giants had a 14–0 lead against an explosive Vikings team led by wide receivers Randy Moss and Cris Carter and quarterbacked by Daunte Culpepper. The only thing in doubt by that point was whether they would shut out that vaunted offense on the celebratory afternoon when the Giants stuck it in the face of all the doubters. Not everyone was surprised that Minnesota didn't score a point. As the story goes, defensive coordinator John Fox called his shot with the defensive masterpiece. General manager Ernie Accorsi's office was right next to the Giants' defensive coordinator. He remembers walking in and telling Fox he hadn't slept a minute that week because all he saw was Minnesota scoring 6,000 touchdowns at night in his head. "And Fox looked at me and said, 'We just may shut them out,'" Accorsi said. "I thought he needed a therapist."

It was typical Fox. He was confident, almost to a fault. It actually left a bad first impression on some of his defensive leaders. Fox was the kind of coach who predicted a shutout seemingly every week. He did it with regularity during his time with the Giants, including in the Super Bowl one week later against the Baltimore Ravens. That one was not quite as successful a prediction. But in the NFC Championship Game against the Vikings, his defense dominated from the start. Culpepper completed 13-of-28 passes for a measly 78 yards with no touchdowns and three interceptions. It was easily the worst game of his season, perhaps of his career. The same held true for the rest of the Minnesota offense. The great Randy Moss had two catches for 18 yards in that nightmare contest for the Vikings.

In reality the game was over before it started. Jim Fassel brought Lawrence Taylor in the night before to speak to the team. This was possible because the sideline for the NFC Championship Game would be filled with Giants legends from Taylor to Harry Carson to Carl Banks to George Martin. They were furiously waving those white towels likes the fans in clear sight of the Giants players. It was a unique, emotional sight.

"It was a lot of the guys that came back," offensive lineman Lomas Brown said. "I wasn't used to that because, coming from Detroit, you've never seen a lot of our veteran guys back in the day. It's different now, but back in the day, you never had a lot of our veteran guys come back for games. And it wasn't like that in Arizona when I was out there with the Cards. It was a little bit like that in Cleveland for the one year I was there, but I was just overwhelmed with how much the alumni for the Giants were involved with the team, how they wanted those guys around, and what they kind of meant to not only the team, but what it meant to the city of New York. So it was huge for those guys to be on the sideline of the game because it almost gives you that extra motivation to not fail to go out there and want to give your best and make sure that we have success. So, yes, I do still remember L.T. talking to us and I remember [the sideline]."

Perhaps it was the little extra boost that this group needed, if they needed it at all. By that point the 2000 Giants had won six straight games in mostly convincing fashion since the Fassel guarantee. In their minds they were ready to join the great Giants teams of the previous generation. They had heard about the exploits of the L.T., Carson, Phill Simms, and Bill Parcells teams of the '80s. The expectation was that they would reach that level of success, too. "Understanding the history helps when looking at people on the sideline who are supporting you and showing up, especially in those big moments, because they've already done that. They've been there and done that. When you see the support from the people, who set the foundation before you, actually supporting you, it gives you a whole lot more confidence," Jason Sehorn said. "It's a whole lot of fun when I looked at the sideline seeing these guys because they're not there very often. They're not there for a regular game. It's the big ones they show up for."

The sideline was enjoying the blowout that day almost as much as the fans. They saw the domination up close and personal and knew where the game was headed from the opening kickoff. Wide receiver Ike Hilliard caught a laser from Kerry Collins down the seam for a 46-yard touchdown less than two minutes into the contest. After Minnesota failed to catch the ensuing kickoff and the Giants recovered, fullback Greg Comella hauled in an 18-yard dart on a wheel route in the right corner of the end zone.

That was a play the Giants had run countless times. Never had Collins even looked in Comella's direction. The fullback's job was simply to clear out the area and occupy the flat defender. Only this time he went uncovered. Comella caught the ball almost in a backpedal and landed hard on his backside. "The thing that I remember most is that he landed on his ass," Barber said. "So he got one foot down, and when I first saw it on the replay, I was like, *Ah, he's out of bounds.* But his ass hits inbound, hits in the end zone, and so it's a touchdown. And when he gets back to the sideline, he's just complaining. He's like, 'Oh, my God, it hurts so bad.' So we get in the locker room, he pulls his pants down, and he has this massive bruise on his ass. And he played the whole second half with it. It was just a funny moment. But I remember when we were driving to the stadium, we looked at each other like, *Gee, this is it.* I was like, *Yeah, man, this is it.*"

The Giants were going to the Super Bowl. After the Comella touchdown grab, the rest of the game was essentially a coronation. The Vikings stood no chance in that atmosphere to threaten that Giants. On the sideline Taylor declared the game over early on. He had already seen enough. The look in the

Vikings' eyes said they were done. "I told these guys in the first quarter, 'The Giants can't be beat, and Minnesota may not score,'" Taylor said.

L.T., the soothsayer, was there to witness the best game of Collins' career with the Giants. The quarterback went 28-of-39 for 381 yards with five touchdown passes. It wasn't an accident either. This was planned. It was exactly what Sean Payton, the mad scientist, envisioned when he began watching tape of the Vikings immediately after the divisional round win against the Philadelphia Eagles. He spotted the deficiency and wanted to attack.

Amani Toomer remembers getting treatment that Monday when Payton stormed into the training room to inform him of the plan. He knew the wide receiver would be excited. "I just watched the film, and I'll tell you what," Payton said. "You better get ready because we're putting the ball up in the air."

The Giants offensive coordinator studied the Vikings cornerbacks and wasn't impressed. That was where he was going to attack—relentlessly. The game plan was going to be to sling it around the yard barring any crazy weather. "I remember being so excited. I had a swollen ankle and did something to my knee, and I remember I said, 'Coach, I'm going to be fine!'" Toomer said. "And I walked off the [training] table and I start hopping on one leg and saying, 'Coach look at this.' It was a spectacular day."

Magically, Toomer was healed, knowing there would be opportunities for a big day in the NFC Championship Game. The Giants were just fine with their fate resting on the quarterback nobody wanted one year earlier (Collins) and their three young receivers (Hilliard, Toomer, and Joe Jurevicius). Toomer had six catches for 88 yards and a touchdown that afternoon.

Barber, the team's best offensive player, might as well have taken that afternoon off, which maybe wasn't the worst thing in the world since he was dealing with a broken forearm. He didn't care at this point. It was his and many of the Giants' first real chance at reaching the Super Bowl. "Sean Payton comes into our meeting room, and he says, 'Look at the tape. We're going to throw for 300 yards in the first half. Their DBs are suspect,'" Barber said. "He thought the reason that they were so good is because Randy Moss and Daunte Culpepper gave them a lead, and then every team had to play catch up. And so their defense got to capitalize on playing from ahead. So it was just get on top of them on the defense side of the ball. If you hit Randy Moss, he will quit. If you hit him, he'll quit. And so we had this perfect game plan on how to beat them and then we went out and executed it, and it was perfect, and you couldn't have scripted it better."

The 39 pass attempts that Collins had in the NFC Championship Game were tied for the third most he had during that season. The 381 yards passing and five touchdowns were both seasons highs. His previous season high of 350 yards passing came in that infamous loss to the Detroit Lions before the Fassel guarantee. That was in large part because the Giants were down big early and threw feverishly as they were trying to complete a comeback.

The amazing part about throwing 39 times for 381 yards in the championship game is that the Giants were blowing out the Vikings basically from the start. It would have been more, way more, had the game not been so lopsided. The Giants led 34–0 at halftime when Collins had already thrown 34 passes and compiled 338 yards and four touchdowns. That was in the first half of the NFC Championship Game alone! If Minnesota had kept pace, Collins might've thrown close to 70 passes in the contest. "Great job, unbelievable," Fassel said to Collins as they celebrated on the field afterward. "Put it on your shoulder, and you put it right on through there."

Just as Payton drew it up. Fortunately, it was 35 degrees, and there were only light winds on that January afternoon. The football Gods worked in the Giants favor, especially considering the old Giants Stadium was known for its winds. That's what made the cannon-armed Collins such a good quarterback for that team and game. He could cut the ball through the Giants Stadium winds as if they didn't exist.

Payton also proved he was the perfect offensive play caller for that team and that day. As per his personality, there was never any doubt it would work. There certainly wasn't a lack of confidence in him or his unit. "Oh, yeah, look, I'm going to tell you how it went with Sean Payton back then," Lomas Brown said. "So he wouldn't say, '*If* we get this first down,' or '*If* we convert this fourth down,' or '*If* we complete this long pass.' He would always say, '*When* we do that.' That's the one thing I always remembered about Sean being my offensive coordinator for those two years...To me that just helps your confidence when you hear a coach speak like that. And I knew he was confident. Some of the play calls that he was calling during that game let you know that he was confident in what we could get done against that defense. And we went out and did it, and we attacked those corners. I think we attacked them from damn near the first play of the game to the last play of the game and really put those guys in a bind. And that's the area we attacked...the secondary. Sean Payton had seen something. He knew we could exploit their secondary. And that's what we did all game."

The celebration on the field afterward was one to remember not only because the Giants were going to the Super Bowl for the first time in a decade, but also because of the way it all unfolded. It began with Fassel putting his chips on the table. The Giants then went on this magical run that nobody saw coming. They ripped off win after win. And the way it all unfolded, it made it that much more memorable. They weren't supposed to beat the Vikings—let alone shut them out. "These guys were just fun. It was magical," Strahan said of the 2000 team. "And that 41–0 game, you know how I knew we were going to win before the game even started? Because Randy Moss was arguing with our security trying to get Lil Wayne and the Cash Money crew onto the field for pregame. I was like, *Who in the world is worried about a rapper right now?* It just kept rolling. Rolling! And [the legends] waving the towels, and they wanted the shutout. 'We want the shutout! We want the shutout!' And we wanted to give it to them. So I'm glad we were able to do that part."

The Vikings came and left bitter. There were complaints about the field. At the time Giants Stadium had plates of grass that didn't hold up well by January. There was talk about how they had to paint the grass trays just to keep it green. Players on both sides wore baseball-type studs on their cleats for the NFC Championship Game. There have even been unfounded whispers over the years about the Giants being able to listen in on Minnesota's headsets that day.

None of it stopped the team and its fans from reveling in the moment, which surprised just about everyone—at least everyone outside that locker room. New York hadn't won a playoff game in seven years entering that season. Then it was headed to the Super Bowl. "This is a Giants team that was referred to as the worst team ever to win the home-field advantage in the National Football League," Wellington Mara told FOX broadcaster Terry Bradshaw while being presented the George

Halas Trophy, given to the NFC champion. "And today on this field of painted mud, we proved we're the worst team to ever win the National Football Conference championship. And I'm happy to say that in two weeks we're going to try to become the worst team to ever win the Super Bowl."

Considering where Mara and the Giants were one year earlier when he addressed the team following a loss to the Vikings that eliminated them from playoff contention, this win had extra meaning. This team wasn't supposed to be there. They were being led by a quarterback nobody wanted, by a coach whose job was in jeopardy, by a defense that never seemed to get enough credit up until that point.

It was truly a special afternoon. John Mara still has a picture in his office of his mom and dad on the field before the game ended, soaking up the moment. That moment remains etched in his memory. "That one for me, seeing my dad actually go on the field before the end of the game, I had never seen that before," John Mara said. "And so just to watch him enjoy that was pretty cool."

The atmosphere that day was otherworldly—like no other game before or after at Giants Stadium, where the stands seemingly hung over the field. There were times when those in attendance thought the stadium was shaking. This was a different time. It was before seat licenses, when Giants games were filled with the hard-working, die-hard, blue-collar fans of the era. It was hardly corporate the way stadiums in general are today. When you went to Giants games at the time, you felt like it was filled with teamsters and union workers, cops, firemen, and longshoremen. That was the Big Blue clientele. Everyone had their seats for decades.

At the start and during timeouts, the anthem of that season was Bon Jovi's "It's My Life." It felt like the ultimate Jersey song, the ultimate Giants song. With the legends on the field pregame for the introductions to the waving white towels amidst the celebration, Giants Stadium was rocking. The atmosphere resembled a rock concert. "I'll never forget L.T. and all the greats waving those white towels when we walked out. It was electric. I had never seen the stadium like that before," Toomer said. "And because of that, we destroyed the Vikings. They still talk about that game. They still talk about 41–0 in Minnesota. It was very special. I'll never forget that. Best home game I can ever remember."

15

A Super Letdown

AMONG THE CHALLENGES THAT COME WITH PREPARING FOR the Super Bowl is to keep things consistent. Back in January 2001, there were two weeks between that great NFC Championship Game win against the Minnesota Vikings and the big game. Not that it seemed to affect the Giants much. They enjoyed the win and the circumstances that came with playing in the big game and did not seem distracted.

They did, however, stray from their ways even if it was hardly noticeable from the outside. The Giants had alternated introducing the offense and defense each game leading up to the Super Bowl. Tiki Barber even remembers fullback Greg Comella saying to him on the way to the NFC Championship Game that if they won that day they would be getting introduced in the Super Bowl in two weeks' time. That meant something to them. Being introduced at the Super Bowl would be this great honor. But out of nowhere, Jim Fassel told the team a few days before the game that the defense, the unit probably most responsible for them being there, would be introduced to the world that afternoon in Tampa.

So it was the offense, which stormed onto the field first after the Baltimore Ravens defense was introduced, that created a tunnel for the defensive players who were afforded the ability to soak in the actual introduction. It concluded with Mike Barrow, Michael Strahan, and the heart of the team, linebacker Jessie Armstead, running onto the field. It may have seemed inconsequential, but it represented that the Giants were perhaps out of their element. They had strayed from what had been working. They changed the routine. There is some thought among the players that they were so concerned by the dominance of the Ravens' defensive front that they tried to get too tricky with their offense.

In a way, the Giants knew they were in trouble. The champagne may not have been completely tapped, and already Super Bowl XXXV was in jeopardy. New York had handled the Vikings and that lethal passing attack, but what awaited them in Tampa in the big game was a completely different beast. Ernie Accorsi and the Giants had slapped together a veteran offensive line with the likes of Lomas Brown, Glenn Parker, Ron Stone, and Dusty Zeigler alongside 1999 first-round pick Luke Petitgout. They were a solid group but hardly the strength of the team. Against these Ravens defenders, they would be put to the ultimate test.

Baltimore had one of the best defenses of all time. The 2000 Ravens still resonate, and their defense is in the conversation with the '85 Chicago Bears, the '70s Pittsburgh Steelers, or the "Purple People Eaters" Vikings from 1969 for the best defense of all time. With 700-plus pounds in the middle of the line with Sam Adams and Tony Siragusa supported at the next level by the greatest linebacker of his generation in Ray Lewis, the Baltimore defense was almost impossible to run against. It allowed just more than 60 yards per game on the ground that year, almost 12 yards better than any other team. The Giants had the second-best run defense during the 2000 season, allowing a modest 72.3 rushing yards per game.

It was just past the midway point of the first quarter when the Giants realized they were in big trouble. That Ravens run defense was legit, and New York wasn't going to be able to do much in this contest. It was at that point during their fourth possession of the Super Bowl that Sean Payton called for "Sprint 39." It was a play this New York offense had seemingly perfected. The crafty offensive line knew how to reach the second level to get to the opposition's linebackers. They would be able to make just enough contact for Barber to shake loose. Well, the Giants called it on a second-and-8 from their own 16-yard line in the first quarter. Immediately, there was penetration up the middle from Adams and Siragusa, forcing Barber even more horizontal than he would have liked. In the process, Zeigler was knocked to the ground. He couldn't get to his defender. Parker had to help in order to assure that Barber wouldn't be tackled in the backfield. This kept Parker and Zeigler from getting to the second level to get a piece of Lewis, who tracked the play all the way to the sideline. He had started at the far side hash marks, but with his speed and instincts, he covered almost 30 yards running stride for stride with Barber.

Lewis dove and clipped Barber's shoestrings for a measly two-yard gain. In a clear passing situation on the next play, Kerry Collins was pressured on third down, and the Giants were forced to punt. It was a bad omen. "We were always successful with this play because it was impossible for the linebacker or the second level to be right, especially if we could get up to the linebacker," Barber said. "I see the hole developing. We had good blocking wide receivers. Amani and Ike and those guys, they blocked well. So there's a hole. And then Ray hits me in my ear hole, and I was like, 'We're screwed.' Because if that play didn't work, we're screwed. That was our bread and butter at the time."

Lewis really could do it all. That postseason alone he led all players with 31 tackles, but he also had nine passes defended, two interceptions, and a fumble recovery. He would equally be a handful in the Super Bowl. The Ravens had allowed just 16 points total in their first three playoff wins. It didn't matter that they had Trent Dilfer at quarterback and the offense was average at best. All they needed was to score double digits, and Baltimore would likely be raising the Lombardi Trophy on January 28, 2001, at Raymond James Stadium.

On his drive home from Giants Stadium to his home in Manhattan immediately after the NFC Championship Game, Accorsi began to worry. "I thought *Uh-oh* because I knew how great their defense was," Accorsi said. "Hell, they didn't score a touchdown in five games, and they beat everybody by 20."

True to form, Lewis was everywhere in that Super Bowl. He had five tackles and four passes defended, including a tipped ball that landed in the arms of fellow linebacker Jamie Sharper for an interception. Baltimore's defense dominated.

Still, the Giants have regrets. It may have been a different game if not for a holding penalty called against defensive lineman Keith Hamilton early in the second quarter with Baltimore up just 7–0. It was a screen pass, and Hamilton's hand scraped across running back Jamal Lewis' chest. It turned Lewis sideways and off his route. Dilfer threw an ill-advised pass into the arms of linebacker Jessie Armstead, who raced 43 yards for the would-be score. Only a questionable penalty negated the play, taking away the would-be touchdown. The *New York Post*'s Kevin Kernan called it "Obstruction of Justice" in the lede of his story the following day. The Giants hated everything about it. "I'm going to my grave bitching about that call," Accorsi said.

Accorsi thought Dilfer could've crumbled if there was no flag on that play. That was the Giants' path to a Super Bowl victory. Instead, Dilfer got a reprieve, the Ravens added a field goal later in the quarter, and the Giants didn't have any points on the scoreboard at halftime.

Tight end Howard Cross believes the penalty was called because Baltimore's game plan that afternoon was for their defensive linemen to tackle the Giants' guards and prevent them from reaching the second level. That would make running "Sprint 39" and other plays unsuccessful. Fassel saw this and was complaining about it from the start. It put the officials on high alert for defensive line holding. "Jim was complaining about it so much," Cross said, "and when he complained about it, they called it on the Giants."

Armstead remembers running down the hash mark unable to see anything. They had handed out disposable Super Bowl XXXV cameras to fans at the game. The cameras were white with a palm tree logo on the left side and yellow circles and triangle to replicate an Xs and Os football play in the background. The selling point for these cameras at the time was the flash. So as Armstead raced into the end zone, all he remembers was the lights from the cameras flashing in his face. When he finally looked back and saw the field come back into focus, he saw the yellow penalty flag. Even the ref closest to him couldn't believe they called that penalty at that time. "One of the refs on the other end—and I was walking back with the ref, and this is the honest truth—the ref said, 'Why would he call something like that?'" Armstead said. "The ref said that, and I was like, 'I don't know! I'm tired as hell, so let me line back up and try to stop them.' And I promise that's exactly what the refs told me."

The Giants ultimately allowed a Jermaine Lewis kickoff return for a touchdown late in the third quarter. Collins threw an interception that was returned 49 yards for a score earlier in the third. New York's only points came courtesy of a Ron Dixon kickoff return for a touchdown, and Baltimore won 34–7 for its first Super Bowl in franchise history.

It left the Giants with regrets. If only that questionable penalty on Hamilton had not been called, it would've been a different game. "I really believe that, but you can't make history go back in time," Armstead said 20-plus years later. "But I just wish they would've played it out and see how the game really would've been."

For as successful as the NFC Championship Game was for Collins, the Super Bowl exposed his flaws. Toomer still calls Collins the "best quarterback I ever played with" because Eli Manning was still young when he worked with him. But he thought Collins threw a better and more accurate ball. His deep-ball accuracy was the best most of his receivers had ever seen. But when things started going bad, Collins had the propensity to start throwing the ball everywhere. He always tried to make things happen—perhaps unnecessarily. That showed in the Super Bowl when he went 15-of-39 passing for 112 yards with no touchdowns and four interceptions. It was a forgettable performance. "It's the most disappointing loss I've ever been involved in," Collins said.

Deep down Accorsi knew he needed to get better at the quarterback position if the Giants were going to get over the top. Collins ultimately lasted three more years and threw 51 touchdowns and 46 interceptions before Accorsi landed

Manning in a draft-day trade in 2004. Collins declined to take a pay cut and asked to be released. The Giants relented.

Leading up to that, Collins and the Giants made the playoffs again in 2002, but they fell apart and blew a 24-point lead against the San Francisco 49ers in the wild-card round. At that point things began spiraling for Fassel and that iteration of the Giants.

Accorsi knew he needed to upgrade at quarterback. He eventually did with Manning. He wanted a big, physical receiver to complement Toomer and Hilliard. That came in the form of Plaxico Burress as a free-agent signing. He needed to add edge rushers to take pressure off Strahan. He drafted Osi Umenyiora and Justin Tuck. The offensive line in 2000 was a makeshift unit. That had to be rebuilt for long-term success, which it was with the drafting of David Diehl in 2003 and Chris Snee in 2004, while Shaun O'Hara and Kareem McKenzie were added as free agents.

Accorsi remembers a practice against the New England Patriots, who would go on to win the ensuing Super Bowl, the summer after the Giants' Super Bowl campaign. "I'm standing on the practice field at Bryant College with [Bill] Belichick, and he said, 'This is good for us because I can show these guys what a Super Bowl team looks like,'" Accorsi said. "And I'm thinking to myself, *This isn't a Super Bowl team.* That's what I kept thinking to myself. *We've got a long way to go.*

It took seven years to get there, and by the time they reached the desired destination, Fassel was long gone. He was fired after going 4–12 in 2003 as things fell apart on and off the field. Among the famous Fassel stories was his car being stolen—for a second time!—outside a gas station on Route 17 near the Meadowlands. He had left the keys in his new Mercedes. Fassel had a cell phone in the car and called the thief. The burglar answered the call and chastised the Giants head coach, an exchange that was equally comical and head-scratching. Some versions of the story include there being a playbook in the back seat. "He started yelling at me that I was stupid for leaving my keys in the car," Fassel told reporters the next day after practice.

This was not exactly a good look for the head football coach of the New York Giants. These kind of things, along with the playoff collapse in 2002 where the Giants blew the 24-point lead, marred the end of Fassel's tenure. In the end he went 58–53–1 as a head coach. It still doesn't minimize how special that 2000 season was. It's one of just five Giants teams to reach the Super Bowl. And the way it all happened was memorable to say the least.

The magical run started with Fassel putting all his chips in the middle of the table. It ended in the season's final game in Tampa Bay. "I mean, just so many greats as coaches, but the players, too, man," said tight end Dan Campbell, who would go on to become the Detroit Lions' head coach. "The great players, the great teammates, the playmakers, the grunt guys, I mean, we had the right balance, man. Kerry was playing damn good. He was an excellent leader. But that offensive line, Ron Stone, Lomas, we got Glenn Parker, some veteran guys. Tiki Barber, smartest running back I've ever been around. I mean, just instinctive, smart, understood the whole game. And Amani, Ike, I mean, we can go down the line. You got Mike Barrow, Strahan, Jessie Armstead. It was the right combination of teammates, playmakers, and we willed ourselves to get where we got and came up short."

PART 4

2007

16

A New, Softer Coughlin

The New York Giants reached the playoffs during the 2005 and 2006 seasons. Yet something was still not quite right. They started 6–2 in '06, had some ugly losses and skids, and barely snuck into the playoffs with an 8–8 record. They lost in the wild-card round of the playoffs to the division rival Philadelphia Eagles on a field goal as time expired. Maybe more prominently, there was a perception (and reality) about discontent among the players with coach Tom Coughlin. He was in their eyes the drill sergeant of football coaches—being five minutes early was actually on time—and all these little rules irked the veteran players.

There were more than a few instances during that 2006 season of Coughlin possibly losing the team. There was Michael

Strahan saying during a radio interview that wide receiver Plaxico Burress was "quitting on everybody" when he pulled up on a pass while the Giants blew a 21–0 lead to the Tennessee Titans for their third straight loss. Strahan then lashed out at a female ESPN reporter in the aftermath several days later.

At the time it appeared Coughlin's Giants were coming apart at the seams. But that was all just the appetizer. There was Eli Manning's sporadic implosions, costing the Giants chances to win some weeks. Manning threw 18 interceptions that season, which tied for fourth most in the NFL. There was tight end Jeremy Shockey's constant explosions, including when he publicly said Coughlin was outcoached following an early-season loss to the Seattle Seahawks after the Giants fell behind by an embarrassing 35 points. Then there was Coughlin's back-and-forth tumultuous relationship with running back Tiki Barber, which escalated during a Week 11 primetime game when Barber called his lack of usage (10 carries) in a 27–10 loss to the Jacksonville Jaguars a "slap in the face." In the aftermath the following day, Coughlin stormed into the meeting room and threw the newspapers in Barber's face. "What the fuck is this?" the irate coach said.

Coughlin then proceeded to kick everyone else out of the running back room but him and Barber. The two then got into an expletive-filled shouting match. It was worse than some of the players had ever seen between a coach and player. The rest of the running backs stood outside and waited, listening by the door to the back and forth. Coughlin couldn't believe that Barber was putting himself above the team. The way Barber viewed it, he was thinking about the team because they needed him to run the ball to operate effectively on offense. "I make this offense fucking go!" running back Brandon Jacobs remembers Barber saying. "If we're not running the ball, we won't win the game. We've got to run the ball."

Coughlin wasn't even the one calling the offensive plays. That responsibility fell on offensive coordinator John Hufnagel, who was demoted several weeks later. Kevin Gilbride took over the play calling, a responsibility he held for the next seven seasons. It didn't matter at that point. Coughlin was the boss, CEO, and coach all rolled into one. He demanded respect. Barber, meanwhile, was the outspoken veteran and offensive star on the team. It created quite the combustible combination. "They're fucking motherfucking each other in there. We're like, *Holy shit*, standing outside the room," Jacobs said. "Well, this was our last meeting before we get to go home. Now we're just in here watching practice, right? So now we're in here watching practice, and he comes in the meeting. So I'm like, *Fuck, I'm going home. I'm not going to stand out here and wait.* I didn't give a fuck about watching the rest of practice after a while. I'm not going to stay here that long. They argued for like 20 minutes in there. The meeting was only 20 minutes. They're motherfucking each other in there. Man, it was crazy."

That was just part of the '06 story. Bottom line, there was a lot going on that season despite the Giants reaching the postseason. The way owner John Mara remembers it, the entire media was calling for Coughlin's job. And that might not be an exaggeration. The *New York Post* and *New York Daily News* were running back page headlines constantly putting a fork in Coughlin's career in New York. The *New York Post*: "Boot Him Now: It's Tom To Go." *Post* columnist Steve Serby even called it the "doomsday scenario" when the team ultimately elected to retain Coughlin's services. *New York Daily News* columnist Gary Myers' column that day was titled, "Coughlin Reign of Error to Continue."

The FOX broadcast took it one step further. Hall of Fame quarterback Terry Bradshaw actually called for Coughlin's firing on air before the wild-card loss to the Eagles, and ESPN analyst Sean Salisbury called for his ouster afterward. "I don't think the Giants stayed in this game because of Tom Coughlin," Salisbury said. "They stayed in the game in spite of him."

Yikes! Add Giants fans to the list of those wanting Coughlin removed from his post after three seasons and two playoff appearances. They were chanting "Fire Coughlin" during a blowout loss to the New Orleans Saints in late December of the 2006 season. Incredibly, this was on Christmas Eve. So much for holiday cheer. More like holiday jeer.

Only all this hot-seat talk wasn't a media creation. Coughlin's job was legitimately in jeopardy entering the 2007 season despite back-to-back playoff appearances. It was as real as it gets as evidenced by the teacher being called to the principal's office. "At the end of the year, I had to visit with John Mara and Jon Tisch and tell 'em about my vision of what the future holds," Coughlin said. "I actually had to go visit with the two owners and convince them that. And we were 8–8, but I'm telling you if you look at the 8–8, look at the injuries, it was crazy. And we had some really, really fine performances, but we also had some terrible losses as well."

After the 2006 season, Coughlin was brought in to speak with ownership and forced to lay out his plan before they made a decision as to whether he would be retained as head coach of the New York Football Giants. Mara and Tisch sat there listening to what everyone seemed to believe was the most stubborn 60-year-old man on the planet, detailing a plan that would ultimately lead to an incredible Super Bowl triumph just about one calendar year later.

The seasoned coach was prepared as usual and came with some ideas. Coughlin knew he had to find a way to improve communication with his players. He would walk out of team meetings in the old Giants Stadium after delivering his message. Immediately afterward, he would have to go out back and address the media. The players would walk by, and he would hear different variations of what he had just explained. Coughlin thought he had outlined the simplest thing in the world, but clearly it wasn't. It led to his message being distorted and convoluted. It led to lackluster performance and execution.

The veteran coach, who had wore his welcome thin with the Jaguars just four years earlier, had to find a way to get his message across more clearly so it could be digested the way he intended. "I sat with him and I said, 'What's going to change? What are you going to do different? Because the way it's working right now, it's not really working,'" Mara recalled. "And one of the things that he said was that he was going to form a leadership council of the top players, that he was going to communicate with them. There were a lot of things like that that he went into. And that really impressed me that he didn't take that attitude of, *Well, I'm not changing.* He was willing to make certain changes. Whether that had as much of an effect as people seem to think it did, I don't know."

It did show that Coughlin maybe wasn't as stubborn as most believed. That was a step in the right direction. The leadership council at the very least created an impression that the players were being heard, which was no small thing. The perception at the time was that he wasn't willing to listen to players. The leadership council had members from each position group. Coughlin had a lot of guys in there—sometimes perhaps too many—because he wanted to hear from them directly. He had his stars, beginning with Strahan, who he called the "greatest natural leader I've ever been around," and even lower-level players who worked hard or were on the roster bubble take part in the meeting. "I wanted them in there because I wanted them to hear exactly what my thoughts were. So that was a good thing," Coughlin said. "That communication was a big thing, but it also gave me a chance to talk in more of an informal way with the guys that were responsible for our football team, not only as leaders, but other players as well."

Having Strahan on his side was key for Coughlin. Manning, too. In fact, none of the players—even Barber—wanted Coughlin gone after that 2006 season. That was a big part of the decision. Ownership asked the players—again, even his adversary Barber, who was retiring—for feedback and if Coughlin should be fired. They wanted Coughlin to change, to soften a bit, but they respected him enough as a coach that they wanted things to remain status quo heading into the 2007 season. They tried to ignore that the media and many fans thought it was a gigantic mistake. "I had a conversation with [Coughlin] in the offseason, and one of the things that bothered me at the time was this perception of him that he wasn't willing to listen to players. It was his way or the highway and [he] didn't have a great relationship with players," Mara said. "I think much of that was grossly exaggerated. There wasn't one player, including Tiki, that felt that we should move on from him, and that carries some weight with me because the perception out there was that players hated him. Well, that was not the case."

They didn't hate him, but they undoubtedly had some complaints. They needed Coughlin to listen more and treat them as professionals, to ease off the gas pedal at times. It couldn't be all gas all the time. They could deal with the idea that being five minutes early was considered on time, that there were no cell phones or hats allowed in meetings, or that he required you to dress a certain way (jacket and tie) with certain socks for road trips. They just needed to see some flexibility. A human element was necessary. There needed to be some give and take.

It couldn't be all football all the time. This was a time when players were becoming more empowered. They no longer were just running through a wall because the coach said so. They would ask why beforehand. Coughlin needed to have some sort of explanation. He realized this just in time. "I may be a dinosaur," Coughlin said at the time. "But I can change."

More than just the creating of a leadership council, he laid out a multi-faceted plan. On a bigger scale, it was about improving his relationships with his players, coaches, and even the media. The new Coughlin cancelled a training camp practice that summer and took his team bowling. They got to see a human side of him, making fun of his gutter balls and approach. It was an effective reprieve from football. It helped the players see Coughlin in a different light, which was no small thing at the time. At the start of his tenure as Giants head coach, he never would have done that. This was a man who once proudly explained that he didn't listen to music on the way to work in the 5:00 AM hour because it would interrupt his football-only thoughts. "Well, I think I did change," Coughlin conceded. "And I changed because of the situation that we were in and some of the things that had taken place. I mean, everybody knows."

It was Charles Way, a former Giants fullback who was serving as director of player development at the time, that really got to the old football coach. He hit him where it hurt the most. "When Charles Way said to me, this struck me really, really as a huge bit of wisdom. Charles said, 'Let the players see you as you are with your grandkids.' That meant a lot to me, and I always cared about my players," Coughlin said. "I didn't always show it, but I always did. But what it really came down to was nobody telling me what I had to do. It was me evaluating along with [Giants vice president of communications Pat] Hanlon, and it started out with the communication between me and the members of the day-to-day beat media. That was No. 1. And the way we did it, took the gloves off, invited those guys in, those that had a sense of humor did well with it."

With the help of Hanlon, Coughlin looked to smooth over his relationship with the press. The media is part of what he viewed as "energy sappers." They were among the things that could distract the team from football. But Coughlin met with each of the reporters who covered the team regularly during the 2007 offseason in hope of bridging the gap. Some meetings were more contentious than others. The thing that seemed to hit home the most was when Coughlin heard that they thought he didn't respect their jobs. That was not what he expected to hear.

The reality was that there was almost nothing Coughlin appreciated more than hard-working individuals. He respected the working class, always felt that was where he identified most. Well, the media was the working class. He realized more than ever they were doing their jobs and going home to families like everybody else. That season Coughlin was more helpful and amenable. He wasn't giving out scoops or anything—that was never his thing; he was equal opportunity—but he became softer with the media and in his press conferences. That in effect showed the fans a slightly softer side of Coughlin. It showed he wasn't a cantankerous tyrant.

These were a few of the many concessions Coughlin made entering that 2007 season, which changed his life and the trajectory of his career. Still, his job was essentially on the line. The Giants had given him a one-year extension when the decision was made for him to return. He still needed to win. That was paramount.

It helped that the Giants were growing into his team at the time. Many of the main players, especially on the offensive side, were his guys, players who were either drafted or brought in under Coughlin the previous three years. They didn't need or seem to even care about all the changes that were made. "By the time '07 came along, we were used to his rules and his style and accepted it," Manning said. "All I knew in the NFL was Coach Coughlin and being five minutes early, and practice is going to be hard. And that's just what I thought was the norm and accepted it. And so I think as a group we kind of just said, 'Hey, this is what we do.' As rookies came in, we showed up five minutes early to all the meetings. We wear certain clothes. It was almost like we were policing it, and we're saying it to the guys more than he had to say it. The first couple of years, he had to say it to get his point across. But by this point, you have [center Shaun] O'Hara and [guard Chris] Snee and [tackle David] Diehl and me and guys on the offensive side. We became the veterans, and we just said that, 'Hey, this is the way we do it. This is what we believe in.' And so we were able to maybe police it. If a guy was going out to practice and didn't have the right stuff on, we would stop [him] and say, 'Go put the right stuff on. Let's not upset Coach. There's certain things that get on his nerves. Let's not spark it. Let's not get him riled up.' And so I think maybe it came across that he was a little bit easier and that he would relax on a few things, but I think it's more that we had just become so accustomed to his style that we accepted it, we believed it, and we were able to implement some of his rules, where it didn't always seem like it was coming from him. It was just coming from the players as well."

Whatever it was, Coughlin was back for at least one more season in 2007. The changes or concessions he agreed to make unequivocally saved his job. "Where it did have an effect was on convincing me that," Mara said, "he's not so stuck in his ways."

17

Spags' Big Blue Crew

IT WAS FOURTH DOWN, AND THE 2007 NEW YORK GIANTS defense needed one more stop at the 1-yard line for its first win of the season. It was a make-or-break moment after already having been slaughtered in the first two games. The Giants under new defensive coordinator Steve Spagnuolo had surrendered 80 points in the first two weeks against the Dallas Cowboys and Green Bay Packers. Down 17–3 at halftime in Week Three to quarterback Jason Campbell and the Washington Redskins, they were off to yet another horrific start. The prospects of their season looked bleak at this point.

But they had battled back and were fighting for their proverbial lives down near the goal line in the final seconds. After linebacker Kawika Mitchell single-handedly stopped

Washington running back Ladell Betts in his tracks on third down with 40 seconds remaining, the clock continued to tick. Washington's legendary coach, Joe Gibbs—the same coach who was once the envy of Bill Parcells and was recently plucked out of retirement—and the Redskins were out of timeouts. There would be one more play from New York's 1-yard line that would determine the game and possibly the Giants' fate. The clock continued ticking after Mitchell's tackle, and Washington quickly got back into the same formation with 28 seconds remaining.

But something didn't seem quite right to Spagnuolo as he watched the Washington sideline and the movement of the players on the field. It was as if they were discombobulated despite having all this time for one final play. "I looked across the sideline, and it looked to me like they were a little bit out of sync as to what they wanted to do," Spagnuolo said years later. "And then I turned and I made the call to our defense. In that game we were still signaling. We didn't have the headset yet. At that moment Tom [Coughlin] grabbed me and said, 'Steve, do we need a timeout?' And I said, 'No, I think they're having trouble getting their play in.' And so we just let it roll, and we ran a defense that was a 'goal-line out,' we call it, and they ran an outside running play right into it. And that's what stopped it."

Washington actually just rushed to the line of scrimmage and ran the same exact play from moments earlier with 20-plus seconds remaining. They rushed for God knows what reason at that point. It was fourth-and-goal from the 1-yard line of a 24–17 game, and they unnecessarily snapped the ball quickly. Spagnuolo believes had the Giants called timeout and given Washington a chance to think about the play, they might have dialed up something with a better chance of success. Or maybe they would have just simply been more composed. But one of the greatest coordinators in NFL history went with his gut. “Let’s let it roll,” he said.

The Giants were overloaded to the right side, the offense’s strong side, of their defensive formation. Cornerback Aaron Ross was aligned near the line of scrimmage and took on the lead blocker in the hole. Ross went low, taking out fullback Mike Sellers at the knees and also getting to Betts in the process. Mitchell and fellow linebacker Antonio Pierce finished off the play at the 1-yard line.

The Giants season had been saved for everyone to see. That game in front of the FOX 4:15 PM (EST) national window allowed everyone in that defensive room—from Michael Strahan, who had sat out training camp while contemplating retirement, to Osi Umenyiora and Pierce (a former Redskin) to the defensive backfield led by veterans Sam Madison and R.W. McQuarters—to all let out a massive exhale. They finally had a win on their resume. New York was 1–2 and could get on with their season. After having rallied from a 14-point halftime deficit in that dramatic Week Three win, they finally had something to build on, and their defense had seemingly put it together in the second half.

That win really did mean everything for both the ’07 Giants and Spagnuolo’s career. He was a first-time coordinator that year, coming from the rival Philadelphia Eagles where he was groomed as the linebackers coach under the legendary Jim Johnson. This was his first crack at leading his own group, and he was bringing with him Johnson’s aggressive, deceptive blitzing approach. Spagnuolo, a man who by football standards is small in stature, was confident by nature and knew that Washington game was a key moment. He was trying to keep the Giants from going off the rails and watching his big chance fizzle. It was imperative that he keep his veterans believing in what he was trying to do.

Coughlin was still on board, but if Spagnuolo lost the most influential players in the defensive meeting room after three games, it was over. There probably wouldn't have been any recovering from that. "We were going into Washington, and Spags has a defensive meeting, and he comes in front of the group," Umenyiora said. "And he's like, 'Listen, this system that I'm running, this stuff works! [Johnson's] run this same system for multiple years. This stuff that I'm teaching you 100 percent works. You just have to believe in me, and you have to give it time and this stuff is going to work for you.' He said it, and he was very, very clear about that."

Spagnuolo is one of the most likable and affable people in football. When he talks, the words slide off his tongue in a disarming manner. Players want to believe him. It's almost as if there isn't a bad or negative bone in his body. Even when he reprimands them, he does it in the nicest way possible while still getting the point across. This confidence and comfort made it feel that his defense in New York would be all right. Spagnuolo is the kind of guy who would later show up when he was interim head coach of the Giants in 2017 after Ben McAdoo was fired for benching Eli Manning and opine on the positives of that day's weather before beginning his daily press dispatch. It's didn't matter if the Giants universe, through no part of his own doing, was crumbling around him.

It was more than talk for Spagnuolo. He is the embodiment of a good man who would regularly mention the love he had for his wife, Maria, and her baking. Maria Spagnuolo was known to drop off bread pudding or cookies in the locker room. She was perhaps even more beloved than he was inside the Giants facility. This friendly, disarming approach from

Spagnuolo has helped him become one of the greatest defensive coordinators and assistants of his generation, having won four Super Bowls as a defensive coordinator through the 2024 season.

But it was his interning under Johnson and knowledge of defense that provided Coughlin full confidence in his new coordinator despite the ridiculously slow start in 2007. Coughlin insists he never wavered or got nervous about the hire—even after the first two games against what ultimately would be the NFC teams with the best records, Dallas and Green Bay, were defensive disasters. "I knew we were doing everything in our power to be the best that we could be. It's kind of like going to bed the night before a Super Bowl. If you feel like you've done everything you could," Coughlin said, "there is some peace there."

It's not as if the slow start came completely out of nowhere. In addition to the Giants having a new scheme under Spagnuolo, they were still learning. There also was uncertainty with Strahan, who was 35 years old at the time. The seven-time Pro Bowl pass rusher was not there throughout the spring while the Giants installed their new defense. He wasn't there at the University of Albany for training camp when the defense tried to establish their identity. Instead, Strahan was at his home in Los Angeles, waiting to make a decision on his future. "There was a lot of doubts. There was some real, serious, serious doubt about whether or not he was going to play," Umenyiora said. "But I wanted him to play. I needed him to play."

Strahan was still a key piece to the Giants defense. Just two years earlier before an injury-filled 2006 season, he had 11.5 sacks. Even though he was in the twilight of his career, he demanded attention. It made life easier for Umenyiora and everyone else out there. But with Strahan entering his 15th season, there was a belief that maybe he just didn't want to go through the rigors of training camp. The Giants took their whole operation on the road two-plus hours away to Albany, where they had to live on campus and sleep in dorms. Back then there were still two-a-days, and Coughlin ran a tough camp. His practices were hard, and rules were still strict despite making some concessions. "I was like, 'I'm not going back.' Tom was driving me nuts," Strahan said. "We're up at, when I first started, Farleigh Dickinson, then we're up in Albany, SUNY Albany, in a dorm room pushing two beds together to make it at least a queen. And you got to lay across so you don't fall in the crack in the middle. I'm a grown man, what am I sleeping like this for? What am I doing? A month a year for 14 years, I spent over a year of my life doing that. I didn't want to do it one more time. So I was like, 'I'm going to retire.'

"And I was somewhat considering it. But I got a call from the guys, and they're like, 'You got to come back.' I'd get a call almost every day. 'You got to come back.' I'm like, why? 'It's different.' They just kept saying, 'It is different.' They couldn't explain why it was different. They just go, 'It's different.' I was like, okay, I know they have limited vocabulary, but okay, it's different? So I had to imagine a bigger thing, and then when I came back, it was because it was the most unselfish team that I've ever been on. And it was a bunch of guys that if somebody goes down the roster, they may not go, 'Oh! Oh! Oh!' But we work well together. We didn't want to lose for each other. We were playing for more than just us individually, and I think that's what made the team special."

It's similar to what you heard from the '86 Giants. Still, the Strahan issue hung over the team all summer. At one point Strahan had to release a statement explaining the situation wasn't about the desire for more money. In fact, he was getting fined for not reporting to camp. When the team left Albany to return to New Jersey, the headline in *The New York Times* read: "Camp Ends For Giants, But Questions About Strahan Don't."

This wasn't ideal for a new, first-time coordinator like Spagnuolo. Strahan, Pierce, and Madison were the leaders of that defense. Strahan was the elder statesman, the longest-tenured Giant, and an all-time great. What he said or did carried weight. And Spagnuolo was having to work around his absence early in his Giants tenure. Spagnuolo had ideas like the four defensive end package, which he had to keep buried in his brain because Strahan wasn't around until September to work on it. It later became a staple of the group and took on the name of the "NASCAR Package." It became Spagnuolo and the Giants' calling card.

Without Strahan the Giants actually contemplated signing Simeon Rice, or maybe it was just a bluff by first-year general manager Jerry Reese to expedite Strahan's return. Nonetheless, Rice actually visited with the Giants early in camp. About a month later, Strahan made his decision to return on September 1. The season opener against the Cowboys was eight days later. He barely knew the defense and needed to get into football shape. It wasn't ideal for Spagnuolo or the Giants. "The only time I saw Michael when I first took that job was I saw him for two days during the mandatory minicamp. I think he came to it, but he didn't practice. I think that was the only time I saw him. And then the next time I saw him was the Monday before the Dallas game," Spagnuolo said. "The only thing that did concern me was that he didn't know the scheme. I wasn't worried at all about him rushing the passer or knowing how to play football or defend the run because he's been doing it for 15 years. But I was concerned that he wasn't going to know our defense. He wasn't getting the terminology. It was all different. And it did take time. Quite frankly, it did take Mike a good month, five weeks, or whatever...five games to kind of know everything. Guys were helping him because it was all new to him."

Strahan didn't get his first sack until a Week Four win against the Philadelphia Eagles. That was a game where the Giants sacked Donovan McNabb 12 times. Umenyiora had his way in that contest with Eagles fill-in right tackle Winston Justice, finishing with a franchise-record six sacks in a game that evening. In a way it was the coming-out party for Spagnuolo's defense.

After first hitting its stride beginning in the second half in Week Three against Washington, the Giants defense allowed 12.4 points per game over the next five games, which were all wins. New York had a dominant front led by Umenyiora and Strahan on the edges, and Fred Robbins on the interior, constantly pressuring the quarterback. They had the physical tandem of Pierce and Mitchell making plays at the second level. They had a good mix of youth (Ross and Corey Webster) and experience (Madison and Gibril Wilson) on the back end. "You got to have [a leader] at every level—one in the secondary, one at the linebacker position, and one in the D-line," Spagnuolo said. "Michael took care of the D-line. Antonio was the linebacker leader. Sam led the secondary, but Antonio was the guy that glued them all together. He could hang with the D-line. They loved him. He could hang with the DBs, the linebackers. Antonio had that about him."

That Giants defense finished seventh in the league in total defense that season. It finished first with 53 sacks, as Umenyiora led the way with 13, and Justin Tuck (10) and Strahan (nine) were not far behind. They were the driving force behind the magical playoff run that was to follow. Nobody, not even the seemingly unstoppable New England Patriots, topped 20 points against the Giants defense that postseason. And to a man, they still look back to that Week Three goal-line stand as the moment it all started to come together.

18

Patriot Act I

It was the day after the New York Giants had just clinched a playoff berth in terrible weather conditions in Buffalo. With Christmas Eve just hours away, all the chatter both in the locker room and around the NFL was about whether coach Tom Coughlin would sit or rest his players for Saturday night's Week 17 game against the undefeated New England Patriots at Giants Stadium.

The Giants were locked into a wild-card game against the Tampa Bay Buccaneers the following weekend. The results of their matchup with the Patriots (15–0) was monumental in that New England had the chance to be the first team since the 1972 Miami Dolphins to make it through the regular season unscathed. From a Giants perspective, however, it would have no ramifications on their playoff opponent or prospects. That was set in stone.

Coughlin spoke publicly on December 24 about how he understood the merits of resting players in what many deemed a "meaningless" game. But he never viewed it that way. In fact, Coughlin was uncomfortable even talking about his team not giving its all to win a game that ultimately was delivered to the audience as an unprecedented three-way national simulcast on a Saturday night by the NFL Network, CBS, and NBC. It really wasn't a difficult decision for the old-school coach. "I'm the head coach of the New York Giants flagship franchise of the National Football League. My responsibility is to lead and guide this football team," Coughlin told his team. "I am not going to allow history to record that a team came into New York undefeated, and we didn't put our best foot forward to try to beat them, to not allow them to have the undefeated season, and everybody agreed. Our team was great about that, and we got ourselves ready to play. We were playing to win. We weren't just playing the game. We were playing to win."

Coughlin sat on the decision until Wednesday morning of that week—even if he probably knew the answer right away. But that is when the players returned from a brief Christmas break to learn how they were going to handle it all entering Week 17 against the Patriots. Internally, the players were going back and forth. Some of the guys, especially Strahan, the veterans, or those that were dealing with injuries, could use rest. Michael Strahan was 36 years old and had played in every game that season despite not having a training camp. Osi Umenyiora remembers sitting next to Strahan at that Wednesday meeting when Coughlin informed them of his intention. They didn't think they were going to play. They were already discussing what they were going to do that week before Coughlin put an end to that line of thinking.

Coughlin burst into the team meeting (five minutes early, of course) with his usual brisk walk. It always seemed as if he was in a rush and didn't have time to waste. There weren't enough hours in a day for the coach who could never get enough football. "The first words out of his mouth, he's like, 'I know some of you are thinking we have nothing to play for, but I'm going to tell you right now—get that out of your mind! We're playing, and we're playing to win,'" Umenyiora recalls. "And right then we're like, 'Hold on. What are you talking about?' He's like, 'Nah, we're playing and we're going to beat this team. That's what we are here for. We're not going to take any time off. We're not taking any days off. All this resting starters—I don't understand. I don't understand that. We're never going to do that here. I'm not coaching that.'"

Coughlin said it with such verve and conviction that his players almost had no choice but to agree. They wanted to compete with the best and beat the best, and this Patriots team was better than any group that had been assembled in recent history. They were trying to do the improbable by getting through the regular season unscathed. Then they would take aim at the impossible—getting through it all undefeated. This New England team could score with the best of them, averaging 36.8 points per game with Tom Brady throwing to Randy Moss. The future Hall of Famers combined for a record 24 touchdowns that season, including the playoffs. That helped the Patriots average eight points more than any other team. That is how dominant they were. New England also had a top five defense and was sound in every facet of the game, and perhaps the greatest head coach of all time, Bill Belichick, guided the squad. The Giants and their fans knew a little something about this Belichick guy, who had made his name with Big Blue as Bill Parcells' defensive coordinator 20 years earlier.

To be the team that beat these Patriots and ruined their undefeated season would be special, the Giants believed. It turned out they were right. Ultimately, it might not have been something they accomplished in Week 17, but they would realize this goal later on down the line—at Super Bowl XLII. But before that even seemed like a possibility, the Giants were still going to put everything they had into that final regular-season game that Coughlin would never label as "meaningless." Even mentioning that sent him into a tizzy. Coughlin told the Giants the approach they were going to take—win at all costs—and dove straight into the preparation. The team bought in immediately. "Guess that is what we're doing," Umenyiora said.

This was so typical Coughlin. The same coach, who considered being three minutes early to a meeting being late and who was particular about what kind of socks his players wore on road trips, wasn't about to concede a regular-season game. Every time you stepped on the field in the regular season mattered, according to Coughlin. Deep down, his players had to know where this was headed the second they rushed out of the nasty weather in Buffalo and onto the buses. There were still some players who were hoping for a mini-miracle and wanted the outcome to be different—perhaps even his son-in-law. "I remember going into that team meeting and thinking I'd be okay if he rested us a little bit. I'll be honest with you. [It's the] last week of the year, I'm kind of beat up a little bit," guard Chris Snee said. "But deep down, knowing my father-in-law and knowing his makeup, I knew we weren't getting the day off. I knew we weren't getting the game off. So when he came in and said we're going to play, it's like, *All right, let's go do this. Let's give this team our best shot.* And sure, that was a hell of a team. We knew that."

It also prevented Coughlin from making some difficult decisions. If he decided to rest some of his veterans or only play them for a drive or two, he would've had to draw a line somewhere. Which players would get the evening off and which wouldn't? At the time there were only 45 players on an active NFL roster. That limited the options.

This was the beauty of Coughlin. He came in and treated everyone equally. It didn't matter if you were Strahan (a future Hall of Famer) or the last man on the roster. The same rules applied. It was the opposite of the Giants' previous coach, Jim Fassel, who was known for playing favorites. In the end it created resentment and blew up in his face. Coughlin wasn't like that, and it applied to everything he did. Even when it came to the media, he never played favorites. Some coaches bypass the local media or pick and choose a beat writer who gets the scoop. That went against every bone in Coughlin's body. So he rarely dished individualized scoops. Instead, he would distribute news to everyone all at once.

This line of thinking applied to Week 17 as well. Everyone was going to play against the Patriots. No special treatment. No favoritism. It spared him some potential problems, too. "There would've been some dissension in the moment with the troops," center Shaun O'Hara said. "It was kind of like, *All right, well who—if we don't play to win—are you going to rest? Who's more valuable, or why does he get the day off? Or why is he not playing?* So it was the right way to do it, and I think we all felt like, look, we got nothing to lose. If we don't win the game, big deal. But it was a great barometer for us...This is the best team in the league, [so] let's go. Let's give it our best shot."

The Giants were a playoff team about to embark on some kind of run. At this point they just didn't know how special it would be. This would let them know where they stood before it all started. It's not like they didn't need the work either. The Giants had one of the best days in franchise history running the football the previous week against the Buffalo Bills (289 yards on the ground), but it was not like they played a perfect game. They fell behind 14–0, and Eli Manning had five fumbles and threw two interceptions in that 38–21 victory in the crummy, wintry Buffalo weather.

Prior to that game, New York had averaged just more than 16 points while splitting their previous six contests. So the offense, in particular, could have used some fine-tuning before the playoffs. "I wanted to play just because offensively we had not played real well toward the end of that season, even though we'd won a couple games," Manning said. "It wasn't always the prettiest even before Buffalo, when it was nasty weather. It was maybe the worst weather game I'd ever played in my career, and we couldn't even throw the ball in the second half. It was just like a disaster. We had a [game a] few weeks earlier in Chicago that wasn't great. So the last half, we weren't playing great football as an offense. And so I really wanted to have a chance to go out there and hopefully play well, do some good things, get something going, and get a little confidence going into the playoffs."

The atmosphere at Giants Stadium—just three days before New Year's for a game that didn't have any playoff implications—was incredible. There was a buzz usually reserved for the postseason. And it had everything to do with the Patriots' perfect season. It began with the Giants marching down the field. Manning hit wide receiver Plaxico Burress on a deep post for a 52-yard gain on the game's second play. Oversized Giants running back Brandon Jacobs then took a short pass and trucked linebacker Tedy Bruschi on his way into the end zone. "You soft! You soft!" Jacobs yelled in the Patriots' direction, according to several players.

The Giants were pumped. They were ready for what the Patriots were bringing. Another play that stood out to players years later was Jacobs picking up a blitz from All-Pro safety Rodney Harrison. He stood Harrison up in a collision that could be heard from the third deck. It was the kind of block you didn't often see from a running back. Then again there weren't many running backs the size of Jacobs, who was listed at 6'4" and 264 pounds. At times throughout his career, that might have been an understatement. "Just sent his ass back to the post office," O'Hara said of the block. "Return to sender. He was like, 'Don't bring that weak ass shit in here.' He did that to a lot of guys. But I think we felt like this is the best team in the league. Even though we didn't win that game, we took it to them. And I don't think we felt like that was the best defense we played all year."

The Giants actually led 21–16 at halftime, but that Patriots offense led by Brady and Moss was too potent. Brady completed 32-of-42 passes for 356 yards with a pair of touchdown passes to Moss in the contest. Moss finished with 100 yards receiving and the two receiving touchdowns. Wes Welker added 122 yards receiving on 12 receptions as the Patriots ever-so-narrowly escaped with a 38–35 win to remain undefeated.

Afterward New England owner Bob Kraft and his wife, Myra, were on the Giants Stadium field. This was not your normal run-of-the-mill win. This victory cemented a perfect regular season. Brady walked off with a football tucked under his arm as a memento. Cornerback Ellis Hobbs, who would factor into the rematch, waved the home team off their own field in a move that was caught by the television cameras.

The Giants were taking notes. They didn't like how some of that evening and the ensuing days and weeks went down. "Talk about a bunch of narcissists, egotistical, front-running bastards," Giants right tackle Kareem McKenzie said to a chorus of laughs from his fellow offensive linemen. "I'll never forget I blocked Junior Seau on a draw play. And all of a sudden, out of nowhere, Rodney Harrison comes up and hits me. I'm like, *What is this? Are you kidding me?* And they were just running him out the whole time. And then after the game, Belichick lets them go ahead and just stay in the city, whatever, and just hang out because they were 16–0 for the season. Like, oh, really? Okay, we'll see them again. We'll see them again because, I mean, it was literally that close. To come in there with the sense of bravado that they had, that it was a foregone conclusion that, of course, they would win, that didn't sit well with any of us. To go ahead and have someone come into our stadium and to be so elitist, so to speak, so, yeah, that definitely didn't sit well with me personally."

The Giants saw enough to make them believe that if they met again, the result would be different. Of course, it would have to be in the Super Bowl with the Giants set to play in the NFC playoffs while the Patriots would run through the AFC. The NFC was no walkover either, especially with the Dallas Cowboys and Green Bay Packers, the two teams that spanked the Giants in the first two weeks, standing in their way.

But Manning and Co. had one of their most efficient offensive games in months in the Week 17 loss to the Patriots. Manning threw for 251 yards with four touchdowns. The four touchdowns was a season high. Jacobs averaged more than four yards per carry against that talented defensive front led by Vince Wilfork and Richard Seymour. It left the Giants' offensive line feeling especially confident entering the postseason. "I thought we kicked their ass up front," O'Hara said.

The Giants may have lost that game to New England, but their confidence rose. They felt they had a very basic defensive game plan for that first matchup (nothing outlandish, no elaborate blitz schemes) and still were able to consistently get after Brady. They had just one sack but eight quarterback hits. It's not something that was lost upon them immediately after the game. The Giants thought the result could have easily been different. Maybe they were onto something. "I remember after that game when Strahan was in the locker room, and I think he said, 'Hey, that was supposedly the best team of all time. And we quite frankly let him off the hook,'" offensive lineman Kevin Boothe said. "'If that was the best team of all time, we're in good shape. We're right there with them.' So I think everybody felt good after that. Not good that we lost, but it was like, okay, we got this."

Strahan insisted afterward that the Patriots didn't want to play the Giants. Umenyiora was equally as confident and prophetic. "Next time we see them," he said, "we're going to beat them."

Unfortunately, there were consequences for going balls-out in Week 17. Playing all the starters didn't come without a cost for Coughlin and the Giants. O'Hara and starting linebacker Kawika Mitchell sprained MCLs in their knees against the Patriots. O'Hara missed the wild-card round against the Bucs. Neither O'Hara nor Mitchell were at 100 percent the remainder of the postseason. Still, Coughlin had no regrets. In fact, he felt immense pride. It was further validated when he rolled into his office at 6:00 AM the following day, a Sunday morning.

He saw his phone was blinking red, a sign that there was a message on the answering machine. It was from the legendary John Madden. "Just called to congratulate you and your team for a great effort last night. Not good, but great," Madden said in the message that Coughlin later played for his coaches and players. "It is one of the best things to happen to the NFL in the last 10 years, and I don't know if they all know it, but they should be very grateful to you and your team for what you did.

I believe so firmly in this—that there is only one way to play the game, and it is a regular-season game, and you go out to win the darn game. I was just so proud being a part of the NFL and what your guys did and the way you did it. You proved that it's a game, and there's only one way to play the game, and you did it. The NFL needed it. We've gotten too much of, 'Well, they're going to rest their players and don't need to win; therefore they won't win.' Well, that's not sports, and that's not competition. I'm a little emotional about it. I'm just so proud."

Decades later Coughlin still gets emotional thinking about that call from Madden. This was more than a pat on the back from a broadcaster or even the commissioner. This was Madden, who in Coughlin's mind, was a coach, just like him. Madden may have been out of the coaching business for almost 30 years at that time, but it didn't matter. Once a part of the coaching fraternity, always part of the coaching fraternity in Coughlin's eyes. Decades later it still resonates. "It's what he said. He said, 'I'm so proud to be a part of the NFL because of what you guys did, you and your team did,'" Coughlin said. He said, 'I couldn't be prouder of what you and your guys did.'"

More importantly for Coughlin and the Giants, that game set the stage for one of the greatest upsets in NFL history.

19

The Playoff Run

THE IDEA THAT QUARTERBACK ELI MANNING WAS A STONE-cold lock in the playoffs was hardly the narrative entering the postseason following the 2007 regular season. It was quite the opposite actually. Manning's first two forays into the post-season left doubt about whether he would ever be a Super Bowl–winning quarterback. He was abysmal in his first playoff appearance in a 23–0 loss to the Carolina Panthers in January 2006, completing just 10 passes for 113 yards and throwing three interceptions. He was then uninspiring for most of a 23–20 loss to the Philadelphia Eagles the following year—even if he did lead a long game-tying drive in the fourth quarter. Manning finished with 161 yards, two touchdowns, and an interception in that wild-card defeat.

The notion that Manning would later earn the designation of being one of the most clutch postseason performers in NFL history was foreign at that point. Hard to believe really. Even during that 2007 season, the young quarterback, who had been drafted No. 1 overall out of Ole Miss three years earlier and acquired in a draft-day trade with the then San Diego Chargers, was inconsistent and unreliable. He threw 23 touchdown passes and led the league with 20 interceptions. On Thanksgiving week the up-and-down young quarterback threw three pick-sixes in the same game, a 41–17 loss to the Minnesota Vikings. It actually reached a point that day where it was laughable for some. "The defense is sitting on the bench, and we were just laughing. You were throwing these picks, and they literally ran back one, then they ran back another, and I think they ran back another," defensive lineman Michael Strahan said while telling the story at an event in 2024 alongside Manning. "It got to the point on defense where we were like, *Keep on throwing them. We're going to sit here on the bench and watch it. Go back out there and do it again.* But it got to the point it was comical."

Manning, of course, didn't enjoy it quite as much. "It wasn't funny," he quipped. "Was not funny."

Through it all though, Manning had the respect of his teammates. Perhaps it was his aw-shucks nature. The unflappable Eli. The unbreakable work ethic. Or all of the above. Regardless, the Giants believed in the 26-year-old quarterback in part because they had seen him take so many public shots that would've sent others into the tank only to bounce back and provide them reason for optimism—like when he went toe to toe with the great Tom Brady and that legendary New England Patriots offense in the regular-season finale.

Perhaps nobody had Manning's back more than wide receiver Plaxico Burress. That was his guy, interceptions be damned. He knew Manning was going to bounce back and sling it in his direction even after the three interceptions were returned for touchdowns in the same game.

"I called Eli after the game. I got home and I was like, *Damn, they are going to destroy him in the media this week,*" Burress said. "So I picked up the phone and I called him, I said, 'Hey, man, don't worry about it. We'll get them next week.' And he was like, 'Yeah, we'll get them next week.'"

Simple as that. Manning led a fourth-quarter comeback the very next week against the Chicago Bears. Never a doubt. Manning was an easy target for the media and opposing players early in his career, even entering that playoff run following the 2007 season. He was the son of the legendary Archie Manning and brother of the Indianapolis Colts' Peyton Manning, one of the best quarterbacks in the NFL at that time. They were the first family of football, having produced three high-level NFL quarterbacks. It only added fuel to the fire when Eli Manning refused to go to the San Diego Chargers in the 2004 draft. Instead, he forced his way to New York.

The early part of Manning's career was filled with inconsistency and the camera panning to the sideline where it zoomed in on the aw-shucks Eli look. It was a combination of traditional resting bitch face and a disheveled Goofy being in awe of what he'd just witnessed. "You get him rattled," Eagles defensive end Trent Cole said days before a 23–20 playoff win against the Giants. "And his game starts going downhill."

It wasn't much different entering the playoffs the following year. There weren't a lot of Manning believers outside of the Giants' building. He was an easy target. Bucs cornerback Ronde Barber, twin brother of Tiki Barber, was among those unconvinced. One could say Tiki was in that same boat at the time. "Eli's got a strong arm. I know he's been really maligned this year," Ronde Barber told the *New York Post* prior to their playoff matchup. "You watch him on film. It seems like he's going through a process the right way, making the right decisions.

Sometimes he just throws some bad balls. I don't know the reasons for that. He can be had, we know that."

It's unheard of for a player of that ilk to say something like that nowadays. This was days before the Giants were about to open the playoffs on the road against Ronde Barber and the Tampa Bay Buccaneers. Manning was still looking for his first career playoff win in three tries. New York was looking for its first postseason win since capturing the NFC Championship Game during the 2000 season.

Manning and the Giants handled the Bucs in the Florida heat that day without starting center Shaun O'Hara and cornerback Sam Madison. Those were the casualties of Coughlin playing the starters against the New England Patriots the previous week. Linebacker Kawika Mitchell was also compromised as he dealt with an MCL sprain in his knee. The Giants put the game away in Tampa with a 15-play drive that covered 92 yards and was capped by an Amani Toomer four-yard touchdown reception early in the fourth quarter to make it 24–7. They had survived without the center on their offensive line against a tough Bucs defense headlined by Hall of Fame middle linebacker Derrick Brooks. "[O'Hara got] the Tampa game off where it was hot as heck, and we're in the middle of a 16-play drive, and I look over. Shaun's got a towel around his neck, drinking Gatorade," lineman Chris Snee said. "And I'm cramping up all over, and I can see him clapping [gently]. I'm thinking to myself, *This guy!*"

It was all in good fun since the Giants were still alive, and Manning didn't make the big mistake. No interceptions. No fumbles. No turnovers. It was the first real hint that the postseason magic was hidden deep inside that tough exterior shell. That was the game plan against a Tampa defense that thrived off turnovers. *Don't make the big mistake!* The Bucs forced the third-most turnovers (35) that season. "My thought process was play it safe against this team," Manning said.

"Eli didn't get rattled today," Giants wide receiver Steve Smith added.

It was just the beginning. The Giants were moving on to the divisional round of the playoffs. That was when it would get serious. They were going to face off with the NFC East champion Dallas Cowboys. New York had won eight straight on the road; its last loss away from home came Week One when Dallas had its way.

20

Stick It to 'Em Boys

The New York Giants were seven-point underdogs heading into their divisional-round matchup with the Dallas Cowboys. That was just fine by them. All the pressure was on the Cowboys. They were the team with a record 13 Pro Bowl players that season. They were the team that rolled through the league with a 13–3 mark in the regular season, won the NFC East, and earned a first-round bye in the playoffs. As if that wasn't enough, quarterback Tony Romo, tight end Jason Witten, and linebacker Bobby Carpenter took a trip to the Mexican resort town of Cabo San Lucas during their bye week. It was national news because Romo was dating singer Jessica Simpson at the time. This was all the rage heading into a matchup with a Giants team that Dallas beat twice in the regular season. It led to a billboard outside a car dealership in Dallas: "Jessica Leave Tony Alone Until After The Super Bowl."

This was all just fine by the Giants. Let the Cowboys and Romo, Simpson, and Terrell Owens attract all the attention. The Giants were just fine flying under the radar. "We definitely embraced the underdog role and just said, 'Hey, we've made it kind of tough all year on ourselves.' It was never easy from starting 0–2 to being down in the third game [vs. Washington] and needing a goal-line stand to win that game, winning seven of eight regular-season road games, and not being as good at home," Eli Manning said. "But the tougher the situation, the better we played. So it was almost like the bigger underdog we are, the better we're going to play. And I think it's not the ideal way, but that's kind of the way it was, and we embraced it and ran with it, and it made us feel confident going in no matter what the circumstances were. No matter what situation we got in, how down we got, or how bad it was at certain times, we can turn around and get hot and make the plays needed to win some of these games."

But these Cowboys were good. They had a top 10 offense and defense. In his first full season as a starter, Romo had what turned out to be the most productive year of his career in 2007 with 36 touchdown passes. Dallas had put up more than 30 points in each of its previous two meetings with the Giants that season. "Yeah, hellacious football team," coach Tom Coughlin said.

The Giants knew what they were in for. Dallas wasn't the top seed in the NFC by accident. It didn't mean the Cowboys were unbeatable, but Dallas was under heavy pressure publicly, especially given the Cabo trip. It was the Giants' boat trip in 2016 with Odell Beckham Jr. and Co. times 20.

The Cowboys were the team that scared the Giants a little bit—not the undefeated New England Patriots nor the potent Green Bay Packers. "The only team I worried about in the playoffs was Dallas," Strahan said. "You could tell I was worried because every game I gave a 'Stomp you out' speech. We get to Dallas, and I'm like, 'It's been an honor playing with you guys. Let's just go out here and put our best foot forward.'"

As if Coughlin needed any more ammunition to motivate his crew, it fell into his lap the day of the game. That is when football operations/projects coordinator Ed Triggs came to him with some intriguing information courtesy of an ESPN report that morning. Cowboys owner Jerry Jones had laid out tickets for some of his players to the NFC Championship Game, even though they were playing that day in the NFC divisional round. There was no guarantee they would be playing the following week at home with a berth in the Super Bowl at stake.

It didn't take long for Coughlin to relay this information to his team. How dare Jones and the Cowboys act as if the Giants didn't exist, as if it was their God-given right to be in the NFC Championship Game that year? "Well, I just smiled. Now, I said, 'I don't know if you guys need to know this, but Jerry's already decided the game's over. I don't even know why we're playing it. Why are we playing this game?'" Coughlin said to his team before the game. "Jerry already handed out the tickets to the NFC Championship Game. It was going to be played right here in Dallas."

If New York needed a little extra nudge heading into the contest, Jones had indirectly provided it to this group, which wasn't shy about doing its fair share of talking. "He certainly provided motivation for our players," John Mara said.

Every little bit mattered for this late Sunday afternoon game, which would come down to the final seconds. The Giants jumped out to an early 7–0 lead when Amani Toomer caught a pass on a curl, slipped through a couple arm tackles, and raced down the left sideline for a 52-yard score on the game's opening drive. Still, it was the Cowboys who looked to be in command late in the second quarter when they scored on a 20-play drive that put them ahead 14–7 with under a minute remaining in the first half. It was more than enough time for Manning, the same quarterback who came into that postseason with questions, to drive New York down the field for a massive score. It took him just 46 seconds to complete four-of-seven passes for 56 yards and another touchdown to Toomer to even the score at halftime. "I remember Dallas having the ball [for what] felt like for 29 of the 30 minutes in the first half," offensive lineman Kevin Boothe said. "I remember just feeling, *Did we even have the ball in the first half?* Like they were on 20-play drives. But when we did get the ball, we scored. And I think that was a big thing."

It was the biggest drive of Manning's young career to date, though he would do better with each forthcoming week. Coughlin and many of the Giants believe that drive before the half broke Dallas' will. The Cowboys looked like the better team most of the first half but went into the locker room even. They had put forth so much hard work, and there was basically nothing to show for it. Dallas kicked a field goal early in the third quarter to reclaim the lead, but the Giants went ahead for good on a Brandon Jacobs one-yard touchdown run early in the fourth quarter. Romo and the Cowboys would have their chances, especially late when they were in Giants territory on each of their final two drives.

It all came down to the final few plays when Dallas took shots at the end zone. On third down Cowboys wide receiver Patrick Clayton inexplicably hesitated mid-route when he beat Corey Webster down the right sideline. The ball ended up overthrown for an incompletion. That was the one that the Cowboys would have liked to have back. It was the fastball right down the middle that they missed. Now they were going to have to hit the perfect pitch. On the final play, Romo tried to hit Terry Glenn in the end zone down the middle of the field on fourth down with just seconds remaining. But cornerback R.W. McQuarters ran stride for stride inside Glenn, turned his head perfectly, and corralled an interception for the biggest play of his career.

The game was over. The Giants had pulled the upset. "I love the way we played the end of the game defensively just because that was a gut check, too," defensive coordinator Steve Spagnuolo said. "That fourth quarter and the way we played that two-minute drill were as good as anything that we had done that year."

It was as if someone had hit the mute button in the building. All of a sudden, Texas Stadium had gone completely silent as if all 63,000 fans had their tracheas removed simultaneously. "Go home! Go home!" Strahan yelled to the crowd.

The Giants were headed to Green Bay for the NFC Championship Game. They were on a heater, handling raucous road environments as if they were silly putty. Strahan and Co. had won nine straight road games. So much for those tickets Jones had distributed for the NFC Championship Game. "I was hoping they had a rebate program," Giants defensive lineman Justin Tuck said.

Manning, meanwhile, was taking the perception that he was a choke artist who could be flustered in big spots and sending it to Mars. He was incredibly efficient that afternoon in Irving, Texas, having completed 12-of-18 passes for 163 yards with two touchdowns, no interceptions, and no fumbles. So much for the idea that he was the Giants' weak link. In fact, he was proving to be a strength. The Giants were flying sky high. Their confidence was through the roof. In their minds nobody, not even the big, bad Patriots, were better than them. “When we won that [Dallas] game, it was over,” Strahan said years later. “The Super Bowl was ours. The Patriots didn’t want to play us.”

But first they had to go to Green Bay, where they had no idea what was in store for them.

21

The Frostbite Game

It was 3:30 pm (CST) when New York Giants quarterback Eli Manning took the field with his receivers at Lambeau Field for early warmups. This was their routine. Manning would throw passes to Amani Toomer, Plaxico Burress, and Co. in order to prepare for the upcoming game. But on this day, January 20, 2008, the weather for the NFC Championship Game between the Giants and Green Bay Packers was unlike anything they had ever experienced. The temperature at kickoff was -1 degrees. With the windchill, it was -23.

Not that it really matters when the weather is that extreme, but Manning was from New Orleans, Toomer was from California, and Burress was from Virginia Beach. They weren't exactly groomed for these conditions. Still, they were all veterans. They had played their fair share of games in cold weather over the years. They thought it was just going to be another one of those days—until they went through their warmups. Their normal routine would include some stretching and warmups before going through the route tree. It would last 30 minutes, and each receiver would run 20 routes or so. Not this day. "I think I threw each one about seven routes," Manning said.

Manning was having trouble feeling the football. The receivers were unable to use their hands. Toomer and Burress were uncharacteristically body-catching everything; they never did that. "I just said, 'Y'all loose?'" Manning said. "They're like, 'Yeah. Yeah!'"

It was the shortest warmup of Manning's career. The freezing winds made their hands numb. The ball felt like throwing and catching a cinderblock. Not only was it hard and frozen, but it also felt heavy and slick. Inevitably, it had to be a problem, right? The Giants were expecting it to be cold. They just weren't quite prepared for that type of cold. How could anybody be? "[I] kind of went out there with not a ton of clothes, didn't go double sweatshirts and everything, just wanted to get a feel for the temperature, what was it like," Manning recalled. "And at that point, [I] learned I just had to keep my hands warm at all costs. My hands had gotten frozen just because when you're out there during that moment, it happens so quick. You don't have TV timeouts, you don't have time between plays to warm up your hands. They're a little exposed. I'm trying to throw it. I'm trying to catch it. I'm like, 'It's hurting my hands to catch it.'"

Back in the locker room, the Giants offensive line squeezed into the training room where they were rubbing Warm Skin All Weather Guard all over each other. Picture that: a group of 300-pound men standing around and rubbing each other down in hopes of remaining warm on a football field in freezing conditions. These same men would take the field moments later without sleeves under their pads and jerseys. It was one of those tough-guy decisions where the testosterone allowed machismo to trump logic. It wasn't the least bit practical given the conditions. "Of course we had all said earlier in the week that we weren't going to wear sleeves," center Shaun O'Hara said, "which is probably not the smartest thing in the world."

The Giants' equipment staff, though, had purple surgeon's gloves available for the players. Many of them wore those under their normal gloves for the first time in their careers. Starting right guard Chris Snee remembers squirting Flexall under the rubber gloves to try to create heat. These were some of the scenes before the game. None of it worked. To a man, they all insist it was the coldest game they've ever been a part of at any level. It remains one of the coldest games ever played in NFL history. During the contest several Giants players talked about how guys were huddling so close to the heater that they were melting their gear or essentially lighting themselves on fire. It was so cold they didn't care. Defensive end Osi Umenyiora remembers the tip of his nose being frostbitten and feeling frozen all the way through. "You shouldn't be playing football in that kind of weather," he said.

When players went back on the field, they had to suck on their mouthpieces for a minute because the saliva was turning to ice cubes and filling the gaps. The offensive linemen saw left tackle David Diehl was profusely sweating and noted that the droplets on the back of his neck had turned to icicles. O'Hara's helmet had frozen and at one point actually cracked upon contact. "That was something I've never seen before," he said.

Manning somehow had to keep his hands warm. That was imperative because the Giants still intended to throw the football. It was a bold strategy but one that ultimately paid off in the end. One would think that might not be possible in these conditions. Somehow, someway, that was not the case on this day. New York's equipment room had concocted some contraption for Manning that looked like an oversized oven mitt. It went up to his elbow. Inside, there were seven or eight heat packs at all times.

Manning made backup quarterback Jared Lorenzen wear it while he was on the field in order for it to remain warm and hot. Anytime Lorenzen could, he came onto the field to give Manning a few seconds with the homemade hand warmer. Manning was cooking. "He would run out there halfway through the huddle and give me a little 10-second warmup on my hand just to keep it warm, so you had a chance to get a good grip and throw the ball," Manning said. "Usually, you get to the sideline, you might get on the phone and talk to the quarterback coach who is up in the booth. I told him after the first series, 'Hey, my hands are freezing just talking to you right now. I got to get back in the heater or I'm not going to be able to throw this possession.' So I said, 'I'll see you at halftime, and we'll make our adjustments, but I can't talk to you again. If you need something, call it down, and I'll talk to you if something's extremely important.'"

Incredibly, Manning made it look easy. The same quarterback, who opposing players were outwardly questioning entering the playoffs, was a difference maker in the worst of conditions. Manning completed 21-of-40 passes for 251 yards in the winds and dangerous temperatures in Green Bay during the NFC Championship Game. The legacy was growing. Throw by throw, he was dispelling all the myths. It was as much winning the mental part of the game as it was physical. That was the beauty of Manning. He studied the game as much as anyone and knew when and where he was supposed to throw the ball—even if at times he could be confused by certain looks. He wasn't confused very often on this frigid Midwest evening. "They wanted to play man-to-man, press [coverage] man-to-man all day on

Plaxico. He ended up having 11 catches," Manning said. "I think nine of them were on just fade-stops where he was going to be pressed. If the guy was off, he ran a five-yard hitch. If the guy pressed him, he was going to run a fade. It was either back shoulder him, or I'd lead him. If he beat him, I was going to lead him down the field. One time he went inside, and it looked like a slant, but it was still the fade-stop. I mean it wasn't complex. This is like...you do this when you're eight years old and playing peewee football. 'Hey, run a hitch or a fade.' And that's all we were running, and we kept doing it, and they couldn't guard it. We just did it up and down the field. That's the game. That's the game you want to play in."

It sounds so easy. Maybe, on a normal day, it would be. Pitch and catch. Fade or hitch. But in these conditions, it shouldn't have been. Just walking onto the field that day was difficult. Gripping the football that day was difficult. Catching the football was equally challenging. Holding onto the frozen leather football was rough. It was a minor miracle that Manning was able to throw the ball as accurately as he did in that NFC Championship Game. The great Brett Favre, who was used to freezing temperatures having played his entire career up until that point in Green Bay, was having trouble that day. Favre ultimately threw for 236 yards with a pair of touchdown passes and two interceptions. His final interception in overtime cost the Packers a chance at reaching another Super Bowl. That was the last pass he would ever throw for the Packers before joining the New York Jets and then Minnesota Vikings.

The Giants didn't think that game should have ever come down to a sudden-death overtime period. On their very first offensive play of the game, they made their presence felt. That is when offensive coordinator Kevin Gilbride called for a handoff off the right tackle. All 264 pounds of running back Brandon

Jacobs was charging to the right side when he was met by All-Pro safety Charles Woodson. Jacobs put his shoulder down and trucked Woodson for another three yards. It was a nasty collision—so violent that FOX analyst Troy Aikman actually said on the broadcast he didn't know how many more times Woodson would want to do that. Who even knew if he could survive that again?

The Giants twice settled for field goals after long drives in the first half, and their final possession ended on downs in Green Bay territory. They dominated but only had a pair of Lawrence Tynes field goals to show for their efforts. One slip on the frozen tundra by cornerback Corey Webster resulted in a 90-yard touchdown by wide receiver Donald Driver, and the Packers led 10–6 at halftime. "I just feel like that game could have been ours in the first half, to be honest with you," Snee said. "I thought we ran the ball well. Eli and Plax played pitch and catch."

At this point Coughlin's face was the color of a ripe Jersey tomato. It was as if his light Irish Catholic skin had too much sunlight, though it was night and -23 degrees with the windchill at kickoff. It only got colder as the night progressed. Coughlin's face only got more chapped as the game deepened. Not that the Giants coach was affected with a trip to the Super Bowl on the line. If you knew Coughlin and what he stood for, he was going to put everything he had into procuring a win. The weather wasn't going to be a factor. "It was cold, but you know what? In the second half, I didn't feel anything," he said years later, his face finally fully thawed. "I was not cold in the second half. I really wasn't. For whatever reason, I wasn't cold."

That was so Coughlin. He was thin and frail but tough and even stronger-minded. There was a reason he played as a wingback in the late '60s at Syracuse alongside Hall of Famers

Larry Csonka and Floyd Little, and it wasn't that he was the most talented of players. He was among the most strong-willed. That trait extended into his coaching career. Almost out of a job 12 months earlier, Coughlin was now on the verge of reaching his first Super Bowl as a head coach. He had gotten close with an expansion team in Jacksonville back in 1996 and 1999, but he had never been there to this point.

His chances eight years later were hurt because the Giants were wasting opportunities in the second half in Green Bay. They had a 48-yard Ahmad Bradshaw touchdown run in the fourth quarter negated by a "phantom hold" on Snee just before the two-minute warning. The Giants thought Packers defensive lineman Ryan Pickett flopped on the play. "That would've haunted me for the rest of my life if we didn't make that third kick," Snee said.

Tynes missed a 36-yard field goal later in that drive as time expired in regulation. He also missed a kick earlier in the fourth quarter. One was a bad snap; the other was a bad kick in terrible conditions. It was becoming harder by the minute to do anything. No kick was a gimme that day. "That ball, I still to this day don't know how Lawrence Tynes kicked it," O'Hara said. "I don't know how Eli was throwing it. I could barely grab it to snap it. It was so hard because you can't keep the balls warm. You can't put them in the heater. You can't put them in a trash can and warm them up. So by the end of the game, that leather was starting to get slippery, and it was so darn hard. I was worried about messing up a shotgun snap or fumbling a snap with it."

Tynes had made his first two kicks—from 29 and 37 yards—in the first half. He missed from 43 and 36 yards (both wide left) in the second half. But the Scotsman would have a chance at redemption moments later. He was not about to shy away from the chance to be a hero. It took only two plays into overtime for the stage to be set. That's when the defensive coordinator Steve Spagnuolo, who didn't look like he would make it through the season after two weeks, picked the perfect play call, and the cornerback who was benched earlier in the campaign made the play of the game.

Webster, the third-year cornerback out of LSU after being a second-round pick in 2005, saw Driver running a quick out route. Webster undercut it and picked off Favre near midfield for the biggest interception he would ever make. It put the Giants in position to get back to the Super Bowl. "It was another call that we ran that we hadn't done a lot," Spagnuolo said. "We brought linebackers up to shoot [the gaps] and played some two-man [zone], and Corey was in great shape playing underneath like he's supposed to. Favre threw the ball away. [It] wasn't the greatest throw, but it was a really good play by Corey."

The Giants got the ball on Green Bay's 34-yard line but gained just five yards on three plays—two Bradshaw runs and an incomplete pass. That left them with a decision—kick a 47-yard field goal or go for it on fourth and 5 from the Packers' 29-yard line. "I look over during the overtime break, and Tynes is huddled on the sideline like he's freezing. He's freezing to death," Coughlin said. "It would be a 47-yard field goal. I don't say anything because remember earlier in the game I had asked Lawrence Tynes if he could kick a 46-yard field goal in this weather. He turned around and walked away. So I'm looking at him. He throws off his cape and he jogs out on the field. I see him do this. I yell, 'Field goal!' The coaches start yelling in my headset, 'No, Coach! Don't let him do it! What if he misses? Field possession!' It could have went 55 yards he kicked it so well. It was straight and true, and that was the call to end the game. There's no doubt about it. He made it. That's what athletics was all about."

The Giants were going to the Super Bowl with a chance for their third Lombardi Trophy in franchise history. They would get what they wanted—the undefeated New England Patriots. That same team of narcissists that they had taken to the brink three weeks earlier.

22
Helmet Catch

If the New York Giants thought they were significant underdogs against the Dallas Cowboys and Green Bay Packers, it was nothing compared to when they would play the New England Patriots in Super Bowl XLII. They were 12-point underdogs in the big game despite playing them tough one month earlier. Just about the only person to pick the Giants to pull the upset and knock the undefeated Patriots from the pedestal of perfection was New York wide receiver Plaxico Burress. He had the underdogs winning 23–17. That prediction made its way back to the Patriots and quarterback Tom Brady. "We're only going to score 17 points?" Brady chuckled during Super Bowl Media Day.

It was as if Brady was insulted by the insinuation that the high-flying Patriots offense wouldn't score more than that. They had scored at least 20 in each of their 18 contests before the Super Bowl and an NFL-record 589 points that season. "Okay, is Plax playing defense?" Brady added. "I wish he had said 45–42 and gave us a little credit for scoring more points."

The Patriots put 38 on the board in the Week 17 meeting with the Giants. That was on the road in a hostile environment. The difference this time is defensive coordinator Steve Spagnuolo would throw everything he had at Brady. The Giants decided not to do that in the regular-season finale.

Burress' prediction created quite the hoopla. When he spoke to the media the Wednesday before the game, the crowd resembled the mob that met Brady earlier that afternoon in Phoenix. It didn't leave his coach happy. Tom Coughlin always preached to his players, "Talk is cheap; play the game." It's the same line he later parroted to New York Jets coach Rex Ryan before their famed Christmas Eve matchup in 2011. But Plaxidomus and his teammates were confident. They didn't think they could handle the Patriots—they knew it. There was no doubt. "I don't think the Patriots really wanted to play us," Burress said. "I really didn't because we could play any brand of football. We were like bullies. We didn't care. We had the guys up front. Those guys were just probably the best offensive line group that I played with in my 13 years. Those guys absolutely were great. We could run it, we could throw it, and we didn't care. We could play physical football, finesse, however you wanted to play."

It's apropos that the pregame media hype centered around Burress. He always seemed to attract the drama. This was the same player that never practiced that season—*never*—to the point that it became a running joke among his teammates. "To put it in perspective, Allen Iverson practiced more than him," quarterback Eli Manning later quipped.

It didn't matter that Burress hurt his ankle in Week Two when he stepped on the foot of Packers cornerback Al Harris.

It didn't stop him from doing damage. Burress had more than 1,000 yards receiving and 12 touchdowns that season despite not practicing and dealing with the bad foot injury. His teammates didn't know, but Burress later said he had a tendon in his right ankle snap early that season. He was left with a decision to let it rest, have surgery, or try to manage the pain. He went with the final choice, the one that in this case was best for the team.

The injury left Burress with little stability in his foot or ankle. It was a problem that would have to be managed to the end. To make matters worse, Burress said he slipped walking out of the shower and hurt his knee the week of the Super Bowl. The Giants truly believed his status for the game was in jeopardy. "I don't even know if he's going to play in the Super Bowl game," Coughlin said. "And he plays, and they got to double him. And I'm telling you, he can hardly run."

Burress ultimately would feel good enough to make an impact in the fourth quarter with the game on the line. That was the kind of gamer he was. He may have had a sometimes contentious relationship with Coughlin—there always seemed to be a push and pull between the two—but when Burress was on the field, his coach seemed to admire his competitive nature. Maybe it's why years later there is a mutual respect. It likely has something to do with the connection they share from February 3, 2008, the day that changed both of their lives. Coughlin would get that elusive Super Bowl. Burress would play the role of hobbled hero. "Fast forward to Sunday, they wrap my knee up, gave me really, really good medicine...I don't know what it was," Burress said in an interview years later with Bleacher Report. "[I felt like I] didn't have a knee, like I bought a knee off eBay. I was feeling fantastic."

The Giants had their top wide receiver for the Super Bowl. And they would need him, especially at the end when they needed a play the most. They would need everyone against one of the greatest teams in NFL history. The Patriots knew they were that good. They were cocky, too. Just as Brady couldn't imagine only scoring 17 points with that loaded offense, New England didn't see a scenario where it could lose to this Giants team. Defensive lineman Richard Seymour even invited New York's offensive linemen to the Super Bowl afterparty during the first quarter of the big game. "That's a hell of a team, but there's a difference between being confident and then just overconfident," Chris Snee said. "I think they were definitely on that line. Some of them were over."

It's rare that the hype lives up to the billing. But it did in the fourth quarter of Super Bowl XLII. That is when 21 of the game's 31 points were scored. The first of three touchdowns in the final quarter came from an improbable source in David Tyree. In his fifth professional season, the former Syracuse University wide receiver had just four catches on five targets the entire season. Tyree, a Pro Bowl special teams ace, was only playing on offense because the Giants were short on healthy wide receivers. In preparation for the game, there was reason for concern. This didn't look like a good idea. Tyree dropped everything thrown in his direction on Friday, the final practice of that week. "Friday you want everything perfect, right?" Coughlin said. "It's not a long practice. It's not a physical practice. It's a hurry here and do this, hurry there and do that. So we're down inside what I call the tight green [zone], and David can't catch anymore. The ball is hitting his helmet. The ball rolled, ricochets off his shoulder pads. The coaches are looking at me, and I'm looking at them, and the practice is over, and Eli goes over, and he puts his arm around David Tyree. He says, 'David, I want you to forget about this practice. I know—we all know—that when the time comes, you will make the plays in the game.' And that was it. No more was said about it."

If it was just Tyree's five-yard touchdown catch that gave the Giants a 10–7 lead with 11:05 remaining in the contest, it would have made for a great story. But that was nothing compared to what was about to happen. That was the appetizer for the most unimaginable main course known to man. After the Patriots reclaimed the lead on a Brady to Randy Moss touchdown pass with 2:42 remaining, all hell broke loose. The Giants got the ball, and legends were about to be born. Manning's Hall of Fame case was about to be plastered on his resume and include an MVP trophy. It helped that Manning had nerves of steel in the biggest of spots.

These were the situations the players dreamed about in their backyard as kids. It all happened on that final drive in Glendale. "[It's] 17–14, fellas. One touchdown and we're world champions," Strahan said to the offense before they went out onto the field. "Believe it, and it will happen."

He was talking directly to the Giants' offensive line. Left tackle David Diehl, Snee, and Rich Seubert nodded and barely blinked. They were locked in, focused to the point that they appeared in a trance of complete concentration. After Amani Toomer caught a pair of early passes, the Giants were faced with a fourth-and-1 with just under two minutes remaining. Brandon Jacobs eked out two yards for a first down. It was a little too close for comfort.

"Chris [Snee] and I blew Wilfork back," center Shaun O'Hara said. "Chris got underneath him and pried him open, and we threw him out of that A-gap. That might've been the best block we had on Wilfork all game long. And I'm still to this day mad that we didn't get more yards. Brandon barely got that first down. But if you go back and watch, we blocked that about as well as you could draw it up."

Wilfork was driven into the ground and out of the A-gap on the play. Jacobs didn't get more yards because the blitzing linebacker muddied the pile in the backfield. But it was still enough to keep the drive going. After Manning scrambled and miraculously held onto the ball as defensive end Adalius Thomas tackled him from behind, he targeted Tyree on the right sideline. Something went wrong. Manning and Tyree weren't on the same page. Cornerback Asante Samuel had a chance on the right sideline to toe tap and grab what would've been a game-ending interception. It clanked off Samuel's right hand, which is unusual because Samuel had such good hands. He had an NFL-best 10 interceptions the previous season and six in 2007. This was a catch he'd made countless times before but not on this afternoon in the biggest of spots.

It opened the door for Manning and Tyree to redeem themselves on the very next play. Manning faced instant pressure from Thomas off the edge. He used a speed rush to beat Diehl. Defensive linemen Jarvis Green and Seymour ran a twist to get O'Hara and Seubert on different levels. Snee, the right guard, was just standing there, not blocking anybody on the other side as Seymour and Green got their hands on Manning's back, and Green grabbed a chunk of his jersey. Referee Mike Carey was about to blow the play dead when Manning magically escaped the grasp of Green even if he was almost facing his own end zone. Manning turned, got his feet set, and fired seemingly recklessly and blindly deep down the middle of the field. "The fact that Eli got out of that," O'Hara said. "I still don't know how he managed that."

It looked like a Hail Mary attempt in the moment. A disheveled quarterback throwing a wobbling ball through the air out of desperation. It was a blind heave in hopes that something positive would happen. It was thrown in the direction of Tyree, the same player who had that miserable Friday practice and wasn't on the same page as his quarterback one play earlier. Tyree leapt on the 25-yard line, his foot exploding off the L on the blue and red Super Bowl XLII logo. His right hand met the ball at its high point and pinned it to his helmet. Physical Patriots safety Rodney Harrison was on his right shoulder, trying viciously to pry the ball as Tyree's back arched on its way down to Earth. The ball miraculously remained wedged between his hand and helmet as they fell to the ground and then wrestled for the ball. Harrison couldn't believe how this situation had played out, how he hadn't knocked the ball free.

Coughlin ran on the field and called timeout with 59 seconds remaining. It was a 32-yard gain and put the Giants in striking distance of a legendary upset. Just like that, the "Helmet Catch" was born. It would not have happened if not for the pocket collapsing so quickly and Tyree defying all odds and securing the catch. The way it all played out, many of the Giants offensive linemen didn't even know he caught the ball with his helmet until they got back to their rooms after celebrating. Still, it would not have been the Helmet Catch as we know it nor would Manning have been the legend he's become without ultimately finishing the drive. It simply would have been an amazing play in a loss—not the legendary moment it has become.

It first took an incredible individual effort by rookie wide receiver Steve Smith on third and 11 to get the Giants into what Coughlin liked to call the "green zone." Smith caught the ball near the right sideline short of the first down. But he was able to stay inbounds and slide up the field just past the first-down marker for a 12-yard gain. The Giants were 13 yards from taking the lead. "What a play that was by Steve Smith," Coughlin said. "Eli just looked quick at the coverage and he went right to the flat. They're defending the first-down marker. He catches the ball four or five yards deep and he just beats the defender across the first-down marker for the first down."

It set up this call from radio announcer Bob Papa: "Manning calling signals, takes the snap, looks left, lobs it left. Burress is wide open. Touchdown Giants in the left corner of the end zone!"

The 6'5" Burress was matched against 5'9" cornerback Ellis Hobbs, who had been waving goodbye to the Giants several weeks back on their home field, in man-to-man coverage. Not that the height really mattered on this play. Burress looked as if he was going to run a slant and went to the corner of the end zone. The ball met him midway through the end zone. Hobbs was nowhere in sight. He had bit on the slant just as the Giants expected. They had seen it on tape and knew they could exploit Hobbs' over-aggression. They didn't even need to use that distinct height advantage in this instance. Burress had enough left in his body to leave Hobbs in the dust of forgettable Super Bowl goats. "Eli looks at Plaxico, and he said, 'If they single cover you, I'm coming to you,'" Coughlin said. "So he knew it, and his fake of the slant, they were just standing there. They weren't even close."

Burress, the man who operated without practicing that season, caught the ball and immediately went to the back pylon, fell down on a knee, and said a quick prayer. Diehl and Seubert met him in the end zone. The celebration was on. The Giants had a 17–14 lead. "That just speaks to the talent [Burress] has," defensive lineman Justin Tuck said. "To not work on anything other than the playbook during the season and come out and give us eight catches, 116 [yards], two touchdowns, man!"

That it was Tyree, who made the incredible catch given his struggles at practice only two days earlier, and Burress, who contributed the game-winning touchdown despite there being questions about whether he was healthy enough to play, only added to the absurdity of the upset. It was all so improbable. "Fourth quarter...knee is killing me," Burress said years later. "It's the Super Bowl. If I gotta jump off this leg like it's not hurting, if I tear my knee up, fuck it. [The] ball couldn't come down fast enough. [I] said to myself, 'Man, if you drop this football, you will not be allowed back in New Jersey.' Still to this day as time goes on, it starts to mean even more."

The Giants still had to stop the NFL's best offense for another 29 seconds after the Burress touchdown catch, which they did, to pull off the unthinkable. They had spoiled the Patriots' unbeaten season and won their third Super Bowl in franchise history: Giants 17, Patriots 14. Burress' prediction wasn't far off. In fact, he had given Brady too many points. Forget topping 21 points. Brady and Co. couldn't even muster more than two touchdowns.

It was only possible because of a perfect game plan from Spagnuolo that was reminiscent of Bill Belichick's 17 years earlier in the Super Bowl against the Buffalo Bills in the "Wide Right" game. Spagnuolo was one of the underrated stars of the Helmet Catch contest. The game plan Belichick concocted for the high-flying Bills in Super Bowl XXV is in the Hall of Fame. What Spagnuolo devised might as well be, too. It was that good. "If we could keep them under 30 points, that was good, and then to have it turn out the way it did was just a testament to the guys that were involved," Spagnuolo said. "I mean, just the grit and determination of that crew, now I'm speaking more specifically just to the defensive guys because of what we were up against and how great they were. I mean, [the Patriots] just blew through everybody and put up some points against us in that 16th game [of the regular season]. But then to go out there in the biggest game of the year and perform the way we did, I mean, to a man defensively, our guys executed things exactly, almost exactly the way we wanted to, and the results speak for themselves."

It set the stage for a ticker-tape parade for the ages down the Canyon of Heroes in Manhattan. An estimated one million fans were in attendance that day for the first Super Bowl parade of this sort in Giants history. That is because in 1986 the city of New York was still bitter about the Giants moving to New Jersey. The mayor at the time, Ed Koch, didn't want to hold a parade for a New Jersey team. "We cannot spend $500,000 on a foreign team," Koch said before the big game. He added, "Let [New Jersey] Governor Kean finance it in Moonachie."

In 1991 the Gulf War was taking place. Wellington Mara didn't think it was appropriate to have a parade while there was a war in progress. So the players on those teams never got to experience what the 21st century champion Giants did. Unfortunately, neither did Wellington Mara. He passed in 2005.

That is part of what made this Super Bowl triumph so special for John Mara. It was the first without his father. John Mara remembers looking around and seeing his kids celebrating, and it really hit home. The parade was the icing on the cake. "It was unbelievable," John Mara said. "It was unbelievable to see that many people...wearing Giant uniforms and the ticker tape. And when you think about the people that have had that type of parade in the past—astronauts, heroes—it was an incredible experience. In particular, I loved watching the players' reaction to all of the people cheering. And that to me was something that'll always stick out in my memory."

The fact that it was with Manning as the quarterback was comforting. Wellington Mara passed during the 2005 season. The last game he ever saw in person was the final game of Manning's rookie year. It was against the Cowboys, and Manning led a game-winning touchdown drive in the final seconds for his first career win. "I can remember walking to the locker room with him afterward and him saying to me, 'I think we found our guy.'" John Mara said years later. "And how right he was."

It was made even sweeter that Manning's first Super Bowl came against the undefeated Patriots. There was the previous matchup in the regular-season finale. There was the improbability of getting through the Cowboys and Packers in the playoffs after the way the first two weeks of the season went down. There was the Helmet Catch. None of those things were likely to happen. The probability rate of that parlay would have been close to zero. This Giants team wasn't supposed to win anything. In the end they pulled off one of the most improbable Super Bowl victories of all time. They were the first NFC team to win it all as a wild card. And to do it as such a massive underdog against the greatest quarterback of all time in Brady and the Patriots made it that much more enjoyable.

But Osi Umenyiora was right. He said it right after the regular season matchup in Week 17. "The Patriots didn't want to play us, and Osi's prophecy was right," Strahan said. "[We were] just a team of guys who really wanted to win for each other, and we were just so happy for each other's success. We supported each other, and that's what a team is about. I mean that's what life is about."

23
The Legendary Line

WHEN TOM COUGHLIN TOOK OVER AS THE HEAD COACH IN 2004, the New York Giants were looking to flip the meandering organization on its head. Coughlin was a hard-nosed coach known for his no-nonsense approach taking over from the player-friendly Jim Fassel, whose star players and favorites seemed to operate under different rules. Things had to change, in Coughlin's mind. He was taking over at Club Med. His job was to toss chairs around the resort and make it look and operate totally different. To create a football *feng shui* of sorts. The days of marinating in the hot tub because of a little boo-boo—while the rest of their teammates practiced—were over. Coughlin wanted a total 180 from what was going on at the end of the Fassel era, when the players were admittedly running the asylum. Coughlin spoke in his introductory press conference of injuries as a "cancer" and "mental thing." There were too many games missed because of injuries, and he didn't believe that atmosphere was conducive to ultimate success.

That is not how Coughlin ran the show previously in Boston College or with the Jacksonville Jaguars. The drill sergeant coach was going to mold and harden what he believed was a group that had gotten too comfortable with their surroundings and restore the pride of a franchise that was more than a decade removed from its last Super Bowl triumph, which he had been part of as the wide receivers coach in 1990 under Bill Parcells. "What we must be all about right now, immediately, is the restoration of pride—self-pride, team pride, the restoration of our professionalism and the dignity with which we conduct our business," Coughlin said sternly at his introductory press conference.

That first offseason with him as the head coach was as much about reshaping the attitude of the Giants as overhauling the roster. At the forefront of the plan was rebuilding the offensive line. One of the Giants' first moves in March 2004 was signing New Jersey native Shaun O'Hara in free agency. He was the first offensive player added to the mix that offseason. Only linebacker Carlos Emmons and defensive tackle Fred Robbins were added days earlier as Coughlin's initial additions. Emmons was a physical linebacker with five years of playoff experience, while Robbins was a 325-pound immovable object whose 11-inch hands could swallow a mortal human.

The character of the individual was almost as important to the Giants as their ability to perform on the field. O'Hara and Robbins would eventually become captains and significant Super Bowl contributors for the Giants later in their careers. "I'll never forget just the first time I met with Coach Coughlin, and he was like, 'Listen, we need players like you, and I want you to come here not just as a player but I got to change this locker room, and I need your help,'" O'Hara recalled. "That was his big thing."

The Giants offensive line was a weakness the previous season in 2003. They tied for allowing the second-most sacks (44) and finished 28th in the NFL in rushing despite having Tiki Barber, the best running back in franchise history, in his prime. There were so many questions about the unit entering that '04 season, Coughlin's first in charge, that then-ESPN analyst and former Washington Redskins quarterback Joe Theismann singled them out during a preseason game (that didn't even involve them) as having the league's worst offensive line. It was a critique they had heard for several years leading up to Coughlin's arrival, and it stretched into the 2005 season.

Leftover from the previous regime, a young David Diehl remained on the roster. He had started 16 games as a rookie at right guard. He was a fifth-round pick out of the University of Illinois and had shown signs of being a keeper as a rookie. Whatever the New York Giants asked Diehl to do, he was down. Whether it was left tackle, right tackle, left guard, right guard, no problem. He did it all throughout his 11-year career—all with the team that drafted him in the fifth round of the 2003 NFL Draft. The final tally: 65 games at left tackle, 42 at left guard, 26 at right tackle. and 27 at right guard. In the postseason, he had 10 starts at left tackle and one at left guard. No matter how you cut it, that's impressive versatility. He loved being part of the Giants. He worked tirelessly and maximized every ounce of talent in his body in addition to being universally respected in the locker room and for his work off the field.

Diehl was a Pro Bowl selection in 2009 and a second-team All Pro in 2008 at left tackle. He was the starter at left tackle on a pair of Super Bowl teams, the second of which he started the season at left guard before Will Beatty went down for the season with an injury. "Diehl played everywhere. He could play every position. That's why he was so awesome," Barber said. "I loved Diehl. He would come up to me before every game and say, 'Hey, find me. Seek me out, Tiki. You can count on me.' And that's just how he was. He was this massive human being at that point. I'm older, I think I'm 28, 29, and he's this second-year player, and his confidence was just awesome. He would say, 'You can count on me!'"

They had scrappy guard Rich Seubert, an overachiever who had worked himself into a starting role. An undrafted free agent out of Western Illinois, he made his NFL debut on September 10, 2001. The world changed the following day. Seubert, a large man with an even bigger personality, was the longest-tenured offensive lineman on the Giants roster during the glory years of the Manning/Coughlin era. He grinded his way onto the active roster and into a starting spot in his second professional season after spending most of his rookie year inactive. Seubert started all 16 games in his second season and was the memorable intended receiver on the now-infamous Trey Junkin botched snap play in the wild 39–38 playoff loss to the San Francisco 49ers during the 2002 season. Officially, he was flagged for "ineligible downfield pass," but the NFL said the following day they made a mistake and Seubert was an eligible receiver. There should have also been a pass interference penalty on the 49ers on that play.

Seubert was dealing with a serious leg injury after breaking his fibula, tibia, and ankle during the '03 season in a gruesome injury that occurred when Philadelphia Eagles defensive lineman N.D. Kalu inadvertently stepped on and crushed his left leg. Seubert wouldn't return until 2005 after months in a hospital and five surgeries. "I heard it," he said. "I didn't know how bad it was. It was scary though. You hear it break."

He is loud and boisterous, the kind of guy who to this day is in the middle of every joke. He can dish it but also take it in return. Always a ball of entertainment. But with the sarcasm and wit came a nasty edge on the field. It was a favorite of Giants fans. Seubert would do anything at the bottom of a pile to recover a fumble and was always in the middle of scrums. He even admittedly made it a point after a few years in the league to start the first fight of training camp every year. "[It] was kind of like the unofficial start of training camp," Kevin Boothe said. "It was just a matter of when."

Excitable linebacker Mathias Kiwanuka was a common target because the offensive line room knew he ran hot and cold. Defensive end Jason Pierre-Paul during his rookie year was another. Seubert is open about how it was always a young player or rookie who was running their mouth. He wasn't dumb enough to mess with Michael Strahan or someone with that type of clout and resume. Either way, the fans ate it up. So did Seubert. It was, perhaps, his favorite hobby. "I wasn't afraid to pick a fight in practice because I knew I had seven guys that were going to have my back," Seubert said. "I'm not dumb. I'm not going after some of these guys without my guys behind me. So I knew if something went down in practice, these guys would do anything for you. And I would do anything for these guys. And that's the way we played."

So many of the offensive line stories seem to revolve around Seubert. There was that time where he had to execute a reach block on defensive lineman Albert Haynesworth, then with the Redskins, on one of the first plays of the game. After a week where his teammates and offensive line coach Pat Flaherty were gassing him up about facing Haynesworth, O'Hara heard Seubert trying to butter up his opponent. "Hey, Albert, just want to let you know I vote for you for the Pro Bowl every year," Seubert said.

"I hear this and I get back hot," O'Hara said. "I'm like, '[Snee], you're not going to freaking believe this. He's out here giving Albert a handjob. And [Seubert's] like, 'What? What? I can't pump him up a little bit.' I'm like, 'What are you doing? You're such a kiss ass!'"

Two series later, Seubert comes over and says to the rest of the line, "Hey, I told you it would work out. The running back was coming out behind me, and Albert helped me up. He was like, 'Hey, watch your legs, watch your legs.' He's looking out for me now. We're boys."

O'Hara was such a critical piece. The Giants finished the '03 season with Ian Allen and Jeff Hatch starting at tackle in their season finale while Diehl and Scott Peters played guard and Chris Bober started at center. O'Hara was signed to play center, his more natural position after flipping between center and guard for the Cleveland Browns his first four years in the NFL. Making O'Hara their center was a decision that didn't move the needle much at the time, but it ultimately turned out to be a difference-maker.

The Hillsborough, New Jersey, native was also an undrafted free agent, but he was out of the hometown college of Rutgers in New Jersey, where the Giants play and practice. O'Hara originally proved himself in the NFL in Cleveland, where he started more games at guard (30) than center (eight). He became a free agent in 2004, fittingly just as the Giants were looking to rebuild their offensive line. The Browns were lowballing him prior to the start of free agency, so his agent, Tony Agnone, who also represented Strahan and Osi Umenyiora, advised him that in order to receive fair-market value, he would have to go elsewhere. New York wasn't even on his radar as he entered free agency that year. Bober was the Giants' center at the time, and O'Hara didn't know what they were going to do with him. Bober was a decent player but a free agent as well.

Despite being advised that a vacation might be a good option prior to the frenzy that can be free agency, O'Hara instead elected to drive home from Cleveland to New Jersey. He had a meeting set up on Sunday, March 7, in Arizona with the Cardinals. He thought there was a good chance that was where he would sign. But that Friday night before the meeting, O'Hara was having dinner at his childhood home with his parents when the phone rang. It was Agnone. "Hey, we just got off the phone with [the Giants]," Agnone said. "We were talking about another player, and your name came up. They asked what you were doing, what your status was."

They wanted O'Hara to come for a visit before meeting with the Cardinals. They asked where he was and if he could get there on short notice. Fortunately for O'Hara, he was already in New Jersey. "Good things happen when you go see mom," O'Hara likes to say in relation to his eventual signing with the Giants.

O'Hara signed a three-year deal that was reported by ESPN to be worth $5.4 million. The lure of playing at home and at his natural position, center, was too good to turn down. He never even made the trip to Arizona. His signing was done by Saturday evening and announced on Sunday. "Center is my more natural position," O'Hara said at the time. "I played center my first two years at Cleveland, and then they switched me to guard. I like playing center. You've got to be smart and you've got to be vocal, and it fits my personality."

Boy was O'Hara right. He was the player most likely to be fined by the rest of the group for blabbing to the media. It was hardly unusual to see O'Hara surrounded by a group of cameras during media availabilities. More importantly, with his gift for gab, O'Hara became a leader on that offensive line, helping direct traffic and make calls. It was a perfect fit. He went on to become a three-time Pro Bowl center (2008–10) and a second-team All Pro in 2008.

O'Hara and Manning were also a perfect match. There is nobody that O'Hara would rather have, in a professional setting, put their hands on his backside than Manning. The two have remained especially close even after their playing careers ended.

The signing ironically may not have happened without Flaherty. He vouched for O'Hara years after questioning whether the young center would even make it in college football. Their relationship stretches back to when O'Hara was at Hillsborough High School and Flaherty was an assistant at Wake Forest. "We don't know if you're going to be big enough to play Division I football," O'Hara recalled Flaherty saying.

O'Hara embedded that in his memory bank, apparently never to be deleted even if Flaherty may have been onto something. O'Hara walked on at Rutgers at 235 pounds. That wouldn't be the case when they met again. It happened during O'Hara's sophomore season at Rutgers when they faced Wake Forest. As O'Hara went through his normal pregame tradition of reading game-day material on the toilet, he noticed Flaherty was still on the Deamon Deacons' staff. He made a point of going to find him before the game. "'Hey, Coach Flaherty, don't know if you remember me, Shaun O'Hara from Hillsborough High School,'" O'Hara recalled. "'You didn't think I was going to be big enough to play Division I football? I'm going to be wearing out your All-American [defensive tackle] all day.' And he was like, 'Oh yeah, I knew you were going to be a good player.'"

It didn't end there. A few years later, the Browns were playing the Redskins in a preseason game. O'Hara was an undrafted free agent trying to make the team in Cleveland when he was going through the same pregame routine from college. Again, he saw Flaherty's name in the program. Again, he made a point to remind him about the misevaluation. "I'm like, I got to find him," O'Hara said. "So I find him on the field. I go up to him, 'Hey, Coach Flaherty, I don't know if you remember me, Shaun O'Hara.' "And he's like, 'Oh, yeah, Shaun, come on. You don't have to keep introducing yourself.' And I'm like, 'Yeah, it's crazy we're both here. You didn't think I'd be big enough to play Division I? You son of a gun.' And he's like, 'You keep holding that against me?'"

The next year Flaherty was the tight ends coach for the Chicago Bears, who the Browns faced in a regular-season game. "Don't even fucking say it!" Flaherty told O'Hara before that game.

It was a marriage that was meant to be. O'Hara had a successful seven-year run with the Giants—all with Flaherty as his offensive line coach. They remain tight to this day.

After officially using their first-round pick in 2004 on quarterback Philip Rivers before trading him in the deal that netted Eli Manning, the Giants selected guard Chris Snee out of Boston College with the 34th overall selection in the second round. A quiet, hard-working monster in the weight room who would eventually become an All-Pro guard, Snee also happened to be the future son-in-law of the head coach. He had a young son with Kate Coughlin before joining the Giants. It didn't matter. Snee could play.

He had another connection to the storied franchise. During his college years at Boston College, he roomed with Mike Fassel, the son of former Giants coach Jim Fassel. He had even more familiarity with the team by 2004, when Coughlin became the coach. Coughlin was hired in early January. Snee was drafted by the team before the end of April.

Snee would later marry and have four kids with Kate. They made their life in New Jersey, where they never left and still reside. It almost never happened. General manager Ernie Accorsi didn't believe in picking a guard in the first round. But Snee had such a high grade that when he was there early in the second, it had to be considered. So Accorsi and Coughlin went outside the draft room for a sidebar conversation. "I said, 'This is up to you,'" Accorsi recalled. "'It's between you and me. No one in that draft room's going to know anything about it. But I have to have credibility with my scouts. He's the highest-rated player by a mile, but if you don't want to coach him, we're not picking him.'"

That is when Coughlin had to loop in the real boss—his wife, Judy. She was always the voice of reason. "He called my mom first just to say, 'This obviously is a rare, very rare, situation,'" Kate Snee once told *The New York Times*. "He asked her, 'Do you think this is the right thing to do? Do you think it's going to work out?'"

Tom Coughlin came back in the room and asked if Snee was the best player.

"By a mile!" Accorsi said.

"Pick him," Tom Coughlin said.

With Judy Coughlin's approval, the Giants drafted Snee in the second round of the 2004 NFL Draft (34th overall) out of Boston College. All he did was become one of the best offensive linemen in franchise history. Snee was inducted into the Giants Ring of Honor in 2015.

Playing for his father-in-law was definitely a unique situation. But they never made it feel that way. Next it was a matter of how it would be received internally and how Snee and Coughlin would handle their relationship. It definitely raised eyebrows with some of the Giants.

But Snee earned everyone's respect by putting his head down and going to work. There was no favoritism from Coughlin, and it was always a player/coach relationship on the field and in the building. Sure, there would be jokes. The offensive line would say something and then warn Snee he better not share that with dad over dinner. Seubert, of course, would have the most fun with it. He also had a lot of free time on his hands as he rehabbed the leg injury. "Hey, what'd Tom make for breakfast?" Seubert used to say.

The amazing part is it would eventually fade. The situation became normal. If you didn't know the connection, you wouldn't have been able to notice when they were at work. It was always "Coach" when he was talking about Coughlin. "Give credit to both of them," Boothe said. "The only time you would see any bits of it would be training camp or something like that where it's Family Day and the grandkids showed up. But outside of that, it was a professional relationship that was no different than anybody else's. And it obviously helps that Chris was really good, too."

Snee started Week One as a rookie. He started all 152 games in his career at right guard, including in two Super Bowls. He was first-team All Pro by 2008. He was a second-team All Pro in 2009 and 2010. He was Manning's trusted protector on the field and roommate on the road.

The organization's priorities were becoming clear. What Coughlin and general manager Accorsi wanted was starting to take shape—a rejiggered culture and locker room *and* a rebuilt offensive line. That would help fix what had gone wrong during the previous 4–12 season, which turned out to be Fassel's last. This was a key offseason for the Giants that would lay the foundation for the success that was on the horizon. O'Hara would be Manning's trusted sidekick and his starting center for the next seven seasons. Snee would blossom into one of the best offensive linemen in franchise history and be an anchor on two Super Bowl–winning lines. Diehl would become a steady performer, sliding around the line before becoming the starter at left tackle in two Super Bowl triumphs. Seubert eventually fought and clawed his way back from that serious leg injury and became an inspirational mainstay on the line.

To complete the regular starting unit, right tackle Kareem McKenzie was signed during the 2005 offseason after spending four years with the crosstown rival New York Jets. McKenzie was the missing piece the Giants didn't even know they needed. But McKenzie really was a complete player. He wasn't just your old-school right tackle who excelled simply in the run game. He was a solid pass blocker that Manning and the rest of the crew could trust. "I don't think Kareem got enough credit for how good of a pass protector he was because when you watched him kick slide, you were not impressed," O'Hara said. "You weren't like, 'Oh my gosh, this guy's really got great fast footwork.' But he was so long, his arms were so long, and he was so good with his punch. He just perfected his craft, and it was like he out-slowed everybody."

McKenzie wasn't in a rush to get to his spot. He'd rather get there efficiently and effectively. Although some tackles rush through their backpedal, almost as if they're having a seizure, McKenzie did it quietly and smoothly. He was unique in just about every way possible.

McKenzie was known as a deep thinker. It's hardly a surprise he now has five different degrees. A lot of guys had books in their lockers, but McKenzie actually read them. He was a Renaissance man of sorts, reading to gain knowledge rather than messing around and playing video games. You didn't mess with Big Bear. He was the only player in the locker room that the offensive line agreed was prank-proof.

Boothe was later claimed off waivers from the Oakland Raiders and became an invaluable handyman for Flaherty's group. He was a sixth-round pick by the Raiders out of Cornell in the 2006 NFL Draft. Boothe is just one of two Cornell alum, along with former Green Bay Packers and Cleveland Browns center JC Tretter, to be drafted this century. Boothe proved to be a versatile piece who would fill in at guard or center. He became a full-time starter midway through the 2011 season and started at left guard for the Giants in Super Bowl XLVI. His ability to slide in seamlessly and fill the void was huge that season.

Individually, these players were not all that impressive. Mostly average/good players. Together is when they were at their best. They created one of the best offensive lines in football during that time and were essential to the team's success on and off the field. "The sum was greater than the individual parts," said defensive lineman Chris Canty, who played against the group when he was with the Dallas Cowboys and then went against them every day at practice with the Giants.

Perhaps most amazing is how long the Giants were able to keep that group together. That starting five was together from 2005 to 2010. A six-season run without any changes on the offensive line is a lifetime. With free agency and the current volatility of today's NFL, it's probably something that can't be replicated. That familiarity provided the Giants an inherent advantage. They had a communication and connectedness that Canty had never seen before. It was especially valuable with a young quarterback, and it helped overhaul the locker room for Coughlin. "That was such a huge thing to have those guys being the leaders, setting the tempo, setting the pace for what we have to do," Manning said. "And they were so focused on the details of playing offensive line, of doing things the right way."

By 2005 the Giants had one of the best offensive lines in football. They finished sixth in rushing that year, averaging 138.1 yards per game. They finished seventh compiling 134.8 yards per game the following year. Heading into that memorable 2007 season that netted their first Super Bowl in 17 years, this was already an established group, one that Coughlin and new offensive coordinator Kevin Gilbride knew they could count on to be one of the league's best units. "What a great combination they became," Coughlin said. "And the one thing is you remember that Eli also fit in there because Eli could take it and dish it out a lot like Michael Strahan."

It didn't take long as this group of young offensive linemen started coming together to figure where they would be on Thursday afternoons in particular. They developed a routine that would have them congregating in the offensive line room after practice and into the evening, grinding tape of practice and their opponents. It became an event they absolutely could not miss.

The entire line and Manning piled in every Thursday. It quickly became a routine in 2004 because the Giants line needed to make sure they were prepared for every possible blitz they might encounter against a particular opponent or scheme.

"Chasing ghosts" was a phrase you might have heard O'Hara mutter during that time. This Giants group of Diehl, Seubert, O'Hara, Snee, and McKenzie, which had come together by the start of the 2005 season, wanted to make certain they were fully prepared for anything and everything. It was an unofficial meeting that ran without coaches and was led primarily by Manning. At times the running backs and wide receivers would pop in. It could go on for hours. But no matter who was there, it was always the core of the offensive line who would bunker down and work, usually with some food obtained courtesy of runs by the younger players. (Five Guys was a popular choice at the time.) Only it never really felt like work. It was more like five to 10 friends chopping it up while simultaneously achieving a common goal. "It's good to hash all those things out," Snee said. "I can't tell you how many hours we spent in that room—breakfast while watching film, lunch while watching film. I get it. In the cafeteria you want to sit there and be social and interact with the rest of your teammates. But we always grabbed our food to go, and we kind of hunkered down with our guys...I just kind of stress the importance of watching tape together. To me that's invaluable."

The tradition began in the dorms at the University at Albany, where the Giants held training camp until 2012. It took place in the white-walled meeting rooms at Giants Stadium, which is where the players did their daily work until they opened a new practice facility across the Meadowlands in 2009. The plush accommodations of the TIMEX Performance Center, which was later rebranded the Quest Diagnostics Training Center, afforded a new room, but it didn't change or even alter the routine. The standard had already been set for this Giants offensive line plus their quarterback. "Thursday after practice we just kind of set our new [code] words, our new calls, how we're going to pick up a certain blitz, what we're going to do to make these things work," Manning said. "And that was big just to get on the same page with them. They loved it. They appreciated it. They want to protect. They want to do their job. And they took great pride in working together as a group. So it was great to have those guys in there, the way they protected me but also the way they took great pride in running the ball. And that's what we wanted to do. We wanted to run the ball first and be tough, and they had to kind of set that mentality."

They ran the ball for at least 250 yards six times from 2005 to 2008. That included a 301-yard effort late in the 2008 season against the Carolina Panthers. Snee believes that was the best and most complete game their offensive line ever played. Derrick Ward rushed for 215 yards on 15 carries that day, and Brandon Jacobs added another 87 yards on 24 carries. It was an absolute offensive line masterpiece. The five starters were moving in unison as if they were composing a symphony. Flaherty served as the proud conductor.

But it was rarely that simple. There was always a push and pull between the offensive line and Gilbride. The Giants' line—similar to just about every offensive line that ever existed—wanted to run the ball more. They were constantly begging Gilbride, who had a run-and-shoot sling-it-around-the-yard background, to run it more. "You knew specifically that if you had a chance to run the ball, you damn well better make it count because if not it's going to be thrown, and we definitely don't want to be in a passing situation," McKenzie said. "Pass for what? Why? What's the need? Run the ball! Simple. Wear 'em down."

This Giants line did it with regularity during that time, including in the playoffs and Super Bowls, and it was Flaherty's job to advocate for his group. They would come off the field after a drive, and he would ask what was going on and what they wanted to call when they returned to the field. The answer was almost always the same. To a man they would answer with only a tinge of sarcasm: "Run the ball!"

The players doing the dirty work in the trenches would give the same input to Gilbride as well. It was met with open ears even if it still wasn't enough for the run-loving linemen. They were 11th in rushing yards and 21st in attempts in 2004. They were sixth in yards and 11th in attempts the following year, then seventh in yards and 16th in attempts, fourth in yards and eighth in attempts in Gilbride's first year as offensive coordinator in '07, and finally first in yards and seventh in attempts, in 2008. That year was the pinnacle of their run-dominating powers.

The data showed there was some merit to the belief that they should run the ball more. Quite frankly, it was because they were quite good at it, and it fit their skill sets, particularly the right side of the line with Snee and McKenzie. They were both known as dominant run blockers—not that they were slouches in pass protection either. Even Seubert and Diehl on the other side and O'Hara orchestrating things from the center all played with power and had a nasty edge to them. Together, it made them a powerful unit. "It was a physical group, and that was really the personality," Flaherty said. "Kevin [Gilbride] did what he needed to do. Most coordinators, they want to throw the football, but he listened to these guys. He listened to me once in a while, but he listened to these guys a little bit more."

When they did run, it was often a thing of beauty. Barber rushed for 1,662 yards in his final season in the NFL in 2006. That was primarily with Luke Petitgout as the left tackle and Diehl at left guard while Seubert worked his way back from the broken leg. It's actually amazing to consider that Barber had 234 yards against the Redskins, rushing behind that line in what would amount to the last regular-season game of his career. He had another 137 yards on 26 carries in his final career game, a 23–20 last-second playoff loss to the rival Eagles.

The following year, the Giants did even better on the ground on a miserable December day in Buffalo. With Barber now retired, it was Jacobs and rookie Ahmad Bradshaw that allowed them to compile 289 rushing yards against the Bills in the crummy weather at Ralph Wilson Stadium. They remember it like it was yesterday. A play called *36-Bob* went for a 43-yard touchdown by Jacobs in the first half. The line matched man to man with the defensive linemen across from them. Fullback Madison Hedgecock picked up blitzing Bills linebacker Keith Ellison, and Seubert cut off the scraping middle linebacker. Buffalo then couldn't stop *15-Bob* in the fourth quarter, which Bradshaw took to the end zone for an 88-yard score. Again, it was Hedgecock who picked up the weakside linebacker and a pulling Seubert who reached and blocked middle linebacker John DiGiorgio. Bradshaw finished with 151 yards rushing on 17 carries, an electrifying performance from the seventh-round rookie. Jacobs added another 143 yards on 25 carries on a day where the Giants had to rush out of the locker room following the game, just to get out of Buffalo before they got stuck there for days.

All of that hard work on the ground helped the Giants clinch a playoff berth in a season where they ended up winning the Super Bowl. Still, that game in Buffalo sticks out years later.

"For somebody who didn't play that game, that was probably the most miserable I've ever been on a sideline," Boothe said. "It was 65 degrees at kickoff, and then it poured in the second quarter, like a downpour, and then the temperature just plummeted after that. I think there was sleet, and then by the end, it was a blizzard."

That kind of inclement weather didn't stop these Giants. After all, this is the same crew that made a pre-determined decision to wear short sleeves during the famous 2008 NFC Championship Game in Green Bay when the temperature was -23 degrees with the windchill at kickoff. It was a statement no doubt—even if it wasn't exactly the smartest of choices.

Snee remembers the '08 game against the Panthers as one of the offensive line's crowning achievements. Forget for a moment that they compiled 301 yards on the ground—at the time the fifth-highest output in franchise history—but the 34–28 win at Giants Stadium clinched the top seed in the NFC that season for the Giants. It was a special win for the team and their dominant offensive line, which earlier that year was praised in *ESPN The Magazine* for being among the league's best units. Not offensive lines, but overall units. "Those are the games that you take pride in," Snee said. "The Carolina game at home, pound the rock against them to clinch the No. 1 seed, might be my favorite game—other than the Super Bowls—ever. That for our front might've been our best game ever played, just the way we ran the ball against that defense with everything that was on the line, coming off a couple of losses, the Plaxico [gunshot] situation. To win that game at home, to lock up the one seed, that was a lot of fun."

Flaherty, who was hired as an offensive line coach in the NFL for the first time in 2004 by Coughlin, quickly earned the trust of his unit. He did it by coaching them hard and honest, by putting in equal, if not more, work than the players. It was something they noticed, and the trust was reciprocated. To this day, Flaherty remains close to his Super Bowl offensive lines. When he talks to youngsters, he still brings up this famed group, their character, and their post-career successes off the field.

As of 2024, Diehl was coaching the offensive line at the University of Memphis. Seubert was a successful head coach at the Watchung Hills High School in New Jersey. O'Hara worked as an analyst for the NFL Network and the Giants. Snee was a senior scout for the Giants, and McKenzie was a professor with masters and PhD degrees. Boothe received an MBA from

George Washington University and worked his way up the ladder with the NFL into a director's position on the management council.

The continuity and unity was integral to their success. Almost 20 years later, the Giants offensive line that was key to two Super Bowl victories still jokes about some of the same things they did during their playing careers. They laugh at the mention of Seubert always asking for the line to "slide left," about Diehl forgetting the play call, about O'Hara having never met a camera he didn't like. They were serious about their football, but it came with an endless supply of jokes and one-liners. Whatever the work/fun split was, it was effective. This was the rare group who liked each other on and off the field. Even when McKenzie and Boothe joined in 2005 and 2007, respectively, they were welcomed with open arms because the way they worked aligned with what was already in place.

The big personality of Seubert kept everybody on their feet even when he was rehabbing the leg injury. In fact, that may have only made it worse since he was always around hassling the young guys and newcomers. Seubert seemed to always be in the middle of every joke, every prank, both then and now. His personality alone made it fun and interesting to come to work every day. "There was a particular guy that maybe instigated them when things were bored," Flaherty said. "I won't bring up his name, but if one guy got into something on that offensive line, they had to take five guys on him. And that says something about what this offensive line was really about."

Manning was essentially part of the group. Some of his closest friends to this day were from that line. O'Hara even serves as his sidekick on *The Eli Manning Show*, which was founded in 2021 and runs on the Giants' team website. Snee remains a close friend. It mattered that the starting quarterback watched film with them privately, went to dinner with them regularly, and was involved in the endless supply of jokes and pranks. It was possible because they spent so much time together and it strengthened the bond. "I was so close to those guys," Manning said. "Having the continuity was huge."

It was no doubt part of the tremendous on-field success for the storied franchise from 2004 to 2011. The best offensive line in franchise history, it was almost as if they could consistently communicate through telepathy on the field. What Manning was thinking, so was his offensive line. They saw a certain look or a certain defensive player line up a specific way and they knew exactly what to do. "Say it was the free safety. *Why am I looking at the free safety? What or how does that play into it?*" McKenzie explained. "But we were able to go ahead and communicate and be able to say, whether you burp, fart, whatever it is, however you communicate, just be able to do that and know what's going on. And being able to do that and having that familiarity of playing next to this same guy on a continual basis, you start to see things through the same lens. And what you see is the offensive line being able to go ahead and do some pretty significant accomplishments overall."

All of those hours they spent studying together made a difference. All those years together were invaluable. All that extra time on Thursday afternoons and evenings in the offensive line room watching tape paid serious dividends. It made this group unforgettable. "Honestly, that's probably what differentiated our offensive line, our group, from so many other lines in the league," O'Hara said. "We literally were to the point where we could run any play at any point in time in the season from any week. And we knew how to block it, we knew how to handle it. We could change a protection in the middle of the game. We could come back and we could talk to Gilbride and talk to Flats and talk to them about, 'Here's what they're doing, and it's not what they showed on film, it's not what they did last time we played. This is what they're doing.' And I think all that comes just from the knowledge of the game and the time that we put in. So I think we also took a lot of pride in that."

PART 5

2011

24
All In

When it comes to the New York Football Giants and eventual Super Bowls, it always seems to begin with [insert coach] being on the hot seat. It happened with Bill Parcells early in his tenure, Jim Fassel in the middle of that Super Bowl season, and Tom Coughlin again in 2007.

In Coughlin's case, it incredibly happened twice! It didn't matter that ownership, led by John Mara, said entering the 2011 season that Coughlin wasn't on the hot seat. By the middle of the 2011 campaign, his butt cheeks were heating up once again. "[Coughlin] knows as well as anyone that he's in a bottom-line business," wrote *Newsday* columnist Bob Glauber. "If his team isn't in the tournament in January, the Giants likely will make a move—and it will be a necessary move."

This was around Thanksgiving in 2011. By the time President's Day arrived in February, Coughlin had another

Super Bowl win on his resume and told everyone to kiss those butt cheeks.

It's too simple to just look at the job security of the head coach and make any overarching assumptions. Coughlin had only received a one-year contract extension through the 2012 season so he wouldn't be a lame-duck coach. And then he stumbled through a year where they were 7–7 through 14 games, including getting smashed 49–24 in New Orleans by a strong Saints team after Thanksgiving. "We had no answer," Coughlin said years later of the Saints and that losing stretch.

The Giants wanted no part of the Saints again. That would come into play later down the road. But at the time, that wasn't even on their minds. This Coughlin-led team had its work cut out just to make the playoffs. If they didn't, his job security would undoubtedly be in question. It seems asinine in retrospect, but it was reality. The coach who had won a Super Bowl four years earlier never had a losing record in New York aside from his first season with the team, made the playoffs again in 2008, missed with a respectable 10–6 record in 2010, was on the hot seat.

It was clear where Coughlin stood on all this. After the final game of the 2010 season, a 17–14 win against the Washington Redskins at FedEx Field, he stood in the locker room and told this team, "Outstanding finish to the ballgame. We did our part, okay? That's all I can ask you to do," he said. "Hey, from the bottom of my heart and everybody's, we have a 10–6 season! A 10-win season in the NFL? And [the critics] can kiss my ass? They can line up and kiss my ass. It's not an easy thing to do."

Except everything that unfolded up until Week 16 in 2011 didn't support Coughlin's case. It was the night before Christmas Eve when the tide seemed to turn. It was at a players' chapel meeting where a young speaker uttered an important message that undoubtedly resonated. Gian Paul Gonzalez was a ninth-grade teacher and speaker in Union City, New Jersey. Nervously standing in front of a large group of players, he provided the message and theme for what was about to be another magical run for six weeks. Gonazlez was a friend of the Giants team chaplain who asked him to speak. That is how Gonzalez instantly became a major figure in New York's Super Bowl run and a part of the team for many years. He talked about what it meant to be "all in," to unselfishly be fully committed to a cause not only for your own self-serving interests, but also for the good of the whole.

The Giants went out the next day on Christmas Eve and manhandled Rex Ryan's New York Jets. That was the day Victor Cruz scored on a 99-yard touchdown that propelled the Giants in the right direction. It was the day everything changed for that 2011 Giants team. Afterward, defensive end and captain Justin Tuck summed up the motivation that would eventually carry them to another Super Bowl. "We were all in today," Tuck said. "Went to chapel last night, and the speaker talked about 'all in.' Today you could just tell the Giants were all in."

From that point on, the 2011 Giants were different. They had a special connection, a unique desire to do this thing together. It's no accident they eventually reached the mountaintop, considering the work that was put into the climb—even if it wasn't always easy. There were the players-led film sessions that were organized after Thursday and Friday practices. Eventually, coaches starting sitting in, too, when they realized it was becoming a regular thing. That was part of the all-in concept. Everyone was on the same page.

It's especially rare, considering Fridays are generally date night for players and coaches. That is the night they block off time for the family, let loose, and have a good time. Saturdays are generally a light day of work (a walk-through and a full 36 hours for your body to recover). In fact, Friday practices are often referred to as "parking lot practices" because when they end players are generally in the parking lot running to their cars immediately after the final whistle.

Coughlin had the players out by 1:00 PM on Fridays throughout that season. At 1:15 PM guys would sit down and watch an extra hour of film, just going through the checks and calls to get ready for the game on Sunday. They were doing it on their own of their own free will without even the slightest mandate from coaches or management. There would still be time for date night or whatever was on the schedule later.

Defensive line dinners became common for Fridays that season as well. Ruth's Chris Steak House was the go-to spot. Occasionally, they would switch it up and go to The River Palm Terrace or Fleming's in Edgewater. Credit card roulette would decide who was picking up the tab. It was more the idea and the company that mattered than the venue. "It was really about us having a commitment to each other to see how good the team can be, to see exactly what we could get done if we're all pulling the rope in the same direction," defensive lineman Chris Canty said. "And I think that was the cool thing about it, the connectedness of it, the love for one another that you're willing to sacrifice time away from family. You're willing to go the extra mile. I know all of these things sound cliche, but it was real, and that is what created the bond that we all now still share."

It wasn't just those extra players-led meetings in the facility. Veteran cornerback Corey Webster used to have the defensive backs at his New Jersey townhouse every week. There would be beverages, wings, and more film to digest. Eventually, some of the linebackers started coming. Then some defensive linemen.

It was a productive way to chop it up and get some extra work, the kind of things that only close-knit teams do. It's also why some of the defensive calls picked up pop culture nomenclature. The byproduct was that on the field they became a more well-organized, cohesive unit. The Giants defense allowed 20 points or fewer in each of their final six games, including the playoffs. It was another selfless unit that was playing for each other, which history shows was a common refrain from all their Super Bowl teams.

Look no further than standout defensive end Osi Umenyiora. He went into the 2011 season unhappy with his contract, looking for a new deal. The Giants actually granted him permission to seek a trade that summer despite having two years left on his contract. After all, Umenyiora and his veteran teammates had just seen aging legendary Giants such as Shaun O'Hara and Rich Seubert cut because of age and injury. This made it that much more curious to Umenyiora why fans would take issue with him wanting a new deal or trade. "What really annoys me is the hypocrisy of people clamoring for my head for asking for a new deal or to be traded, saying I have two years left on my deal," Umenyiora said. "Where is O'Hara? Where is Seubert? True inspirational football players. They were cut after being injured."

Umenyiora had a procedure done on his knee to repair his meniscus that summer and would miss the first three games. He returned and had seven sacks in his first six games. But late in the season, he suffered a high ankle sprain in the blowout loss in New Orleans. It was "real bad," a source told the *New York Daily News*' Ralph Vacchiano at the time.

Umenyiora had a decision to make. The Giants were 6–5, mired in mediocrity, and his contract situation remain unresolved. He could shut it down, consider it a lost season, and turn his attention to 2012, which would be a contract year. Not exactly a terrible option considering New York didn't seem to be headed anywhere special. Or Umenyiora could get injections into his ankle and try to play through the discomfort and pain. The two-time All Pro and Pro Bowl pass rusher went to an unlikely source for advice—Parcells. The legendary Giants coach was recently retired after a final stint in the front office of the Miami Dolphins. "I remember calling him, and he said something really interesting to me," Umenyiora said. "He said, 'Osi, whatever you do, don't be the victim.' I was too afraid to be like, *What the fuck does that even mean? Don't be the victim? I couldn't understand it. Don't ever be the victim?* And I kind of took him meaning don't feel sorry for yourself. No, oh-woe-is-me, kind of deal. Don't do that. Take control of the situation and go out there and see what happens."

Umenyiora returned for a win-and-get-in game against the Dallas Cowboys in Week 17. He had two sacks in the contest, which were his first after missing four games. And he once again was a major factor in the postseason. Umenyiora had 3.5 sacks and a forced fumble in the playoff run. The Giants probably wouldn't have another Lombardi Trophy in their lobby if he had taken the easy way out. Hat tip to Parcells. "That advice—when I was trying to decide what I was going to do—it just kept on playing in my head. It was like, *Don't be the victim here, man. Don't be the victim!*" Umenyiora said. "Can you imagine if you are like, no, I'm not going to do this? I'm going to bow out and I'm not going to play anymore, and then the team goes on this run without you."

Umenyiora fortunately didn't miss the ride. That was lucky for him and the Giants because this one was perhaps even more improbable than 2007. The 2011 Giants were 7–7, heading into their Christmas Eve matchup with the crosstown rival Jets. They had the 32nd-ranked rushing attack. Their defense had allowed 49, 38, and 34 points, respectively, in a three-week stretch late in the season. It didn't look all that promising up until the final few weeks and the playoffs. Then they went all in.

This was why veterans like safety Antrel Rolle came to the Giants. They thought this team, this organization knew how to win. They expected everyone to be all in. "So when we started having big signed guys like Trell, who weren't there previously and who were upset that we weren't doing everything that we were supposed to do, and saying that in the media, that propelled the rest of us who were still there to be like, 'Oh, fuck that!" "I'm the old guy, and we're not going to be the hard-working team?' So you saw a lot of rejuvenated energy later in that season."

With this kind of approach, there was no way they were going to lose to the Dallas Cowboys in Week 17 at MetLife Stadium with the NFC East title and playoffs at stake. That put the Giants on the right track with two straight wins heading into the playoffs, where nobody was going to be able to slow them down.

25

Cruuuuuuuuuz!

It was the summer of 2011, and Victor Cruz hadn't done anything up until this point other than impress the New York Jets and Rex Ryan in a preseason game the prior year. Cruz had spent his rookie season on injured reserve after that breakout performance in the preseason. The New York Giants really placed him on IR rather than the active roster because they needed a roster spot for a second kicker when Lawrence Tynes was dealing with an injury. "I knew what was going on," Cruz said with a chuckle years later.

Cruz had a minor hamstring injury and said he would be able to return the following week. But the Giants didn't need him at the time. They placed him on injured reserve, making it like a redshirt year for Cruz. It was one of those wink-wink moves, but because Cruz had made public his intention to return, it forced the NFL to investigate the legitimacy of the transaction.

The league said it was fine. The Giants were off the hook, and Cruz's rookie year would end with three games and no catches. So it was with zero career receptions on his resume that the hometown hero, a Paterson, New Jersey, native, received the break of a lifetime during the NFL lockout that next offseason. Cruz spent the early part of 2011 at home in New Jersey. One day he looked at his phone and saw "Eli Manning" flash across the screen. "I'm like, *What is this a joke? Who's pranking me right now?*" Cruz said. "*What is this?*"

Manning was at his home in New Jersey, staying in his Hoboken penthouse rather than heading back to Louisiana or Mississippi that offseason. That was because his wife, Abby, was pregnant with their first child. It was a huge moment for the quarterback and an equally momentous break for Cruz. Manning needed someone to catch passes for him during offseason workouts. He needed to get in some throwing sessions, and because it was the lockout, none of the other receivers were in town. In addition players weren't allowed in team facilities—not even to work out on their own. "We didn't have all the normal [Organized Team Activities]," Manning said. "We didn't have the normal practices and everything that you normally have to get an up-and-coming young guy ready for the season, to get on the field and throw routes and have the coaching and go over everything."

This was all just fine with Cruz. He would've dropped anything and everything for that one-on-one time with Manning. This was a soon-to-be second-year receiver who was trying to make his mark in the league. The Super Bowl–winning MVP told Cruz to meet at his condo building. Cruz figured Manning would be taking him to some plush field or facility to throw. Instead, they met in the lobby of his building and walked out to a park.

It was 8:00 AM, and there they were in Hoboken, throwing at a dog park. "There 100 percent were people walking their dogs and looking at us. They were looking at us like, *Is this a joke?*" Cruz said. "You look in this dog park, and Eli's throwing footballs with this random Black guy over here in the corner. It was weird because no one really came by and was saying hello to him, but I think they were also kind of used to seeing him in Hoboken because he lived there for so long. So no one really bothered him. But you could definitely feel the eyes of people walking their dogs a little bit closer and just coming a little bit closer than they probably normally would. You can definitely feel that."

Cruz posted up maybe 15 yards away, then dropped to 25, and then 35 yards and was just playing catch. Incrementally, they were going over all kinds of throws from varying distances. Eventually, they ran a wide array of routes. All the while Manning went over specifics of the Giants' offense. It was invaluable work for the undrafted wide receiver out of UMass. The lockout in a way was a stroke of luck for Cruz. He got to spend all that time with Manning. It wasn't always at the dog park; they went to Hoboken High School and other local fields sometimes. Still, it helped build trust between quarterback and receiver. "He's telling me about certain things he likes to see. I'm taking a couple steps left, a couple steps right over the shoulder, all these different types of throws," Cruz said. "And he's explaining to me the offense and things he likes to see and feel when I'm running routes, when one of his receivers is running routes. And I was like, 'Okay!' I felt in that moment like this is something that is not happening by accident. This is a movie scene."

It's only fitting because Cruz's career was a made-for-TV fairytale. He went undrafted in 2010 out of the University of

Massachusetts despite thinking there was a chance he could be selected on the third and final day. As the draft was concluding, Cruz was getting some calls either for invites to minicamp or training camp. It came down to the Seattle Seahawks, Washington Redskins, or the Giants. Cruz and his agent had prepared for this scenario. They had mapped out how many receivers each team had on their roster, who was on contract years, and where he had the best chance to stick. But there really wasn't much of a choice to make. "When the Giants reached out, I was like, *Ooooh, I would love to stay home.* But I looked at the roster and I was like, *Damn, they got nine receivers.* They were deep at that time, but they were also the only ones that agreed to bring me all the way through to training camp," Cruz said. "So the others just invited me to rookie minicamp. If I did well there, they would continue to bring me along. The Giants were going to take a nice long look at me in training camp, rookie minicamp, and all of those things. And I was like, *Oh, I like that. That's what I want.* That's the type of opportunity that I was looking for."

Cruz immediately chose the Giants while on that call with his agent. He instantly received a call from New York's Northeast scout Chris Pettit, who also happened to be a UMass grad and had developed a relationship with Cruz. They became friends over the years. It didn't matter to Cruz at this point that he wasn't drafted. He had gotten a call from the Giants, the hometown team right there in his own backyard. He went and grabbed the hat he had received in the gift package at their local Pro Day earlier that spring. He put it on and walked outside. "I remember wearing the hat and walking outside, and everyone in my neighborhood was waiting for me to come outside and see what was happening," Cruz said. "I came outside with the hat on, and everybody was cheering and going crazy. I went and met up with all my friends, and we were going nuts. So that's how it happened. And then obviously I got into that training camp and minicamp and just continued to do good things."

Cruz made the Giants as an undrafted free agent as a rookie. That was a big deal. He did it in large part because of one of the greatest preseason performances of all time. It didn't come completely out of nowhere. Cruz was having a nice training camp, but he still hadn't come close to solidifying his spot on the team. Then he faced the cross-town rival Jets. The Jets and Giants play in the preseason every year at MetLife Stadium in what they used to call the Snoopy Bowl. It was called that because MetLife used to use Snoopy as its logo and in ads. The Snoopy Bowl in 2010 was the perfect convergence of events. Not only did Cruz catch three touchdown passes from former Wisconsin quarterback Jim Sorgi, but he also caught one of them one-handed with his left hand and raced down the sideline for a 64-yard score. That play alone attracted the attention of Jets head coach Rex Ryan. And it was all for the cameras to see since the Jets were the subject of HBO's *Hard Knocks* that summer. "Who is No. 3? Is that a wideout?" the Jets assistant coaches were shown asking in the booth early in the game.

"Yeah," another coach responded.

"Just making sure we didn't have an option quarterback in there," the coach said.

They had no idea who Cruz was at the start of the game. They would know by the time the game was finished. First, there was the one-handed catch for a touchdown. "That's a hell of a play by that kid," Ryan said in a scene that played out on *Hard Knocks* several days later. "I got an idea. Let's stay on top of 3, No. 3," he said after the second score.

When it was all said and done, Ryan was shown meeting Giants coach Tom Coughlin at midfield after the game in awe of what he had just witnessed from this previously unknown wide receiver. "Aye, good game, Coach," Ryan said. "I don't know who the fuck No. 3 is but...holy shit!

"Good player, huh?" Coughlin said with a smile about the rookie Cruz.

"I'm telling ya!" Ryan said.

Cruz and the Giants rookies went back to the University at Albany, where they held training camp that year. The veterans got to stay home for a day. So the rookies were passing the time in Albany by watching *Hard Knocks*. It was Cruz, defensive tackle Nate Collins, and a few other guys piled into a dorm room. At this point they had no idea what they were going to show—if anything at all—pertaining to the Giants since this was a show focused on the Jets. They had the microscope on them. Then, all of a sudden, it shifted to No. 3 in the white Giants jersey. "There is just a whole segment on this moment of my coming-out party, so to speak. So I was like, *Oh shit, this is really happening,*" Cruz said. "And then the crazy story is if you look as they pan to the booth and they ask if I was a quarterback or something, there's a Black guy that's next to the defensive coordinator [Mike Pettine]. He was my college receiving coach, Brian Smith. And so he knew who I was. They were like, 'Who's No. 3? Is that a quarterback?' He's like, 'No, that's Victor Cruz.' I always thought that was interesting that no one really knew that, but he was my receiver coach. And I was like, *Wow, this is pretty insane.*"

Smith was the wide receivers coach at UMass from 2005 to 2006 when Cruz was at the school but struggled to get on the field as he dealt with academic issues. After that scene ran on *Hard Knocks,* Cruz's phone immediately started blowing up. The reaction was incredible. He was now on the map—and effectively on the Giants roster even if that was just the first of four preseason games that season.

It still wasn't until more than a year later when Cruz really started to take off. It almost looked as if it might not happen, even though he was given a chance to be their starting slot receiver in 2011. On the opening drive of that season against the Washington Redskins, a wide-open Cruz dropped an easy third-down pass from Manning. He saw one more ball the rest of the afternoon and finished with no catches. *Uh-oh*, he thought. He had wasted his opportunity.

The Giants actually signed veteran slot wide receiver Brandon Stokley, who previously played with Eli's brother Peyton, the following week. That clearly wasn't a good sign for Cruz. But Stokely tore his quad early in a Week Three game against the Philadelphia Eagles. That meant Cruz would get thrown into the action, and this time he wouldn't miss. The second-year receiver would not be denied. He caught three passes for 110 yards and two touchdowns that afternoon while earning the full trust of Manning. On one of the plays, he caught a short pass late in the first quarter, made three defenders miss—including two that ran into each other—and raced down the sideline for a 74-yard score for the first touchdown of his career.

That is when he took it all to another level by busting out the salsa dance as his touchdown celebration. It was at the behest of quarterbacks coach Mike Sullivan, who was pushing that week for Cruz to represent his culture. The salsa was an ode to Cruz's Puerto Rican heritage. It also made him an instant superstar. "It wasn't until I'm running. Literally, I'm eluding dudes and I'm up the sideline. I'm like, *Holy shit, I'm about to score a touchdown here. What am I going to do?* I got to dance. The only thing to do is dance," Cruz said. "And I put the ball down and I started dancing, and it just took off. And I think it was around maybe a few games later when I kept scoring and I kept doing it and I was like, *Holy smokes, this is really taking off.* When I would pull up and little kids would be dancing when they see me, or old white dudes would be dancing when they see me, it was like, *Okay, this is taking on a life of its own a little bit here.*"

Cruz's career didn't just get off and running at that point. It was shot to the moon. He led the Giants with 82 receptions, 1,536 yards, and nine touchdowns that season. His 99-yarder against the Jets on Christmas Eve day is one of the most memorable regular-season plays in franchise history. It's tied for the longest touchdown catch in NFL history. Cruz had 10 catches for 142 yards in the NFC Championship Game win against the San Francisco 49ers, getting revenge on Pro Bowl cornerback Carlos Rogers for mocking his salsa in the previous meeting during the regular season. Cruz even added a touchdown in the Super Bowl and earned a ring—all in his first full season playing.

He was an instant sensation, the biggest star on that team not named Manning by the end of the year. Nobody, not even Manning after their offseason workouts, saw that kind of success coming. "I had no idea," the two-time Super Bowl MVP quarterback said. "It was a big gamble for us just to say, 'Hey, this guy's going to be our slot receiver.' He's unproven, hadn't done much, had that kind of big preseason game the year before, but that's it."

26

Merry Christmas, Jets!

The New York Giants and Jets play in the same town. They share the same stadium. First it was Giants Stadium (a slap in the face that the Jets had to play in a place donning their crosstown rivals' name) and then MetLife Stadium. One franchise is among the most successful franchises in history with four Super Bowl wins, and the other has been a fledgling organization for much of the modern era. The Jets won their only Super Bowl in 1968 with playboy Joe Namath at quarterback. They haven't gone back since. Their success over the next five decades has been modest at best. The Jets had reached just four AFC Championship Games and won two AFC East titles entering the 2011 season.

Perhaps their biggest accomplishment during that 43-year stretch was making four AFC Championship Games, including in the 2009 and 2010 seasons. They were knocking on the door with the boisterous Rex Ryan as the coach and a daunting defense that was challenging to be the league's best each year. They thought for sure this was their year in 2011. The Giants may have won the Super Bowl four years earlier, but it was the Jets who were making the most noise entering 2011 with their trash-talking bluster—just the way Ryan wanted it. "I have news for you," Ryan wrote in his book, *Play Like You Mean It,* entering that season. "We are the better team. We're the big brother. People might say they are the big, bad Giants, but we are not the same old Jets."

The Jets' success at the time still could only take them so far when it came to the back pages of the New York tabloids and the hearts of the local fans. The Giants were the New York area's primary team—always were, still are to this day. Ryan and the Jets were fighting the good fight, but they always have been the little brother. It is what it is. They are New York's second team, especially given the history and success of the Giants. But Ryan was doing everything possible to change that perception—yelling, taunting, going chest to chest, mouth to mouth with anyone that stood in his way, including the big, bad Bill Belichick and the New England Patriots. Ryan had some success, and at the time, it looked like he was actually making progress. The reality is that Ryan took the Jets into Foxboro and beat Belichick and the Patriots in the playoffs the previous year. He kicked them in the teeth, outplayed them physically, and outcoached Belichick and the Patriots mentally.

The argument could be made entering 2011 that Ryan and the Jets were making serious inroads. That was the famous "Can't Wait" game where linebacker Bart Scott barked the now famous phrase in an interview with ESPN's Sal Paolantonio. "For all you non-believers, disrespect us, talk crap about the defense like we're not the third-best defense in the league," Scott said. "All we hear about is [the Patriots] defense. They can't stop a nosebleed, 25th in the league, and we're the ones who get disrespected."

"Congratulations. See you in Pittsburgh," Paolantonio responded.

"Can't wait!" barked Scott with rare intensity, authority, and also a glimmer of bemusement.

This was the chatty, trash-talking team that would face the Giants in Week 16 the following year with the playoffs on the line for both teams. Right on brand, they would talk their way into the game. Jets wide receiver Santonio Holmes trashed the Giants secondary, saying (among other things) that they have "poor-tackling guys" and "there are plays to be made over their head." All-Pro cornerback Darrelle Revis responded to some comments from Victor Cruz by saying he didn't even know who the young receiver was. And then there was Ryan with his usual bravado, poking coach Tom Coughlin and the Giants by mentioning they hadn't made the postseason each of the two previous years and plastering a picture of Eli Manning getting crushed by Jets outside linebacker Calvin Pace during a preseason game on the front of their defensive playbook that week. It set the stage for big brother to assert his dominance and for the Jets to experience another letdown while the team playing in the same backyard got to celebrate. "Talk is cheap. Play the game," Coughlin told his team, a line he patented over the years.

It was Christmas Eve, Giants at Jets, at the new MetLife Stadium with everything at stake. Both teams desperately needed a win. Only a few days earlier at a chapel meeting, Giants players were presented with the "all-in" moniker. The Jets were 8–6 entering the contest and had the advantage of being the home team. The Giants were 7–7, hanging on to their playoff dreams by a thread. They had to beat the Washington Redskins the previous week to keep those dreams alive heading into this massive contest against their crosstown rival. "We *had* to win," Coughlin said. "We *had* to beat the Jets."

If not, he would predictably hear the calls for his job. The Giants missing the playoffs for a third straight season would not be well received. This was an organization with high standards. Heck, it was only four years earlier that Coughlin had to head into that meeting with John Mara and Jon Tisch and state his case to keep his job...after two playoff appearances!

This was going to be the biggest, most important game between the two "New York" teams in their shared stadium. The Jets had the ever-so-slight advantage of being the home team. It was, presumably, their fans in the stadium. The Giants were visitors in their own building. Leave it to Ryan to try to make them feel that way. Ryan pulled out all the stops, including ordering for the mural of the Giants' Super Bowl trophies outside their own locker room to be covered by a black curtain. Two metal poles stretched 50 feet or so with the curtain to cover the painted cinderblocks. Giants players led by offensive lineman David Diehl, running back Brandon Jacobs, and defensive end Justin Tuck pulled down the curtains when they returned from early warmups. While they were in the locker room, the curtains found a way back up. It was met with even more rage from Diehl, Jacobs, Tuck, and other Giants on their way back to the field before the game. It was as if the curtains were the ones hurling those insults throughout the week.

Like the Jets, they stood no chance. This was simply the final straw to a week where Ryan and the Jets' trash talk seemingly pushed every Big Blue button. They nudged them ever so forcefully to the brink of their composure. "So [Ryan's] saying all of this disrespectful stuff, and then you covered up our Super

Bowls? You covered up our trophies. Why did you cover up our trophies?" Jacobs said. "Your visitors are coming out of that side. That's your visiting team coming out that side. Why would you do that? You have nothing to do with that whole tunnel. You are all the way on the other side of the stadium. Why would you do that? We ripped that shit down. Somebody came, covered it up again, then we ripped it down again when it went up. We took it all the way down before we went to the field."

It wouldn't stop there. Jacobs went over before the game to talk with former teammate Plaxico Burress. The wide receiver, who once was a Super Bowl hero for the Giants, was playing for the Jets at the time. Ryan walked over and started chirping at Jacobs. "You just watch!" he said. "We're going to win the Super Bowl."

"Well, go win the Super Bowl," Jacobs fired back.

That is when the talk escalated. Ryan kept reiterating the Jets were going to win the Super Bowl. Jacobs wanted none of it. He mocked the sentiment. That is when they went face to face.

"He bumped into me and shit with his belly and said, 'I'll fucking kick your ass.' I said, 'I'm the wrong one of these Giants to mess with,'" Jacobs said. "'All these other guys are going to give you a pass. I'm going to punch you in your shit. I'm going to lay you out.'"

At that point Burress tried to play peacemaker between his current coach and friend. "Don't do that, B," Burress said. "Come on, walk off."

As they continued to spit fire at each other, Jacobs, one of the biggest trash talkers on the Giants, started calling Ryan "fat boy." "Hey, fat boy, what you gonna do fat boy?" he said.

It was an insult that would resurface later between the two. In the meantime there was an actual game to be played. The contest will forever be remembered for Cruz's 99-yard touchdown reception late in the second quarter. Throwing out of his own end zone, Eli Manning hit Cruz on the right side. He split a pair of Jets defenders after making the catch and raced down the right sideline. Cruz outran Jets safety Eric Smith to the end zone for the record-breaking score. It gave the Giants a 10–7 lead at halftime and altered both teams' playoff fate. "They know my name now, right?" Cruz said after the touchdown.

The Giants never looked back. Ahmad Bradshaw ran for a pair of touchdowns in the second half. Defensive lineman Chris Canty, who once thought he was going for a free-agent visit with the Jets before finding out it was surprisingly the Giants, had a safety. The Giants won 29–14 as the road team made it known afterward they didn't like the talk. Jacobs called Ryan a "disrespectful bitch" in his postgame interview on the field with Paolantonio. Cruz made sure Revis knew who he was. All this cemented that it wasn't just another win on the road to another Super Bowl. This was a forever win in a rivalry game. "Does that make it that much sweeter when you are able to beat the Jets, that other team, and because of the whole Rex thing that was going on? I think it did," Mara said. "He was trying to really pump them up to be like, 'Oh, we're not the little brothers of the city. We're the team. This is our city.'"

It only reiterated that New York was the Giants' city. They were the ones with all the Lombardi Trophies and the fan base with the long wait list even if they hadn't experienced as much success in the previous two seasons as the Jets did. Their resume was longer and had way more experience. This is what Canty thought when he joined Giants as a free agent from the Dallas Cowboys prior to the 2009 season. "You know what? It's funny, them blocking out the championships. I guess the murals on the wall in the stadium didn't bother me as much. What bothered me was the two years that I was here prior to us going on the

Super Bowl run, just all the talk about the New York Jets," Canty said, "because they made the conference championship game in '09 and '10, and everybody was talking about the Jets on the doorstep of winning the championship. The Jets are closer to winning a Super Bowl! And I'm just sitting there like, *The Jets haven't won a Super Bowl in 40 years. What the hell are they talking about? Why we keep talking about that? The Giants literally just won it in 2007. What are we talking about?* And so it got to the point where it was just obnoxious and overbearing because it was so much talk and so much bluster."

It's conceivable that Canty could have been on the other side of the matchup. The 6'7" defensive lineman was a Bronx native and lived there until he was a teenager. The prospects of coming home when he was a free agent in 2009 were enticing. The Giants, however, weren't on the radar "at all." They already had a strong defensive line, and it didn't appear they were going to shop in Canty's price range. The division-rival Washington Redskins were interested. They were talking on the opening night of free agency, and owner Daniel Snyder's plane was supposed to scoop up Canty and his father in Charlotte, North Carolina, the following day. The vibes were so high that Canty remembers looking at some Washington, D.C., real estate. But by the time they woke up the next day, Snyder and the Redskins had committed $100 million to defensive lineman Albert Haynesworth.

That is when Canty's agent, Brad Blank, called and told him New York was interested and wanted him to come up that afternoon. Okay, perfect. Canty just assumed it was the New York Jets. They played an odd-front, the kind of 3-4 defense where he had spent his entire career, and had a need to bolster their defensive line. "It wasn't until I got off the plane, and my agent calls and says, 'The guy from the Giants should be there,'"

Canty said. "I'm just like, 'The Giants?' I thought I was coming to see the Jets."

So former Giants linebacker Jessie Armstead, who was working in the front office, picked up Canty and they headed to the Chart House in Weehawken where they chopped it up. Armstead then took him on a tour of the new practice facility that was being built at the time. He was the perfect recruiter because he talked about his experiences with the team and city. Armstead played nine seasons with the Giants and was part of the 2000 Super Bowl team. He also spent two seasons in Washington, so he knew the difference. They talked about how the Giants had key pieces and were retooling for another run. A key component was a Super Bowl–winning quarterback in Manning. That was important to Canty. He wanted to taste that type of winning since he was on the other side of that divisional round playoff game in 2008 with the Cowboys. So he signed with the Giants—not the Cowboys or the Jets—inking a six-year, $42 million deal in 2009.

And two years later—on Christmas Eve in 2011—order had finally been restored in New York.

27
Eli Equals Elite

The tone of the entire 2011 New York Giants season was set on an overcast afternoon in August. That is when quarterback Eli Manning sat down for *The Michael Kay Show* on what was then ESPN New York 1050 and emerged from his general monotone shell. "Is Eli Manning an elite quarterback? Are you a top five, top 10 quarterback?" Kay asked during an interview at the team's facility during training camp.

"Yeah, I think I am," Manning said confidently.

"Are you in the Tom Brady class?" was the follow-up question from Kay.

"Yeah, I consider myself in that class," Manning said. "Tom Brady is a great quarterback, he's a great player, and what you've seen with him is he's gotten better every year. He started off winning championships, and I think he's a better quarterback now than what he was—in all honesty—when he was winning those championships. I think now he's grown up and gotten better every year, and that's what I'm trying to do. I kind of hope these next seven years of my quarterback days are my best."

This was the caterpillar shedding its skin for the entire world to see. It was out of character for the Giants starting quarterback, who was coming off a disappointing season of throwing a league-leading 25 interceptions. To talk so bluntly and confidently about himself publicly was not something you saw from Manning often. It's probably why these comments—and the "Is Eli Elite?" debate—drew so much attention. Manning was generally the master of deflection and self-deprecation. He knew how to turn just about everything into an answer on how it's more about the team than himself. After a lifetime of training, it was his reflex. If that wasn't an option, he would talk in generalities. Nothing splashy, trying to avoid headlines. That was almost always the approach. But this question by Kay was so direct it elicited an answer that sparked permanent debate. Manning spontaneously decided to address it head on. In a way he was feeling himself: a quarterback in his prime (30 years old at the time) who was confident a big year was on the horizon.

It set up a storyline that would follow the team throughout the season right up until the point that Manning ended it with his performance on the field. Perhaps it was the organic nature of it all that made it so intriguing. This was the kind of conversation that was going on in bars, but rarely do the players themselves chime in with such an emphatic answer of their own. "It wasn't meant to be a gotcha question," Kay said. "I thought he'd say something like, 'Well, that's certainly what I'm aspiring to.' But he said, 'Yes, I am' and explained himself. I had no idea that it would take off like that. I mean, there was a whole segment on that during the Super Bowl pregame show. So it became a running thing, and certainly he wins the Super Bowl. He was elite in the Super Bowl for sure."

Manning backed up his talk in the biggest way possible. Even the staunchest doubters had to eat crow. Manning had his best season to date that year in 2011 after his comments. It can be argued even to this day (rather easily) that was the best season of his career. Manning would throw for a career-best 4,993 yards that season. He tossed 29 touchdown passes and cut the interceptions to 16. His 8.4 yards per attempt was the highest of his career, and the five fourth-quarter comebacks and six game-winning drives easily were new career bests. They were the type of numbers that would make just about any quarterback envious. His NFC Championship Game performance that season is also considered by many to be the greatest game he played in a 16-year career. He then capped it with a second Super Bowl triumph and second Super Bowl MVP.

That is one way to settle any debate about whether he was truly elite. In the playoffs there was not even the slightest rebuttal. It led to the popular saying that, "You can't spell ELIte without Eli." Manning meanwhile knew what his preseason declaration meant. There would be pressure on him to live up to his own hype. "You have to back up your words," Manning would say years later.

The Manning story really had its twists and turns. He was going to be the No. 1 overall pick in 2004 but made it known that he didn't want to play for the San Diego Chargers. He was drafted by the Chargers and eventually traded to the Giants, who had selected Philip Rivers with the fourth pick. It created one of the most awkward moments in draft history as an unhappy Manning took the stage and snapped pictures with the Chargers jersey. Eventually a trade would be executed that sent Manning to New York while Rivers and a first-, third-, and fifth-round pick went to San Diego.

The Giants were set on either Manning or Miami of Ohio's Ben Roethlisberger, who was selected 11th by the Pittsburgh Steelers and had a Hall of Fame career of his own. But general manager Ernie Accorsi was obsessed with Manning. He was intent on making that deal happen even if it took hard negotiating. "He was definitely enamored with him," owner John Mara said.

The differentiator between Manning and Roethlisberger was that the former played collegiately in the SEC. Manning went to Ole Miss while Roethlisberger was playing at Miami (Ohio). Manning was doing it against the top competition in college football without a great supporting cast. That seemed to resonate with Accorsi. Roethlisberger was a great college player and prospect the Giants liked, but he played in the Mid-American Conference, affectionately known as the MAC. It wasn't the big, bad SEC. The talent he faced every week wasn't the same.

Here's Accorsi's famed scouting report on Manning:

> "Wears left knee brace...During pregame warmup, didn't look like he had a rocket arm... As game progressed, I saw excellent arm strength under pressure and the ability to get velocity on the ball on most throws. Good deep ball range. Good touch. Good vision and poise.
>
> "Sees the field...In shotgun on most plays and his only running option is a draw...his offensive line is poor. Redshirt freshman left tackle. Eli doesn't trust his protection. Can't. No way he can take any form of a deep drop and look downfield. With no running game (10 yards rushing the first half) and no real top receivers, he's stuck with the three-step drops and waiting til the last second to see if a receiver can get free. No tight end either. No flaring back. So he's taking some big hits. Taking them well. Carried an overmatched team entirely on his shoulders. I imagine,

except for Vanderbilt, his team is overmatched in every SEC game...He's big, never gets rattled. Rallied his team from a 14–3 halftime deficit basically all by himself. Led them on two successive third quarter drives to go ahead, 17–16. The first touchdown, a 40-yard streak down the left sideline, he dropped the ball over the receiver's right shoulder. Called the next touchdown pass himself, checking off to a 12-yard slant...Makes a lot of decisions on play calls at the line of scrimmage, but they ask too much of him. They don't just let him play. This is a guy you should just let play...When he's inaccurate, he's usually high, but rarely off target to either side...Plays smart and with complete confidence. Doesn't scold his teammates, but lets them know when they line up wrong or run the wrong pattern... Threw three interceptions. Two were his fault. Trying to force something both times. He could have run on one of them, a fourth down play. He has a lot to learn.

"Summary: I think he's the complete package. He's not going to be a fast runner, but a little like Joe Montana, he has enough athletic ability to get out of trouble. Remember how Archie ran? In that department, Eli doesn't have the best genes, although I never timed mom Olivia in the 40. But he has a feel for the pocket. Feels the rush.

"Throws the ball, takes the hit, gets right back up...Has courage and poise. In my opinion, most of all, he has that quality you can't define. Call it magic...Peyton had much better talent around him at Tennessee. But I honestly give this guy a chance to be better than his brother. Eli doesn't get much help from the coaching staff. If he comes out early, we should move up to take him. These guys are rare, you know."

The way Accorsi viewed it, if you didn't have a quarterback who you can envision holding up the Lombardi Trophy, you didn't have a quarterback at all. Manning and Roethlisberger looked like those guys. In retrospect he was right. Both won a pair of titles. Rivers finished with none and didn't make a Super Bowl, even though he had a Hall of Fame career.

When the Giants got on the clock in that quarterback-heavy draft, it still looked like landing Manning might not happen. The sticking point was Chargers general manager A.J. Smith's insistence in plying edge rusher Osi Umenyiora from the Giants' vice grip. But Accorsi was not going to include the pass rusher who was the perfect complement to Michael Strahan. It was a smart line to draw because Umenyiora went on to become an integral Pro Bowl piece on two Super Bowl teams. Accorsi and the Giants still hoped the deal could get done even if it was at the last minute. The first round of the draft back in these days was on a Saturday. They were supposed to hear from Smith and the Chargers on Friday. Crickets.

New York heard through legendary *Sports Illustrated* reporter Peter King that the way the Chargers were going to play this was that they would call halfway through their time on the clock with the fourth pick. That proved accurate. Smith called midway through the 15-minute window. He made one last Hail Mary effort for Umenyiora to no avail. "A.J. calls, and he starts playing games," Accorsi said. "'So you want Eli?' I said, 'Get to the point!' He said, 'Well, you can have him if you give me Osi.' I said, 'I can speak Italian. I don't know what language you want me to use. You're not getting Osi. I'm not giving up a pass rusher.' So he said, 'What about next year's No. 1?' Well, we had already met on what we said we would give up. It wasn't like I had a meeting at that point. We had already decided we would give up next year's No. 1 and whatever the other pick

I gave up in next year's draft. I said, 'Yes, I will do that.' Well, now we just had to get it in."

At this point there was a time crunch. There were only a few minutes left on the clock for the Giants. If they didn't get the pick in on time, it would roll right into the Washington Redskins who were scheduled to select fifth. So Accorsi and Smith got on the phone together with the league and quickly verbally confirmed the deal. They had a trade. Manning had his wish. The San Diego fans were left jaded even if they received Rivers and draft picks that would eventually turn into kicker Nate Kaeding, outside linebacker Shawne Merriman, and offensive lineman Roman Oben. It was a good haul, but it also didn't ultimately equate to any Super Bowls.

Chargers fans never forgot. They booed Manning relentlessly every time he touched the ball in their 2005 matchup in San Diego. When he returned eight years later, Manning was greeted with a huge cutout of his face but decked out with accessories that made him look like an elderly woman—massive bedazzled earrings, bright red lipstick, and makeup, including enough red blush to make him look like a grandma with blue eye shadow that accentuated his bushy eyebrows.

The Giants got the next Manning quarterback. By this time Peyton Manning was a two-time NFL MVP with the Indianapolis Colts. Their dad, Archie Manning, was a legendary figure for the New Orleans Saints, having made a pair of Pro Bowls for the team in 1978 and '79. Eli Manning was going to be the missing piece at quarterback the Giants had been searching for since Phil Simms was famously cut in 1994 by general manager George Young and coach Dan Reeves. It prompted owner Wellington Mara to cry when discussing the difficult decision.

Manning didn't cry early in his time in New York, though at times it looked like he might. It definitely wasn't always smooth.

Even his first ever practice with the team was rocky. "Eli's first workout with the Giants is a bust" was the headline...from the generally straightlaced Associated Press!

"Manning Fumbles His Debut" was the dispatch from the *New York Post.*

The practice with at least 50 media members watching his every move famously concluded with a pass that clanked off a blue tackling dummy. The Giants downplayed it at the time, but it undoubtedly wasn't the greatest first impression. His new teammates noticed. It caught their attention, too. "Eli, he's not a very impressive guy first appearances...He comes in, and you're kind of like, *This kid looks a little goofy. What's going on?*" center Shaun O'Hara said. "He looks a little gangly. So I think we were all kind of just wondering, *What are we getting out of this kid? Is he the spoiled brat of Archie and the younger brother of Peyton?* I think we all found out really quick he is the anti-Peyton. He is the complete opposite of Peyton personality-wise and just the way that he's wired."

It was behind the scenes where Manning originally won over his teammates. He handled all the media attention and criticism like a professional. He never threw a teammate under the bus and always put the blame on his own shoulders. One of the more amazing things about Manning was that he would voluntarily make himself available to the media every Monday after losses in order to shield his teammates and take full responsibility for the team's failures. After a Giants win, he would let his teammates do the talking. He let them soak in the glory and praise. That is the kind of man and teammate he was for the Giants.

These types of little things were noticed. They helped earn the respect of his teammates even if his play on the field early in his career was uneven. There were a lot of interceptions (including leading the league in interceptions twice in his first six seasons as a starter) and head-scratching mistakes. But he knew the game. "I will never forget: one of the things I always did when I was in Cleveland was we would always watch film after practice on Wednesdays and Thursdays with the quarterbacks to go over the third-down looks, blitz fronts, make sure we were all on the same page with protections in the run game, just making sure we had the safety rotations figured out and how we're going to handle that at the line," O'Hara said. "Kurt [Warner] never stayed for it. So the first week Kurt was like, 'I'll watch film at home.' And so the first week it was Jesse Palmer and Eli. So I'm in the room, and I've got the remote in my hand, and I'm like, 'All right, we're going to start watching some of the film.' And Eli comes in and he is like, 'Give me the remote!' And I never got it back. I was like, 'Oh, okay, all right, young buck.' And then he started fast-forwarding through all the runs, which drove me nuts. He's like, 'No, don't, the run game's not important.' So he would go right to the coverages, and then he would write it down. He'd write down our coverages to all the third downs, and Tim Hasselbeck would sit in there, and so they would kind of go back and forth with coverages. I went from thinking I was going to be babysitting him and having to teach him about all this stuff, and I ended up learning more from him than I think he ever learned from me."

It was still a bumpy road to that first Super Bowl. Manning started his rookie season behind Warner. When he finally got in, there were growing pains. He didn't even make it through a loss to the Baltimore Ravens, when he completed just 4-of-18 passes for 27 yards with three turnovers and was sent to the bench in the second half. But Manning provided a glimmer of hope with a big performance in the season-closing win against the Dallas Cowboys when he had three touchdown passes and led a game-winning drive in the final minutes of a 28–24 victory. That was the momentum they needed for the future.

There was still a bevy of ups and downs before the 2007 Super Bowl. There were times when fans weren't sure Manning was the answer. He threw three pick-sixes in the same game against the Minnesota Vikings and was an easy public target. One *Newsday* headline in 2007 read: "Unfortunately, Eli's as Good as He's Going to Get." Another read: "Eli's O.K.—That's the Giants' Problem"

The Super Bowl win later that season surely would have answered those questions, right? Not quite. Manning still had a bumpy road to the 2011 season. Even as he improved, there always seemed to be that lingering belief that he had gotten lucky, hit a hot streak at the right time during the 2007 playoffs, and rode it right to the bank with the family name on the account.

So Manning had to do it all again to win over the final doubters.

28

The Greatest Game Eli Ever Played

Eli Manning's career spanned 16 seasons. He played in 248 career games, including the playoffs. There were two Super Bowl victories squeezed in there alongside 37 game-winning drives and 27 fourth-quarter comebacks. A nice resume, for sure. Clearly mixed in there were some great performances and moments. There were some great games, too, but none is quite comparable to the 2011 NFC Championship Game in Candlestick Park. The way Manning stood in there against a ferocious San Francisco 49ers defense and fired darts while in a labyrinth of pressure was unlike any other day in his legendary career.

It all happened on a typical San Francisco winter day. It was crisp and wet. There was a steady drizzle that made the field wet and muddy. Manning would be more than familiar with that soggy turf by the end of the afternoon, and the winner would make its way to Indianapolis for a matchup with the New England Patriots in Super Bowl XLVI. That 49ers defense was nasty. It was talented. It allowed just 14.3 points per game that season behind a relentless pass rush that consisted of Aldon Smith, Justin Smith, Ahmad Brooks, and Ray McDonald. Behind them was the fierce linebacking duo of NaVorro Bowman and Patrick Willis. They comprised the league's best front seven at the time. Incredibly, this is what the Giants wanted. They wanted no part of the New Orleans Saints that year. They were whipped by the Saints down in the Superdome. Drew Brees and Co. hung 49 points on them in a blowout. The Giants were hoping to get another matchup with San Francisco, where they had played (and lost) earlier that season.

The Giants may have wanted the 49ers, but they still had their hands full. Their offensive line wasn't what it once was. Center Shaun O'Hara and guard Rich Seubert were cut before the start of the season. It would be the end of their careers. Right guard Chris Snee and left tackle David Diehl only had a few years left. Right tackle Kareem McKenzie was in what would ultimately be his last professional season. This would actually unknowingly be the second-to-last game of his career. This version of the Giants offensive line had David Baas at center and utilityman Kevin Boothe at left guard. They had trouble running the ball all throughout that season. In fact, the Giants were dead last in the regular season with the 32nd-ranked rushing attack even if it did come to life in the postseason.

The running game struggles would come into play on this January 22, 2012, day in the championship game against the 49ers. Even in the rain, the Giants were going to lean heavily on the toughness and right arm of Manning to get them to the Super Bowl. They dropped back to pass a franchise playoff record 64 times on that brisk and wet afternoon. New York ran the ball 13 times for just 35 yards in the first half. That worked out to 2.7 yards per carry. Not good enough. Their longest run was a seven-yard gain by Ahmad Bradshaw. The only way they were going to move the ball consistently was by putting the onus on Manning, which they did with little regard for his safety.

There was a running joke that the Giants had to beg offensive coordinator Kevin Gilbride to run the ball. According to the offensive line, he never did it. Gilbride loved to sling it around the yard if he could. He came from a run-and-shoot background with the Houston Oilers in the early '90s, and their philosophy was spread it out and throw—early, often, late, anytime they could. Although the Giants were hardly that, there always seemed to be a push and pull from New York's physical offensive line to run the ball. Offensive line coach Pat Flaherty was the middleman. He did the bidding for his group with Gilbride for good reason. The group's ability to run block was their calling card when the line was at its peak during the Coughlin era. But this was not that time. This was clearly not the situation. Not against this 49ers defensive front. The Giants weren't getting push at the point of attack, and Willis and Bowman were too physical and fast to attack the edges. "We got to about the third quarter of that game, and [Flaherty] came over to us and he's like, 'Hey, what do you guys want? What type of plays do you want to run?' And I think at that point we were like, 'Whatever Gilbride wants to call,'" Boothe said. "We'll try to make whatever he calls work because that was a long game. I don't know. We don't have answers. So we're just going to give it our best and we'll see what happens."

They tried to pass, pass, pass. And then dropped back to pass some more. It gave the Giants their best chance to win even if Manning would take a beating. The final stat sheet showed that he absorbed 12 quarterback hits, a crazy large number. He was hit three times by San Francisco defenders when they met earlier that season in a 27–20 win by the 49ers at Candlestick Park. This was four times that on the big stage, as Manning took an unbelievable beating for the world to witness. This game would be vastly different than that first matchup. There were more than a few plays in the NFC Championship Game where Manning had to pick himself off the turf with his helmet pushed up on his forehead, his chinstrap straddling his nose, and his left shoulder pad dangling from the white Giants jersey with the No. 10 on the shoulder. "I remember just every time walking back to the huddle or walking back from a sack, and he's like chinstrap was on his eye, and dirt is on his helmet, man," wide receiver Victor Cruz said. "And he just gets up like an old man. We wipe him off and fix his chinstrap, and he never blamed anyone."

Manning would shake it off, get back to the huddle, and call the next play without ever offering a negative word for his offensive line or mention of the beating that he endured. "It is kind of one of those old-school NFL tough games," Manning said. "What are you going to do? You're fighting to go to a Super Bowl. There is no, *Hey, I'm giving up or I'm getting hit, I'm going to get the ball out a little early now and stop taking hits.* I said, 'No, you just got to keep hanging in there and getting up, and you know what the goal is.' It's right there in front of you. You're not going to give up or you're not going to lay down at any point when you're so close to accomplishing it and getting to your goal. But, yeah, they were unbelievable on defense, just Patrick Willis and Bowman and both Smiths."

Manning was sacked six times in the contest. Each time he was scraped off the grass like a forklift grabbing scrap iron. On one play late in the fourth quarter on the Giants' final drive of regulation, Manning rolled out left to create time. He drifted toward the sideline, waiting for a receiver to come uncovered. Eventually, Manning threw down the left sideline to Bradshaw for a 30-yard gain with 1:14 remaining. But he was buried into the ground by three Niners defenders. On the very next play, Aldon Smith leveled Manning just as he finished his dropback. Manning somehow got the ball out to Bradshaw for a short gain and quickly called timeout despite being all out of sorts. "Facemask's all messed, chin strap is all up my nose, big clump of grass in my helmet, my shoulder pads half out," he said. "The linemen were always there. They're picking me up. They're dusting me off. I never got on them or said anything. I knew they were a good defense. I knew they were trying to block these guys. And so [I was] just waiting for the opportunity; [I] knew going into that game our defense was playing outstanding. They were playing great. I couldn't give them anything. I couldn't let the pressure make me make a bad decision where all of a sudden you force something, or you throw it early or you kind of hope. You just got to say, 'Hey, I got to keep taking sacks if I have to. I can't force it, and eventually we're going to get the opportunity.'"

Manning didn't have a turnover in the contest. He fumbled once after a first-quarter sack, but that was recovered by McKenzie. The same quarterback who led the NFL in interceptions with 25 the previous season didn't throw one that day despite being under tremendous duress in the crummy San Francisco weather. That was the beauty of Manning, what made him ELIte. When it mattered most, he always seemed to somehow elevate his game. Manning threw nine touchdown passes and just one interception during the playoff run that season. His final stat line in San Francisco: 32-of-58 passing for 316 yards with two touchdowns and no interceptions. An absolute masterpiece. "That was just a physical game, man. Eli got up off the ground at the end of every play and delivered the ball," running back Brandon Jacobs said. "He was the man out there that game."

Manning showed his toughness. It was one of the things that made Ernie Accorsi so certain this was the right guy when he scouted him at Ole Miss. It made it almost comical that a lack of toughness was one of the critiques earlier in his career. Ditto the concept that Manning could be rattled and wilt under pressure in big spots when in fact it turned out to be the opposite. During the NFC Championship Game in San Francisco, his toughness could never come into question. After all the hits and times he needed to landscape the mud clumps out of his helmet, Manning didn't feel a thing when he was celebrating a second trip to the Super Bowl. "Yeah, such a good high," he said. "[I] got two weeks to get healthy and prepare and get the soreness off so you don't care at that moment. But I woke up Monday morning a little more sore than other days."

Everyone out there knew what they had witnessed. It wasn't something they needed the film to confirm. He had taken a beating and kept getting up. He was New York's Rocky Balboa. Flaherty took some heat for all the hits. He was hearing it from his wife on the phone after the game. It was there for the world to see on the television broadcast just how big a beating Manning had taken. "She gets on the phone and is like, 'I can't believe the way you got Eli beat up!' But finally Eli's standing right there," he said. "I said, 'Eli, can you come talk to Mrs. Flats here and tell her you're all right?' But he was digging dirt out his facemask. They were good. They were good. Holy, they were good."

Like usual, Manning didn't do it all on his own that day. Football is a team game. The full 46-man active roster contributes. Everyone except backup quarterback David Carr played at least one snap that afternoon. And the two biggest plays down the stretch might have come via special teams, and a difference-maker was rookie Jacquian Williams, a sixth-round draft pick. The South Florida product flew down the field and forced a fumble in overtime from San Francisco returner Kyle Williams. Jacquian Williams was flying past the fill-in punt returner, who was a replacement for the injured Ted Ginn Jr. Jacquian's right hand poked the ball free. It was Kyle Williams' second miscue of the contest. He had a previous punt clank off his knee that was recovered by Giants receiver Devin Thomas.

Jacquian Williams was the epitome of what it meant to be a Giant that season. "Jacquian, specifically his foot, was fucked up. I do remember him damn near limping into that year maybe. But that game and being proud of him as a man, as a human being, and knowing what he had been through and all the drama surrounding his injury and all those things, that type of unselfishness and whatever culminated by making a play. That is part of the reason you play the game, right?" linebacker Mathias Kiwanuka said. "It's a meritocracy. If you put in the work, you're going to get better and something good is going to happen."

Jacquian Williams became a hero in the NFC Championship Game. And Thomas, who was cut the previous year by the Washington Redskins, was as well. He recovered two fumbled punts. The second fumbled punt immediately put the Giants in scoring territory on their third possession of overtime. After two runs by Bradshaw, they were inside the 49ers' 20-yard line, which Tom Coughlin called "the green zone." The Giants still needed one more little break to book their Super Bowl trip.

Coughlin decided to kick the short game-winning field goal in overtime on third down. By the time the Giants got their kicking team on the field and everything was settled, the play clock hit zero. Zak DeOssie snapped the ball only milliseconds after. Lined up between DeOssie and Snee, Aldon Smith had timed it perfectly in the middle of the formation. He used his hands to keep DeOssie and Snee down and leapt perfectly over them. Had the whistle not been blowing, Smith would've had a chance to block the kick. "Smith was in the A gap on my right as I faced out. He literally jumped over my shoulder pad and Chris' knee pad and had a clear block at the ball," DeOssie said. "So if we got that ball off a second earlier and it wasn't a delay of game, I argue we could've lost because that guy had a clear, concise path right for the ball. And then it wasn't a function of technique. The whistle blew. We didn't put our hands up. The guy jumped over. But who knows?"

The reality was that the whistle had blown. The play was dead. The five-yard penalty was hardly a penalty at all. It made it a 31-yard field goal for reliable kicker Lawrence Tynes. That was nothing considering what he had done in Green Bay four years earlier. It actually worked to Tynes' advantage. The ball was in a waterlogged spot prior to the delay of game. "I was really actually relieved when we did get that five-yard penalty," Tynes said. "We were able to move it back. That five yards back really gave us a beautiful green grass spot, and it was perfect."

Still, the Giants needed another unsung hero to advance. DeOssie's snap was far from perfect. It came in low and hot to holder Steve Weatherford. It skipped off the wet grass. Weatherford was able to scoop the ball off the slick turf and stand it perfectly with the laces out for Tynes to drill it through the uprights and deliver the Giants a 20–17 overtime victory.

Weatherford himself had a monster game. Jacquian Williams was a hero. So was Devin Thomas. Justin Tuck added 1.5 sacks on that memorable afternoon. There were so many major contributors to the Giants getting back to their second Super Bowl in four years. But this was Manning's masterpiece. It was the latest piece of evidence to validate his claim of being among the elite. With the left shoulder of his jersey having been completely colored green by the grass, with his light gray pants now having changed to a much darker shade thanks to being rolled in the mud, with his helmet scuffed from one side to the other, this was arguably the greatest game of his career. "No matter what the numbers are, he took a beating in that game. He kept getting up and making plays. He took a beating and he just kept going, and that was unbelievable to me," owner John Mara said. "That to me statistically might not have been his best game, but I think that was his best game."

29
The Manningham Catch

That plane ride home from San Francisco was something special. Smiles stretched from one coast to the next as the celebratory cocktails flowed. It was a party. The New York Football Giants were going back to the Super Bowl for the fifth time—and second in four years. This run was not quite—but almost—as improbable as the playoff jaunt in 2007. The Giants were an average team with a .500 record entering Week 16 during the 2011 season. They didn't look anything like a championship team even if they believed they had the requisite talent.

When the party ended and quarterback Eli Manning finished picking the dirt out of his facemask from the win against the San Francisco 49ers in the NFC Championship Game, there were two weeks until the Super Bowl. That gave the Giants some time to heal and prepare. No messing around. They were going to play Tom Brady and the New England Patriots again in the Super Bowl. It was upon leaving for Indianapolis that Manning set the tone. This wasn't a two-week bender that concluded with a game that the whole world would be watching. It was work. The day before the team traveled to Indianapolis, where the big game would be played, Manning did something some had never seen. He stepped to the front of a team meeting. Players and coaches were transfixed by his every word, and he told them how this week would go. "Hey, this is still a business trip!" Manning said.

He went on to tell his teammates that there would be curfews. It was 11:00 PM every day.

"I was like, 'Eli, you haven't spoke all year. You're talking about curfew?'" said Prince Amukamara, a rookie cornerback at the time.

Curfew is unique because it's not something that exists during a normal week at home for the regular season or even the playoffs. Players go home after work and do whatever they please.

Tuesdays are usually an off day. So Monday nights can be a late night. Fridays are generally a big party night for players because Saturdays are usually just a light practice or walk-through. There are no curfews on Fridays. The idea is just to be responsible enough to stay out of trouble and come to work on time with enough energy to perform. That is what most coaches demand.

This was the Super Bowl. So there was a lot of fun to be had on those prime nights even if it was in Indianapolis, which isn't exactly the greatest party city. Amukamara said that was the only time he remembers Manning giving the team a speech during their five seasons together. Wide receiver Victor Cruz said the same. Maybe it was talked about by the team's leadership council, but it was still special coming from the generally soft-spoken Manning. He had put it all on the line for the team a week earlier in San Francisco. How could anyone repay him by not giving their absolute all in the lead-up to the biggest game of their lives? "He really emphasized how serious this trip was going to be and stuff like that," Amukamara said. "We're a little rambunctious in there, we're loud, we're talking, we're excited. And right at the end, Eli gets up and he is like, 'Guys, I'm letting you know right now: stay focused on this game, forget all the partying, forget all of that stuff. Take care of your family. Take care of that early so you don't have to worry about any of that stuff when you get there. But I promise you, if we lock in and we win this football game, we'll have the best party you'll ever have in your lives after the game.'"

The room went dead silent for a few seconds when Manning finished. Then they exploded. They knew then it was time to lock in. As it turned out, Amukamara needed to allocate as much as time as possible to his assignment that week. He would be tasked with eliminating New England special teams ace Matthew Slater. That was on special teams. He also needed to know the defense inside and out. It's a good thing he did because when Aaron Ross went down mid-game with an injury, Amukamara had to step in at cornerback. He was targeted once—a seven-yard reception that went to tight end Rob Gronkowski. The ball did not come his way again.

That was hardly the highlight of this Super Bowl, which again went down to the final play. Manning somehow almost outdid himself from the last time he was in the Super Bowl and produced the Helmet Catch. That was incredible from an individual standpoint because of the improbability that he escaped the pressure. The throw wasn't actually special. It was almost just a heave that happened to work out. More a great play and a great catch than a great throw. But in Super Bowl XLVI against the Patriots, Manning made one of the best throws you will ever see in one of the biggest spots. The catch by wide receiver Mario Manningham was equally impressive. Maybe not quite to the level of David Tyree...but close.

It came on the first play after New York got the ball back with 3:46 remaining. The score was 17–15 at the time—the final score of the previous Super Bowl between the two teams—but this time in favor of New England. It looked as if this might be a flip of the previous script. Except Manning was getting the ball again late with a chance to be a hero. He never shied away from playing that role in the biggest of spots. In fact, somehow he embraced it even if it wasn't something he could explain. How the heck did he perform *better* in the bigger moments? "I wish I had the answer," he said. "If I knew, I would've done it more."

In this case it was the first play of what would turn into another legendary drive that the Giants were beginning at their own 12-yard line. Manning dropped back, reset the pocket when some push came up the middle, and fired deep down the left sideline to Manningham. The ball was perfectly placed 42 yards downfield between cornerback Sterling Moore and safety Patrick Chung. Still, it was not going to be an easy catch because Chung was on top of the receiver and Moore was underneath. Manningham needed to contort his body, corral the ball while looking back over his left shoulder, and still tap his toes (of both feet) inbounds right in front of the New England sideline. It all happened while NBC announcer Al Michael famously bellowed "Eeeeeeeeeeeeeeeeeeeeeeeli, throwing into traffic on the sideline!"

It was a dart put in the perfect location for Manningham to make the play. "Just putting the ball in a spot where, hey, your guy can get it or nobody. It's kind of a semi-throw away. The No. 1 [option] they took away, and we only had a three-man route," Manning said. "They took away our other two guys, and I just came back to my throw-away shot and put it in a spot where Manningham could catch it. He made an unbelievable catch way over the outside shoulder, trying to keep two feet inbounds while taking a hit. It was just a great, unbelievable individual effort by him."

The Patriots and coach Bill Belichick challenged the call of a completion only to be left disappointed by the result. It was a catch, one of the best in Super Bowl history. Even more so, it was one of the best throws you will see. And Manning did it in one of the biggest spots against one of the greatest dynasties in football history with Brady and Belichick left helpless just feet away on the sideline. "That's the greatest throw in the world because if that safety's helmet goes in front of the ball in front of Manningham, he knocks that ball out," Tom Coughlin said. "His helmet went behind, and so it allowed Manningham to make the great hands-above-the-shoulder-pads catch right in front of Belichick."

For Manningham to do it in front of Belichick was the ultimate slap in his face. That is because Belichick in a way was dumping on Manningham on the sideline right before it happened. "This is still a Cruz and [Hakeem] Nicks game," Belichick told his team before the eventual game-winning drive. "I know we're right on them. It's tight, but those are still the guys. Make them go to Manningham. Make them go to [tight end Bear] Pascoe. Let's make sure we get Cruz and Nicks."

Cruz and Nicks were the Giants' top two receivers. But it's not like Manningham was a scrub. The player they called "Rio" had close to 1,000 yards receiving the previous season. He had 21 touchdown receptions, including three in the postseason that year, in his first four professional seasons after being a third-round pick out of Michigan. The path wasn't always smooth though. Manningham was a star at Michigan, but he had some off-the-field stuff and did not perform particularly well at the NFL Scouting Combine, which was on the same field in Indianapolis, or his Pro Day. He ran the 40-yard dash in a puzzling 4.62 seconds. That left teams unimpressed. So Manningham sat there until one of the final picks of the third round in the 2008 NFL Draft. That is when the Giants decided to take a shot at a player who would ultimately make the biggest play of Super Bowl XLVI almost four years later. "It was like, *All right at this point, this guy's a first-round talent. We got to take a chance now,*" said Marc Ross, the Giants' director of college scouting at the time. "I mean, this is the sweet spot of the bottom of the third. He's a first-round talent. We got the infrastructure to help the guy. That's what you talk about, all those things with him."

It was a good thing the Giants took the risk. Manningham was a solid player for the Giants. He was hardly a problem. At 25 years old, he started 10 games at wide receiver for the Giants that year. But he missed four weeks because of a knee injury. As Manningham explained during the season, there was something "floating" in his knee. He played through it late in the campaign, setting himself up to be a hobbled Super Bowl hero. Manningham made the catch in what would ultimately be the last game he ever played for the Giants. He signed with the 49ers as a free agent—along with Brandon Jacobs—after the season.

Knee problems would end up cutting his career short after two seasons with the 49ers. Manningham tore the ACL and PCL in his left knee the following year in San Francisco. He was done playing football at 27 years old but with a forever Super Bowl moment on his resume. "He was a damn good player, a damn good player," Coughlin said. "A tough, tough kid, too."

The Manningham catch goes down right behind the Helmet Catch as one of the greatest plays in Giants history. That is because Manning was surgical after that. He connected twice more with Manningham to get them into New England territory. He connected with Nicks on both sides of the two-minute warning. There were also some effective runs by Ahmad Bradshaw mixed in, including his six-yard gallop where he toppled into the end zone to give New York a 21–17 lead with 1:04 remaining.

All these years later, it's that Manningham catch that still sticks out to those on the team. That was *the* play. "I just remember thinking to myself, *You could do that a hundred more times and not come up with the completion.* But he came up with the completion the one time he needed to," Chris Canty said. "It was just un-fucking-believable."

Canty and the defense still had to do its part. It was Brady, and there was still more than a minute remaining. But the Giants defense, like usual in these Super Bowls, made life miserable for the legendary quarterback. Justin Tuck sacked Brady again on that final drive. It was his fourth sack of Brady in the two Super Bowl matchups with the Patriots. Brady still got his team near midfield and had one last Hail Mary attempt. The ball seemed to hang in the air for days before safety Kenny Phillips knocked it to the ground just before Gronkowski could scoop it off the turf.

The Giants had beaten the Patriots *again* to win the Super Bowl. Manning had led another game-winning drive that included a legendary play. *Ho-hum.* It was almost a carbon copy of the previous blueprint to beat Brady and Belichick. Only this was the veteran Manning who had done it before. "I mean, I think they're both very different drives," Manning said years later of his Super Bowl dramatics. "I think both drives, if you look at both two-minute drives, it just shows a difference between a four-year quarterback and an eight-year quarterback, where that first drive or the first Super Bowl there was a couple plays that could have been intercepted, some sacks, some negative plays. There was some luck. I was getting sacked in the middle of the field, just so many oh-my-goodness moments it gave you heartache, a heart attack, watching that thing. And then four years later, I mean that two-minute drive was just like textbook from going the first play and getting a chunk. They went blitz zero, I checked to a slant. They played cover two, I checked to a run. Just [for] everything we had an answer, and it just felt very comfortable within that offense with those guys and what they were doing."

The Tyree play was improvising at its finest. The Manningham throw was quarterbacking at its finest. They were both equally great plays for Manning and the New York Football Giants. They are now part of football lore as the plays that helped the Giants win another Super Bowl, their fourth in franchise history.

Acknowledgments

WHEN TAKING ON A PROJECT LIKE THIS, IT'S IMPOSSIBLE TO do it by yourself. I'm lucky enough to have a professional network that was willing to help, guide, and donate their time and memories. To me, you are all friends, and I consider myself incredibly fortunate to cross paths.

To all the former players and coaches who took time to speak with me for this project, I am deeply indebted. Who would've thought when I first started covering the Giants that Tom Coughlin and I would still be on speaking terms some 15 years later? Not this guy. It was so much fun rehashing the past and listening to everybody's stories. They are undoubtedly the backbone of this book.

To have former Giants reporters and columnists like Bill Pennington, Bob Glauber, Gary Myers, Peter King, and Mike Garafolo as resources was also invaluable. They helped me fill in the blanks and provided advice when needed. Thanks for picking up my calls. I could always count on you to make sure I was headed in the right direction.

I'm also appreciative of the Giants' support. Both John Mara and Jonathan Tisch were kind enough to sit down and relive the past. For that, I am grateful. Pat Hanlon, thanks for setting it all up.

A big thanks also needs to be given to Victor Cruz, who spoke with me at length about that incredible 2011 season and agreed to write the foreword. Next round of golf on me. Vic, you've always been good to me. For that I am thankful. You proved once again that all the success that has come your way is warranted.

It really was an honor that the people at Triumph entrusted me with this project. The fact that they would seek me out to handle the Giants version of The Franchise was humbling. Bill Ames, thanks for thinking of me. To my editor, Jeff Fedotin, you made the process easy. It really was rather seamless thanks to everyone at Triumph.

This was my second go-around at this, and there was some apprehension at first. But more than anything, I'm lucky to have a great internal support system. My wife, Abby, has always been supportive of my career even when it wasn't exactly thriving. My parents are always there to help and support no matter what. And my kids, Kylie and Brody, you are my motivation. I'd do anything for you.

Sources

Books

Bowden, Mark. *The Best Game Ever: Giants vs. Colts, 1958, and the Birth of the Modern NFL.* Atlantic Monthly Press, 2008.

Palladino, Ernie. *If These Walls Could Talk: New York Giants: Stories From the New York Giants' Sidelines, Locker Room, and Press Box.* Triumph Books, 2013.

Parcells, Bill, and Mike Lupica. *Parcells: Autobiography of the Biggest Giant of Them All.* Bonus Books, 1987.

Newspapers, Magazines, and Wire Services

Associated Press

Newsday

New York Daily News

New York Post

Sports Illustrated

The New York Times

The Washington Post

Websites

espn.com

profootballhof.com

pro-football-reference.com